BRAHAMANISM

BRAHAMANISM

Editor-in-Chief
Swami Chidatman Jee Maharaj

ANMOL PUBLICATIONS PVT. LTD.
NEW DELHI - 110 002 (INDIA)

ANMOL PUBLICATIONS PVT. LTD.
H.O.: 4374/4B, Ansari Road, Daryaganj,
New Delhi-110 002 (India)
Ph.: 23278000, 23261597
B.O.: No. 1015, Ist Main Road, BSK IIIrd Stage
IIIrd Phase, IIIrd Block,
Bangalore - 560 085 (India)
Visit us at: www.anmolpublications.com

Brahamanism

First Published, 2009
ISBN 978-81-261-3612-4

PRINTED IN INDIA

Printed at Mehra Offset Press, Delhi.

Contents

Preface

India colourful and vibrant, a land as diverse as its people. A mosaic of faiths, cultures, customs and languages that blend harmoniously to form a composite whole. One of the world's oldest living civilizations—which gave to the world—the concept of zero, the primordial sound Aum..., Yoga and Buddhism.

She is old. She is young. The two diametrically opposite, different yet unique and dynamic faces of India coexist even at this turn of the millennium. With a history of heritage, learning and civilisation dating back to almost 5000 years or perhaps even more, the modern India presents itself as an ideal country. From snow clad mountains to breezy sparkling blue sea side. From arid deserts with shifting sand dunes to lush green country sides. From ancient relics and architectural ruins dating back into antiquity to modern cities, India has it all.

To the north it is bordered by the world's highest mountain chain, where foothill valleys cover the northernmost of the country's maximum states. Further south, plateaus, tropical rain forests and sandy deserts are bordered by palm fringed beaches. Its southernmost tip is the meeting point of three Oceans.

India is a land of staggering contrast with a mingling of the tradition and modernity that is an unique experience to be in India. One will forever remember the stay in this wonderful Homeland-a land truly of mystery and enchantment. Only India can offer such an astonishing variety of contrasts.

She has given birth to numerous spiritual leaders and founders of some of the popular religions of the present day world. India probably has the most religious diversity in any country. It's the birthplace of Hinduism, Buddhism, Sikhism and Jainism and is among the few places to have a resident

Zoroastrian population. India with her veritable treasure trove of culture, mysticism, philosophy, art, music and architecture to name a few. Much of India's classical music is devotional and the North Indian Hindustani and South Indian Carnatic streams are distinct and both have a complex 'raga' framework. The legacy of dance in India is tremendous. The classical dances of India are numerous such as Kathakali of Kerala, Bharatnatyam of Tamil Nadu, Kuchipudi of Andhra Pradesh, Manipuri and Odissi from Orissa are the prominent dance forms in this country that sways to an altogether novel beat. The Yakshagana, nautanki and puppetry are ancient folk forms that live on till date. The earliest specimens of Indian painting are the ones on the walls of the Ajanta Caves dating back to 2nd century BC. The Mughals had a huge impact on Indian art. The influence of Persian art brought placid garden scenes, illustrations from myths, legends and history into Indian art. Word craft, handicrafts, architecture and sculpture all contribute to this rich and varied domain. Indian literature, both in English and in the vernacular, is ever more popular around the world.

The book aims at presenting perspectives of different aspects of Indian culture. It has topics on Indian classical music and dance, painting, ayurveda and yoga which are traditional and indigenous system of physical and mental wellbeing, language, philosophy and excellence achievements by Indian in the different branches of science and social sciences. It also includes our ancient religious and classic literature.

It is hoped that this book will be welcomed by the general readers as also scholars who are interested in the Indian heritage.

—Editors

1

Essence of Brahmanism

Hinduism emphasizes the necessity of escaping from material life and of extinguishing desire. Hinduism is very ritualistic and includes extreme self denial and self punishment. Cows are considered sacred as are rivers. Most Hindus believe in the transmigration of souls (reincarnation), where when a person dies, his soul enters the body of a newborn child or even the body of an animal. Over and over. Therefore, devout Hindus will not kill even a fly. They are vegetarians, lest by eating meat they become cannibals.

The caste system in India is directly related to their religious beliefs. About 2500 years before Christ, a white people called the Aryans came to India (probably from Persia.)

The Aryans formed a caste system in order to maintain the purity of their blood and to maintain white supremacy. Originally, they recognized only four castes:

- Brahmans, (highest) priests and scholars
- Kshatriyas, (next) nobles and warriors
- Vaisyas, (next) farmers and merchants
- Sudras, (lowest) serfs and slaves

Later, these four castes multiplied until today where there are thousands of castes in India. Only Hindus practice the caste system; it is abandoned if a Hindu becomes a Mohammedan or a Christian.

The castes became hereditary which meant that all sons are necessarily members of the same caste as their fathers and that he has to follow his father's occupation. The 7000 modern castes even include a caste of thieves! If someone is expelled from his caste or has no caste by birth, he is known as an Untouchable, a pariah, and such a person is in a hopeless and pitiable condition. There are currently more than 60,000,000 untouchables in India.

Hinduism teaches that anyone born into a lower caste or an Untouchable is being punished for the sins committed in his past life. If such a person is calmly resigned to his fate and lives rightly, he will be elevated in caste in his next life. This premise tends to make the members of the lower castes and the untouchables submissive to the terrible economic and social conditions under which they live.

Brahma is the chief god, the omnipresent one who is father of the Brahman Trinity. He has four heads, three of which (representing their Trinity) can be seen from any point of view.

- Brahma(the creator)
- Vishnu(the preserver)
- Shiva (the destroyer of evil)

Advanced Information

Hinduism, one of the great religions of the world, is the major religion of India, where nearly 85 percent of the population is classified as Hindu. Hinduism has developed over about 4,000 years and has no single founder or creed; rather, it consists of a vast variety of beliefs and practices. Organization is minimal and hierarchy nonexistent. In its diversity, Hinduism hardly fits most Western definitions of religion; rather, it suggests commitment to or respect for an ideal way of life, known as Dharma.

Beliefs and Practices

Caste System: The ideal way of life is sometimes referred to in classical sources and by Hindus as the "duties of one's class and station" (varnasramadharma). The term "class" (varna) is one of the words connoting the Caste system peculiar to India. The ancient texts suggest four great classes, or castes: the Brahmins, or priests; the Ksatriyas, or warriors and rulers; the Vaisyas, or merchants and farmers; and the Sudras, or peasants and labourers. A fifth class, Panchamas, or Untouchables, includes those whose occupations require them to handle unclean objects. It is speculated that the Untouchables were originally assigned such lowly tasks because of their non Aryan origins. This classification system hardly does justice to the modern complexity of the caste system, however. The classical works on dharma specify distinct duties for different classes, in keeping with the distinct roles each is expected to play in the ideal society.

Stages of Life

The classical works also outline four ideal stages (asrama), or stations of life, each with its own duties. The first of these is studentship (brahmacarya), from initiation at 5 to 8 years of age until marriage; the second, householdership (grihasthya), when one marries, raises a family, and takes part in society; the third, forest dwelling (vanaprasthya), after one's children have grown; and the fourth, renunciation (samnyasa), when one gives up attachment to all worldly things and seeks spiritual liberation.

Besides the duties that are derived from an individual's class and station, general duties (sanatanadharma) are also incumbent on all moral beings. These include honesty, courage, service, faith, self control, purity, and nonviolence.

These ideal classes and stations encompass males only. The position of women in Hinduism has always been ambiguous; they are, on the one hand, venerated as a symbol of the divine, on the other, treated as inferior beings. Women were traditionally expected to serve their husbands and to have no independent interests. Recent movements within Hinduism, however, such as the Brahmo Samaj, have succeeded in altering this situation.

Aims of Life

Dharma is only one of the four aims of life (purusartha) distinguished within Hinduism. It is thought of as superior to two others-kama, or enjoyment of desires, and artha, or material prosperity. These three constitute the aims of those in the world (pravritti). The fourth aim is liberation (moksa), the aim of those who renounce the world (nivritti), and this is classically viewed as the supreme end of man.

Karma and Rebirth

A widespread feature of classical Hinduism is the belief in Transmigration of Souls, or samsara, the passage of a soul from body to body as determined by the force of one's actions, or Karma. The strict karma theory specifies that one's type of birth, length of life, and kinds of experiences are determined by one's previous acts.

This is modified in popular understanding, but it probably has remained a strong influence on most Hindus throughout history. Liberation is release from this cycle of rebirth. It is typically to be achieved by working out those karmic residues which have already begun to mature, as well as by following certain practices to ensure that no further residues are produced to cause future rebirths. The practices by which one can achieve this are frequently termed Yoga, and the theory of liberation is the core of Indian philosophy.

Philosophy

Hinduism is usually said to include six philosophical systems. The systems called Nyaya, Vaisheshika, Samkhya, and Yoga emphasize yogic practices coupled with an understanding of basic principles of metaphysics and epistemology. Nyaya, in addition, includes an analysis of logic. The systems called Mimamsa identify the performance of ritual-the Vedic sacrifice, or actions performed in that spirit-as the means to liberation.

The many Vedanta systems, taking their inspiration from the Upanishads, tend to emphasize understanding of the relationship between the self (Atman) and ultimate reality (Brahman) as the critical aspect of any path to liberation. Philosophies associated with sectarian movements, such as the Bhakti cults, frequently localized in a linguistic or cultural area within the subcontinent, emphasize the path of theistic devotion.

Hindu Deities

The two great theistic movements within Hinduism are Vaishnavism, the cult of Vishnu, and Shaivism, the cult of Shiva. Hindu belief, however, usually holds that the universe is populated by a multitude of gods. These gods share to some extent the features of the Godhead but are seen as behaving much as humans do and as being related to each other as humans are.

This view is similar to that of the ancient Greeks. For example, the supreme gods Brahma, Vishnu, and Shiva and some of the other gods are often viewed as activated through their relationships with female deities. These female consorts to the deities are called Shakti. Other well known gods are said to be relatives of a supreme god, such as Ganesha, the elephant-headed god, a son of Shiva and Parvati. Kali, or Durga, the consort of Shiva, is worshiped widely throughout India in the autumn. Hanuman, the monkey-faced god, is depicted in many shrines, and along with Lakshmi, Vishnu's wife, is among the most important deities associated with Vaishnavism. The sets of gods recognized by different sects are by no means mutually exclusive, however.

Forms of Worship

Hindu worship takes many forms. One of the least frequent is the congregational form so familiar in the West. Vedic sacrifices were conducted in any open place properly consecrated. Typical Hindu daily worship (puja) includes a stop at several shrines, a visit to a temple, and home worship. A Hindu may be devoted to several gods: the image of one god, frequently a family deity, is commonly installed in a small shrine in the home; a second god, worshiped at a nearby temple, may be the divinity to which the person's caste is committed; and still another may be the god to whom the individual makes obeisance as his Guru (teacher) or his guru's tutor.

Because everything is sacred in a Hindu's eyes, almost anything may be considered worthy of devotion; rivers, cowpens, and the retreats of holy men are among the holy places frequented by the devout.

Home Worship

Home worship typically involves purification of the area through fire, water, and the drawing of symbolic diagrams. Depending on one's class and station, the frequency with which a Hindu is expected to perform the rites, and the role performed in them, will differ. The rites involve offering food, flowers, or incense to the deity, together with appropriate recitations of sacred words or texts. An especially important ritual is known as sraddha, in which Hindu males symbolically support their father, grandfathers, and great-grandfathers in other worlds by offering water and balls of rice; this ritual dates from Vedic times. The worshiper requires the services of a priest on this occasion, as for other life cycle ceremonies such as birth, initiation, marriage, and death.

Temple Worship

The priests also carry out temple worship, although the devotee may participate in the reading of certain hymns or prayers and may give flowers or money to the god directly. The image of a god is believed to be the god, and the cycle of worship in a temple centers on the daily life of the god, involving preparation of the god for worship-waking him up with bells, purifying him with incense, bathing him, dressing him, and feeding him. The worshiper comes to the temple to view (darshana) the god and to receive the food (prasada) that the god has touched. As in the cycle of an ordinary person, special days occur in the cycle of the god of the temple, and on these days special ceremonies are held. These are frequently the times of festivals and may involve elaborate ceremonies: pilgrimages of vast numbers of devotees, processions bearing the god's image throughout the city or countryside, and special music, plays, and dances for the occasion.

Sacred Cities and Festivals

The seven sacred cities of Hinduism are the following: Varanasi (Benares), Hardwar, Ayodhya, Dwarka, Mathura, Kanchipuram (Conjeeveram), and Ujjain. Other important pilgrimage spots include Madurai, Gaya, Prayaga (Allahabad), Tirupati, and Puri.

Each of these places has one or more temples where annual festivals are celebrated that attract large numbers of pilgrims.

Certain festival days are celebrated throughout India on a day fixed according to the Hindu lunisolar calendar. Prominent among these is Dipavali, the "Festival of Lights," occurring in October and November, at which lamps are placed around the house to welcome Lakshmi, the goddess of prosperity. Holi, a spring festival in February or March, is a day of riotous funmaking; this frequently involves temporary suspension of caste and social distinctions, and practical jokes are the order of the day. In the fall (September and October) a ten day period is set aside to honour the Mother Goddess, culminating in Dashara, the tenth day, a day of processions and celebrations. This festival is extremely important in Bengal, where it is known as Durga Puja.

History and Literature

Scholars sometimes distinguish Vedism, the religion of ancient India based on the Vedas, from Hinduism, although it is difficult to pinpoint a time that demarcates them. The Vedas were hymns of the Aryans, who invaded in the 2d millennium BC.

Vedism stressed hope for a future existence in heaven and lacked the concepts of karma and rebirth; Hinduism characteristically includes karma and rebirth, and the greatest hope is for eventual release from their sway.

The Vedic deities were somewhat different from those which dominate in Hinduism, although scholars have traced the origins of Vishnu and Shiva back to Vedic counterparts. Later Vedism is sometimes called Brahmanism because of the authority accorded the Brahmins, or priests, who performed the ritual Vedic sacrifice. However, the challenge of non-Vedic religions, notably Buddhism and Jainism, led to the replacement of the rigid Brahmanical rules by more relaxed and varied forms of worship.

Although the Vedas continue to be spoken of as the final authority in Hinduism, other texts of equal importance exist. Thus, a literature was developed for each of the four aims of life: various Dharmasastras, such as the Code of Manu, which detail the duties of class and station; Kamasastras, such as the Kamasutras of Vatsyayana, handbooks of pleasure, erotic and otherwise; the Arthasastra, attributed to Kautilya (fl. 300 BC), which, like Machiavelli's The Prince, offers advice to a ruler as to how to keep the throne; and the philosophical literature of the various systems, which deals with liberation and how to achieve it.

In addition, certain collections of tales came to be widely known in popular life, especially the two great epics, the Mahabarata and the Ramayana. The Mahabharata tells of five princes who were cheated out of their kingdom and who, after a period of banishment in the forest, returned to fight a victorious and righteous war to regain it. An especially beloved portion of this epic is the section called the Bhagavad Gita, in which Arjuna, one of the brothers, is counseled by his charioteer Krishna, an incarnation of Lord Vishnu. The Ramayana tells the story of the ideal Hindu man, Rama, whose wife Sita is abducted by a demon, and of Rama's journey to Sri Lanka to recapture her. Both epics are filled with didactic tales, edifying poems, and fables. It is probably through their constant retelling in the village that Hinduism is most efficiently disseminated from generation to generation. Another source of Hindu lore is the Puranas, collections of legends and myths.

The period from roughly 500 BC to 1000 AD is sometimes spoken of as that of classical Hinduism. It was during this period that the major literature was composed, the great philosophical systems developed, and the basic Vaishnava and Shaiva sects organized. After 1000, beginning in south India somewhat earlier, a spirit of devotional fervor coupled with social reform swept through India, and the period from that time until near the present is known as the bhakti period. During this time the forms of religious worship changed and diversified further. Singing of devotional songs and poems in the vernacular rather than in Sanskrit, the language in which practically all classical Hindu literature was written, is one example. Direct approach to the god was emphasized, and the mediating role of the priest somewhat curtailed. Love, a sentiment common to all but particularly to the most ordinary villager, is now celebrated as the way to the highest end; some bhakti philosophies hold that liberation is not the supreme goal and that loving service to God is a higher one.

Recent developments in Hinduism are indicative of a movement away from certain aspects of classical practice, such as Suttee, a widow's suicide at her husband's funeral; caste distinctions; and even karma and rebirth.

Shiva

General Information

Shiva (Sanskrit for "auspicious one"), also called Shiva, is the Hindu god who personifies both the destructive and the procreative forces of the universe. As the destroyer, he is represented wearing a necklace of skulls and surrounded by demons. His reproductive aspect is symbolized by the lingam, a phallic emblem. Shiva is also the god of asceticism and of art, especially dancing. He rides on the bull Nandi, and his consort is the mother goddess Uma, or Kali. Some Hindus worship Shiva as the supreme deity and consider him a benevolent god of salvation as well as a god of destruction.

Some Important Hindu Religious Documents Follow:

The Song Celestial 400 BC or Bhagavad-Gita

Chapter I

Dhritirashtra. Ranged thus for battle on the sacred plain-

On Kurukshetra-say, Sanjaya! say

What wrought my people, and the Pandavas?

Sanjaya. When he beheld the host of Pandavas,

Raja Duryodhana to Drona drew,

And spake these words: "Ah, Guru! see this line,

How vast it is of Pandu fighting men,

Embattled by the son of Drupada,

Thy scholar in the war! Therein stand ranked

Chiefs like Arjuna, like to Bhima chiefs,
Benders of bows; Virata, Yuyudhan,
Drupada, eminent upon his car,
Dhrishtaket, Chekitan, Kasi's stout lord,
Purujit, Kuntibhoj, and Saivya,
With Yudhamanyu, and Uttamauj
Subhadra's child; and Drupadi's;-all famed!
All mounted on their shining chariots!
On our side, too,-thou best of Brahmans! see
Excellent chiefs, commanders of my line,
Whose names I joy to count: thyself the first,
Then Bhishma, Karna, Kripa fierce in fight,
Vikarna, Aswatthaman; next to these
Strong Saumadatti, with full many more
Valiant and tried, ready this day to die
For me their king, each with his weapon grasped,
Each skilful in the field. Weakest-meseems-
Our battle shows where Bhishma holds command,
And Bhima, fronting him, something too strong!
Have care our captains nigh to Bhishma's ranks
Prepare what help they may! Now, blow my shell!"
Then, at the signal of the aged king,
With blare to wake the blood, rolling around
Like to a lion's roar, the trumpeter
Blew the great Conch; and, at the noise of it,
Trumpets and drums, cymbals and gongs and horns
Burst into sudden clamour; as the blasts
Of loosened tempest, such the tumult seemed!
Then might be seen, upon their car of gold
Yoked with white steeds, blowing their battle shells,
Krishna the God, Arjuna at his side:
Krishna, with knotted locks, blew his great conch
Carved of the "Giant's bone;" Arjuna blew

Indra's loud gift; Bhima the terrible-
Wolf-bellied Bhima-blew a long reed-conch;
And Yudhisthira, Kunti's blameless son,
Winded a mighty shell, "Victory's Voice;"
And Nakula blew shrill upon his conch
Named the "Sweet sounding," Sahadev on his
Called "Gem bedecked," and Kasi's Prince on his.
Sikhandi on his car, Dhrishtadyumn,
Virata, Satyaki the Unsubdued,
Drupada, with his sons, (O Lord of Earth!)
Long armed Subhadra's children, all blew loud,
So that the clangour shook their foemen's hearts,
With quaking earth and thundering heav'n.
Then 'twas-
Beholding Dhritirashtra's battle set,
Weapons unsheathing, bows drawn forth, the war
Instant to break-Arjun, whose ensign badge
Was Hanuman the monkey, spake this thing
To Krishna the Divine, his charioteer:
"Drive, Dauntless One! to yonder open ground
Betwixt the armies; I would see more nigh
These who will fight with us, those we must slay
Today, in war's arbitrament; for, sure,
On bloodshed all are bent who throng this plain,
Obeying Dhritirashtra's sinful son."
Thus, by Arjuna prayed, (O Bharata!)
Between the hosts that heavenly Charioteer
Drove the bright car, reining its milk white steeds
Where Bhishma led, and Drona, and their Lords.
"See!" spake he to Arjuna, "where they stand,
Thy kindred of the Kurus:" and the Prince
Marked on each hand the kinsmen of his house,
Grandsires and sires, uncles and brothers and sons,

Cousins and sons-in-law and nephews, mixed
With friends and honoured elders; some this side,
Some that side ranged: and, seeing those opposed,
Such kith grown enemies-Arjuna's heart
Melted with pity, while he uttered this:
Arjuna. Krishna! as I behold, come here to shed
Their common blood, yon concourse of our kin,
My members fail, my tongue dries in my mouth,
A shudder thrills my body, and my hair
Bristles with horror; from my weak hand slips
Gandiv, the goodly bow; a fever burns
My skin to parching; hardly may I stand;
The life within me seems to swim and faint;
Nothing do I foresee save woe and wail!
It is not good, O Keshav! nought of good
Can spring from mutual slaughter! Lo, I hate
Triumph and domination, wealth and ease,
Thus sadly won! Aho! what victory
Can bring delight, Govinda! what rich spoils
Could profit; what rule recompense; what span
Of life itself seem sweet, bought with such blood?
Seeing that these stand here, ready to die,
For whose sake life was fair, and pleasure pleased,
And power grew precious:-grandsires, sires, and sons,
Brothers, and fathers-in-law, and sons-in-law,
Elders and friends! Shall I deal death on these
Even though they seek to slay us? Not one blow,
O Madhusudan! will I strike to gain
The rule of all Three Worlds; then, how much less
To seize an earthly kingdom! Killing these
Must breed but anguish, Krishna! If they be
Guilty, we shall grow guilty by their deaths;

Their sins will light on us, if we shall slay
Those sons of Dhritirashtra, and our kin;
What peace could come of that, O Madhava?
For if indeed, blinded by lust and wrath,
These cannot see, or will not see, the sin
Of kingly lines o'erthrown and kinsmen slain,
How should not we, who see, shun such a crime-
We who perceive the guilt and feel the shame-
O thou Delight of Men, Janardana?
By overthrow of houses perisheth
Their sweet continuous household piety,
And-rites neglected, piety extinct-
Enters impiety upon that home;
Its women grow unwomaned, whence there spring
Mad passions, and the mingling up of castes,
Sending a Hellward road that family,
And whoso wrought its doom by wicked wrath.
Nay, and the souls of honoured ancestors
Fall from their place of peace, being bereft
Of funeral cakes and the wan death water.
So teach our holy hymns. Thus, if we slay
Kinsfolk and friends for love of earthly power,
Ahovat! what an evil fault it were!
Better I deem it, if my kinsmen strike,
To face them weaponless, and bare my breast
To shaft and spear, than answer blow with blow.
So speaking, in the face of those two hosts,
Arjuna sank upon his chariot seat,
And let fall bow and arrows, sick at heart.
Here Endeth Chapter I of the
Bhagavad-Gita,
Entitled "Arjun-Vishad,"
Or "The Book of the Distress of Arjuna."

Chapter II

Sanjaya. Him, filled with such compassion and such grief,
With eyes tear dimmed, despondent, in stern words
The Driver, Madhusudan, thus addressed:
Krishna. How hath this weakness taken thee?
Whence springs
The inglorious trouble, shameful to the brave,
Barring the path of virtue? Nay, Arjun!
Forbid thyself to feebleness! it mars
Thy warrior name! cast off the coward-fit!
Wake! Be thyself! Arise, Scourge of thy Foes!
Arjuna. How can I, in the battle, shoot with shafts
On Bhishma, or on Drona-O thou Chief!-
Both worshipful, both honourable men?
Better to live on beggar's bread
With those we love alive,
Than taste their blood in rich feasts spread,
And guiltily survive!
Ah! were it worse-who knows?-to be
Victor or vanquished here,
When those confront us angrily
Whose death leaves living drear?
In pity lost, by doubtings tossed,
My thoughts-distracted-turn
To Thee, the Guide I reverence most,
That I may counsel learn:
I know not what would heal the grief
Burned into soul and sense,
If I were earth's unchallenged chief-
A god-and these gone thence!
Sanjaya. So spake Arjuna to the Lord of Hearts,
And sighing, "I will not fight!" held silence then.

To whom, with tender smile, (O Bharata!)
While the Prince wept despairing 'twixt those hosts,
Krishna made answer in divinest verse:
Krishna. Thou grievest where no grief should be! thou speak'st
Words lacking wisdom! for the wise in heart
Mourn not for those that live, nor those that die.
Nor I, nor thou, nor any one of these,
Ever was not, nor ever will not be,
For ever and for ever afterwards.
All, that doth live, lives always! To man's frame
As there come infancy and youth and age,
So come there raisings-up and layings-down
Of other and of other life-abodes,
Which the wise know, and fear not. This that irks-
Thy sense-life, thrilling to the elements-
Bringing thee heat and cold, sorrows and joys,
'Tis brief and mutable! Bear with it, Prince!
As the wise bear. The soul which is not moved,
The soul that with a strong and constant calm
Takes sorrow and takes joy indifferently,
Lives in the life undying! That which is
Can never cease to be; that which is not
Will not exist. To see this truth of both
Is theirs who part essence from accident,
Substance from shadow. Indestructible,
Learn thou! the Life is, spreading life through all;
It cannot anywhere, by any means,
Be anywise diminished, stayed, or changed.
But for these fleeting frames which it informs
With spirit deathless, endless, infinite,
They perish. Let them perish, Prince! and fight!
He who shall say, "Lo! I have slain a man!"
He who shall think, "Lo! I am slain!" those both

Know naught! Life cannot slay. Life is not slain!
Never the spirit was born; the spirit shall cease to be never;
Never was time it was not; End and Beginning are dreams!
Birthless and deathless and changeless remaineth the spirit for ever;
Death hath not touched it at all, dead though the house of it seems!
Who knoweth it exhaustless, self sustained,
Immortal, indestructible,-shall such
Say, "I have killed a man, or caused to kill?"
Nay, but as when one layeth
His worn out robes away,
And, taking new ones, sayeth,
"These will I wear today!"
So putteth by the spirit
Lightly its garb of flesh,
And passeth to inherit
A residence afresh.
I say to thee weapons reach not the Life;
Flame burns it not, waters cannot o'erwhelm,
Nor dry winds wither it. Impenetrable,
Unentered, unassailed, unharmed, untouched,
Immortal, all-arriving, stable, sure,
Invisible, ineffable, by word
And thought uncompassed, ever all itself,
Thus is the Soul declared! How wilt thou, then,-
Knowing it so,-grieve when thou shouldst not grieve?
How, if thou hearest that the man new-dead
Is, like the man new-born, still living man-
One same, existent Spirit-wilt thou weep?
The end of birth is death; the end of death
Is birth: this is ordained! and mournest thou,

Chief of the stalwart arm! for what befalls
Which could not otherwise befall? The birth
Of living things comes unperceived; the death
Comes unperceived; between them, beings perceive:
What is there sorrowful herein, dear Prince?
Wonderful, wistful, to contemplate!
Difficult, doubtful, to speak upon!
Strange and great for tongue to relate,
Mystical hearing for every one!
Nor wotteth man this, what a marvel it is,
When seeing, and saying, and hearing are done!
This Life within all living things, my Prince!
Hides beyond harm; scorn thou to suffer, then,
For that which cannot suffer. Do thy part!
Be mindful of thy name, and tremble not!
Nought better can betide a martial soul
Than lawful war; happy the warrior
To whom comes joy of battle-comes, as now,
Glorious and fair, unsought; opening for him
A gateway unto Heav'n. But, if thou shunn'st
This honourable field-a Kshattriya-
If, knowing thy duty and thy task, thou bidd'st
Duty and task go by-that shall be sin!
And those to come shall speak thee infamy
From age to age; but infamy is worse
For men of noble blood to bear than death!
The chiefs upon their battle chariots
Will deem 'twas fear that drove thee from the fray.

Brahminism

Catholic Information

By Brahminism is meant the complex religion and social system which grew out of the polytheistic nature-worship of the ancient Aryan conquerors of northern India, and came, with the spread of their dominion, to be extended over the whole country, maintaining itself, not without profound modifications, down to the present day. In its intricate modern phases it is generally known as Hinduism.

Brahmin Texts

Our knowledge of Brahminism in its earlier stages is derived from its primitive sacred books, originally oral compositions, belonging to the period between 1500-400 B.C.

First of all, there are four Vedas (veda means wisdom) dating from 1500 to 800 B.C., and consisting of a collection of ancient hymns (riks),the so-called Rig-Veda, in praise of the many gods; of the Sama-veda, compiled from parts of the Rig-Veda as a song-service for the soma-sacrifice; of the Yajur-Veda, a liturgy composed partly of ancient hymns and partly of other prayers and benedictions to be used in the various forms of sacrifice; and of the Atharva-Veda, a collection of popular exorcisms and magical incantations largely inherited from primitive Aryan days.

Next in order are the Brahmanas (about 1000-600 B.C.). They are a series of verbose and miscellaneous explanations of the texts, rites, and customs found in each of the four Vedas, composed expressly for the use of the Brahmins, or priests. They are followed (800-500 B.C.) by the so-called Upanishads, concerned chiefly with pantheistic speculations on the nature of deity and the end of man; and lastly, by the Sutras (600-400 B.C.), which are compendious guides to the proper observance of the rites and customs.

The most important are the Grhya-Sutras, or house-guides, treating of domestic rites, and the Dharma-sutras, or law-guides, which were manuals of religious and social customs. Being meant for layman as well as priest, they reflect the popular, practical side of Brahminism, whereas the Brahmanas and Upanishads show us the religion on its priestly, speculative side. Closely related to the law-guides is the justly famed metrical treatise, Manava-Dharma-Sastra, known in English as the Laws of Manu. It belongs probably to the fifth century

B.C. These, together with the two sacred epics of a later age, the "Ramayana," and the "Mahabharata," embrace what is most important in sacred Brahmin literature.

Early Brahminism or Vedism

The religion of the Vedic period proper was comparatively simple. It consisted in the worship of many deities, great and small, the personified forces of nature. Prominent among these were

Varuna, the all-embracing heaven, maker and lord of all things and upholder of the moral law; the sun-god, variously known as Surya, the enemy of darkness and bringer of blessings; as Pushan the nourisher; Mitra, the omniscient friends of the good, and the avenger of deceit; as Savitar the enlightener, arousing men to daily activity, and as Vishnu, said to have measured the earth in three great strides and to have given the rich pastures to mortals; the god of the air, Indra, like Mars, also, the mighty god of war, who set free from the cloud-serpent Ahi (or Vritra), the quickening rain; Rudra, later known as Shiva, the blessed one, the god of the destructive thunderstorm, an object of dread to evil-doers, but a friend to the good; Agni, the fire-god, the friend and benefactor of man, dwelling on their hearths, and bearing to the gods their prayers and sacrificial offerings; Soma, the god of that mysterious plant whose inebriating juice was so dear to the gods and to man, warding off disease, imparting strength and securing immortality.

There were no temples in this early period. On a small mound of earth or of stones the offering was made to the gods, often by the head of the family, but in the more important and complicated sacrifices by the priest, or Brahmin, in union with the householder. The object of every sacrifice was to supply strengthening food to the gods and to secure blessings in return. Human victims, though rare, were not wholly unknown, but animal victims were at this period in daily use. First in importance was the horse, then the ox or cow, the sheep, and the goat. Offerings of clarified butter, rice, wheat, and other kinds of grain were also very common. But dearer to the gods than any of these gifts, and rivaling the horse-sacrifice in solemnity, was the offering of the inebriating juice of the Soma-plant, the so-called Soma-sacrifice. Hymns of praise and petitions, chiefly for the good things of life, children, health, wealth, and success in undertakings, accompanied these sacrificial offerings. But the higher needs of the soul were not forgotten. In hymns of Varuna, Mitra, and the other gods there are striking texts expressing a sense of guilt and asking for forgiveness. At a time when the earlier Hebrew scriptures were silent as to the rewards and punishments awaiting man in the future life, we find the ancient rik-bards giving repeated expression to their belief in a heaven of endless bliss for the just, and in an abyss of darkness for the wicked.

Devotion to the Pitris (Fathers), or dead relatives, was also a prominent element in their religion. Although the Pitris mounted to the heavenly abode of bliss, their happiness was not altogether independent of the acts of devotion shown them by the living. It could be greatly increased by offerings of Soma, rice, and water; for like the gods they were thought to have bodies of air-like texture, and to enjoy the subtile essence of food. Hence, the surviving children felt it a sacred duty to make feast-offerings, called Sraddhas, at stated times to their departed Pitris. In return for these acts of filial piety, the grateful Pitris protected them from harm and promoted their welfare. Lower forms of nature-worship also obtained. The cow was held in reverence. Worship was given to trees and serpents. Formulae abounded for healing the diseased, driving off demons, and averting evil omens. Witchcraft was dreaded, and recourse to ordeals was common for the detection of guilt.

Popular Brahminism

In the period that saw the production of the Brahmanas and the Upanishads, the Vedic religion underwent a twofold change. On the practical side there was an exuberant growth of religious rites and of social restrictions and duties, while on the theoretical side, Vedic belief in the efficacy of personal deities was subordinated to a pantheistic scheme of salvation. Thus the earlier religion developed on the one hand into popular, exoteric Brahminism, and on the other hand into priestly, esoteric Brahminism. The former is reflected in the Brahmanas and the Sutras; the latter in the Upanishads.

The transformation to popular Brahminism was largely due to the influence of the Brahmins, or priests. Owing to their excessive fondness for symbolic words and forms, the details of ritual became more and more intricate, some assuming so elaborate a character as to require the services of sixteen priests. The sacrifice partook of the nature of a sacramental rite, the due performance of which was sure to produce the desired end, and thus became an all-important center around which the visible and invisible world revolved. Hence it merited liberal fees to the officiating priests. Still it was not a mere perfunctory rite, for if performed by an unworthy priest it was accounted as both useless and sacrilegious.

In keeping with this complicated liturgy was the multitude of prayers and rites which entered into the daily life of both priest and layman. The daily recitation of parts of the Vedas, now venerated as divine revelation, was of first importance, especially for the Brahmins. It was a sacred duty for every individual to recite, morning and evening, the Savitri, a short prayer in honour of the vivifying sun. A scrupulous regard for ceremonial purity, surpassing even that of the Jewish Pharisee, gave rise to an endless succession of purifactory rites, such as baths, sprinkling with water, smearing with ashes or cow-dung, sippings of water, suppressions of breath—all sacramental in character and efficacious for the remission of sin. There is reason to believe that the consciousness of guilt for sin committed was keen and vivid, and that in the performance of these rites, so liable to abuse, a penitential disposition of soul was largely cultivated.

In popular Brahminism of this period the idea of retribution for sin was made to embrace the most rigorous and far-reaching consequences, from which, save by timely penance, there was no escape. As every good action was certain of future recompense, so every evil one was destined to bear its fruit of misery in time to come. This was the doctrine of karma (action) with which the new idea of rebirth was closely connected. While the lasting bliss of heaven was still held out to the just, different fates after death were reserved for the wicked, varying, according to the nature and amount of guilt, from long periods of torture in a graded series of hells, to a more or less extensive series of rebirths in the forms of plants, animals, and men. From the grade to which the culprit was condemned, he had to pass by slow transition through the rest of the ascending scale till his rebirth as a man of honourable estate was attained.

This doctrine gave rise to restrictive rules of conduct that bordered on the absurd. Insects, however repulsive and noxious, might not be killed; water might not be drunk till it was first strained, lest minute forms of life be destroyed; carpentry, basket-making, working in leather, and other similar occupations were held in disrepute, because they could not be carried on without a certain loss of animal and plant life. Some zealots went so far as to question the blamelessness of tilling the ground on account of the unavoidable injury done to worms and insects.

But on the other hand, the Brahmin ethical teaching in the legitimate sphere of right conduct is remarkably high. Truthfulness, obedience to parents and superiors, temperance, chastity, and almsgiving were strongly inculcated. Though allowing, like other religions of antiquity, polygamy and divorce, it strongly forbade adultery and all forms of unchastity. It also reprobated suicide, abortion, perjury, slander, drunkenness, gambling, oppressive usury, and wanton cruelty to animals. Its Christianlike aim to soften the hard side of human nature is seen in its many lessons of mildness, charity towards the sick, feeble, and aged, and in its insistence on the duty of forgiving injuries and returning good for evil. Nor did this high standard of right conduct apply simply to external acts. The threefold division of good and bad acts into thought, words, and deeds finds frequent expression in Brahmanic teaching.

Intimately bound up in the religious teaching of Brahminism was the division of society into rigidly defined castes. In the earlier, Vedic period there had been class distinctions according to which the warrior class (Kshatriyas, or Rajanas) stood first in dignity and importance, next the priestly class (Brahmins), then the farmer class (Vaisyas), and last of all, the servile class of conquered natives (Sudras). With the development of Brahminism, these four divisions of society became stereotyped into exclusive castes, the highest place of dignity being usurped by the Brahmins. As teachers of the sacred Vedas, and as priests of the all-important sacrifices, they professed to be the very representatives of the gods and the peerage of the human race. No honour was too great for them, and to lay hands on them was a sacrilege.

One of their chief sources of power and influence lay in their exclusive privilege to teach the youth of the three upper castes, for education then consisted largely in the acquisition of Vedic lore, which only priests could teach. Thus the three upper castes alone had the right to know the Vedas and to take part in the sacrifices, and Brahminism, far from being a religion open to all, was exclusively a privilege of birth, from which the despised caste of Sudras was excluded.

The rite of initiation into Brahminism was conferred on male children only, when they began their studies under a Brahmin teacher, which took place generally in the eighth year of the Brahmin, and in the eleventh and twelfth years for the Kshatriya and the Vaisya respectively. It consisted in the investiture of the sacred cord, a string of white cotton yarn tired together at the ends, and worn like a deacon's stole, suspended on the left shoulder. The investiture was a sort of sacrament in virtue of which the youth was freed from guilt contracted from his parents and became Dvi-ja, twice-born, with the right to learn the sacred Vedic texts and to take part in the sacrifices.

The period of studentship was not long for members of the warrior and farmer castes, but for the young Brahmin, who had to learn all the Vedas by heart, it consumed nine years or more. During this period, the student was subjected to severe moral discipline. He had to rise before the sun, and was not allow to recline until after sunset. He was denied rich and dainty foods, and what he ate at his two daily meals he had to beg. He was expected to observe the strictest chastity. He was bound to avoid music, dancing, gambling, falsehood, disrespect to superiors and to the aged, covetousness, anger, and injury to animals.

Marriage was held to be a religious duty for every twice-born. It was generally entered upon early in life, not long after the completion of the time of studentship. Like the initiation rite, it was a solemn sacramental ceremony. It was an imperative law that the bride and groom should be of the same caste in the principal marriage; for, as polygamy was tolerated, a man might take one or more secondary wives from the lower castes. For certain grave reasons, the household might repudiate his wife and marry another, but a wife on her part had no corresponding right of divorce.

If her husband died, she was expected to remain for the rest of her life in chaste widowhood, if she would be honoured on earth, and happy with him in heaven. The later Hindu practice known as the Suttee, in which the bereaved wife threw herself on the funeral pyre of her husband, seems at this period to have been unknown. All knowledge of the Vedic texts was withheld from woman, but she had the right to participate with her husband in the sacrifices performed for him by some officiating priest. One important sacrifice remained in his own hands—the morning and evening offering of hot milk, butter, and grain to the fire on the hearth, which was sacred to Agni, and was kept always burning.

A strong tendency to asceticism asserted itself in the Brahminism of this period. It found expression in the fasts preceding the great sacrifices, in the severe penances prescribed for various kinds of sin, in the austere life exacted of the student, in the conjugal abstinence to be observed for the first three days following marriage and on certain specified days of the month, but, above all, in the rigorous life of retirement and privation to which not a few devoted their declining years.

An ever increasing number of householders, chiefly Brahmins, when their sons had grown to man's estate, abandoned their homes and spent the rest of their lives as ascetics, living apart from the villages in rude huts, or under the shelter of trees, eating only the simplest kinds of food, which they obtained by begging, and subjecting themselves to extraordinary fasts and mortifications. They were known as Sannyasis, or Yogis, and their severity of life was not so much a penitential life for past offenses as a means of acquiring abundant religious merits and superhuman powers. Coupled with these mortifications was the practice of Yogi (union). They would sit motionless with legs crossed, and, fixing their gaze intently on an object before them, would concentrate their thought on some abstract subject until they lapsed into a trance. In this state they fancied they were united with the deity, and the fruit of these contemplations was the pantheistic view of religion which found expression in the Upanishads, and left a permanent impress on the Brahmin mind.

Pantheistic Brahminism

The marked monotheistic tendency in the later Vedic hymns had made itself more and more keenly felt in the higher Brahmin circles till it gave rise to a new deity, a creation of Brahmin priests. This was Prabjapati, lord of creatures, omnipotent and supreme, later known as Brahma, the personal creator of all things. But in thus looking up to a supreme lord and creator, they were far removed from Christian monotheism.

The gods of the ancient pantheon were not repudiated, but were worshipped still as the various manifestations of Brahma. It was an axiom then, as it has been ever since with the Hindu mind, that creation out of nothing is impossible. Another Brahmin principle is that every form of conscious individuality, whether human or Divine, implies a union of spirit and matter. And so, outside the small school of thinkers who held matter to be eternal, those who stood for the supreme personal god explained the world of visible things and invisible gods as the emanations of Brahma.

They arrived at a personal pantheism. But speculation did not end here. To the prevailing school of dreamy Brahmin ascetics, whose teachings are found in the Upanishads, the ultimate source of all things was not the personal Brahma, but the formless, characterless, unconscious spirit known at Atman (self), or, more commonly Brahma. (Brahma is neuter, whereas

Brahma, personal god, is masculine.) The heavens and the earth, men and gods, even the personal deity, Brahma, were but transitory emanations of Brahma, destined in time to lose their individuality and be absorbed into the great, all-pervading, impersonal spirit. The manifold external world thus had no real existence. It was Maya, illusion. Brahma alone existed. It alone was eternal, imperishable.

This impersonal pantheism of the Brahmin ascetics led to a new conception of the end of man and of the way of salvation. The old way was to escape rebirths and their attendant misery by storing up merits of good deeds so as to obtain an eternal life of conscious bliss in heaven. This was a mistake. For so long as man was ignorant of his identity with Brahma and did not see that his true end consisted in being absorbed into the impersonal all-god from which he sprang; so long as he set his heart on a merely personal existence, no amount of good works would secure his freedom from rebirth.

By virtue of his good deeds he would, indeed, mount to heaven, perhaps win a place among the gods. but after a while his store of merits would give out like oil in a lamp, and he would have to return once more to life to taste in a new birth the bitterness of earthly existence. The only way to escape this misery was through the saving recognition of one's identity with Brahma. As so as one could say from conviction, "I am Brahma," the bonds were broken that held him fast to the illusion of personal immortality and consequently to rebirth. Thus, cultivating, by a mortified life, freedom form all desires, man spent his years in peaceful contemplation till death put an end to the seeming duality and he was absorbed in Brahma like a raindrop in the ocean.

Early Hinduism

The pantheistic scheme of salvation just described, generally known as the Vedanta teaching, found great favour with the Brahmins and has been maintained as orthodox Brahmin doctrine down to the present day. But it made little progress outside the Brahmin caste. The mass of the people had little interest in an impersonal Brahma who was incapable of hearing their prayers, nor had they any relish for a final end which meant the loss forever of conscious existence. And so, while the priestly ascetic was chiefly concerned with meditation on his identity with Brahma, and with the practice of mortification to secure freedom from all desires, the popular mind was still bent on prayer, sacrifices, and other good works in honour of the Vedic deities.

But at the same time, their faith in the efficacy of these traditional gods could not be but weakened by the Brahmin teaching that freedom from rebirth was not to be obtained by acts of worship to personal deities who were powerless to secure even for themselves eternal conscious bliss. The result was popular development of special cults of two of the old gods, now raised to the position of supreme deity, and credited with the power to secure a lasting life of happiness in heaven.

It was in the priestly conception of the supreme personal Brahma that the popular mind found its model for its new deities. Brahma was not a traditional god, and seems never to have been a favourite object of cult with the people. Even today, there are but two temples to Brahma in all India. His subordination to the great impersonal all-god did not help to recommend him to the popular mind. Instead we find two of the traditional gods honoured with special cults, which seem to have taken rise independently in two different parts of the country and, after acquiring a local celebrity, to have spread in rivalry over the whole land.

One of these gods was the ancient storm-god Rudra, destructive in tempest and lightning, renewing life in the showers of rain, sweeping in lonely solitude over mountain and barren waste. As the destroyer, the reproducer, and the type of the lonely ascetic, this deity rapidly rose in popular esteem under the name of Shiva, the blessed.

The other was Vishnu, originally one of the forms of the son-god, a mild beneficent deity, whose genial rays brought gladness and growth to living creatures. His solar origin was lost sight of as he was raised to the position of supreme deity, but one of his symbols, the discus, points to his earlier character.

These two rival cults seem to have arisen in the fourth or fifth century B.C. As in the case of the personal god Brahma, neither the worship of Shiva nor of Vishnu did away with the honouring of the traditional gods and goddesses, spirits, heroes, sacred rivers and mountains and trees, serpents, earth, heaven, sun, moon, and stars. The pantheism in which the Hindu mind is inevitably cast saw in all these things emanations of the supreme deity, Shiva or Vishnu. In worshiping any or all, he was but honouring his supreme god. Each deity was credited with a special heaven, where his devotees would find after death an unending life of conscious happiness.

The rapid rise in popular esteem of these cults, tending more and more to thrust Brahminism proper in to the background, was viewed by the priestly caste with no little concern. To quench these cults was out of the question; and so, in order to hold them in at least nominal allegiance to Brahminism, the supreme god Brahma was associated with Vishnu and Shiva as a triad of equal and more or less interchangeable deities in which Brahma held the office of creator, or rather evolver, Vishnu of preserver, and Shiva of dissolver. This is the so-called Tri-murti (tri-form), or trinity, altogether different from the Christian concept of three eternally distinct persons in one Godhead, and hence offering no legitimate ground for suggesting a Hindu origin for the Christian doctrine.

More remarkable was the intimate association of other new deities—the creations of the religious fancies of the common people—with the gods Shiva and Vishnu. With Shiva two popular gods came to be associated as sons. One was Ganesha, lord of troops and mischievous imps, who has remained ever since a favourite object of worship and is invoked at the beginning of every undertaking to ensure success. The other was Scanda, who seems in great measure to have replaced Indra as the god of battle.

Beyond the doubtful derivation of the name Scanda from Alexander, there is nothing to indicate that either of these reputed sons of Shiva had ever lived the lives of men. Not so the gods that enlarged the sphere of Vishnu's influence. In keeping with Vishnu's position as god of the people, two of the legendary heroes of the remote past, Rama and Krishna, whom popular enthusiasm had raised to the rank of gods, came to be associated with him not as sons, but as his very incarnations. The incarnation of a god descending from heaven to assume a human of animal form as a sort of savior, and to achieve some signal benefit for mankind, is known as an avatar.

The idea antedates Buddhism and, while applied to Shiva and other gods, became above all a characteristic of Vishnu. Popular fancy loved to dwell on his avatar as a fish to save Manu from the devastating flood, as a tortoise to recover from the depths of the sea precious possessions for gods and men, as a boar to raise the submerged earth above the surface of the waters, but most of all as the god-men Rama and Krishna, each of whom delivered the people from the yoke of a tyrant. So popular became the cults of Rama and Krishna that Vishnu himself was largely lost sight of.

In time the Vishnuites became divided into two rival schisms:the Ramaites, who worshipped Rama as supreme deity, and the Krishnaites, who gave this honour rather to Krishna, a division that has persisted down to the present day. The evidence of the early existence of these innovations on Brahmin belief is to be found in the two great epics known as the "Ramayana" and the "Mahabharata." Both are revered by Brahmins, Shivaites and Vishnuites alike, particularly the latter poem, which is held to be directly revealed. In the "Ramayana," which belongs to the period 400-300 B.C., the legendary tales of the trials and the triumphs of the hero Rama and his faithful wife Sita were worked into a highly artificial romanbtic poem, largely in the interests of Vishnu worship.

The "Mahabharata," the work of many hands, was begun about the fifth century B.C. under Brahmin influence, and in the folowing centuries received additions and modifications, in the interests now of Vishnuism now of Shivaism, till it assumed its final shape in the sixth century of the Christian Era. It is a huge conglomeration of stirring adventure, popular legend, myth, and religious speculation. The myth centers chiefly around the many-sided struggle for supremacy between the evil tyrants of the land and the hero Arjuna, aided by his four brothers.

The role that Krishna plays is not an integral part of the story and seems to have been interpolated after the substance of the epic had been written. He is the charioteer of Arjuna and at the same time acts as his religious advisor. Of his numerous religious instructions, the most important is his metrical treatise known as the "Bhagavad-gita," the Song of the Blessed One, a writing that has exercised a profound influence on religious thought in India.

It dates from the second or third century of the Christian era, being a poetic version of a late Upanishad, with its pantheistic doctrine so modified as to pass for a personal revelation of Krishna. While embodying the noblest features of Brahmin ethics, and insisting on the faithful performance of caste-duties, it proclaims Krishna to be the superior personal all-god who, by the bestowal of special grace helps on his votaries to the attainment of eternal bliss.

As an important means to this end, it inculcates the virtue of Bhakti, that is a loving devotion to the deity, analogous to the Christian virtue of charity. Unhappily for the later development of Vishnuism, the Krishna of the "Bhagavad-gita" was not the popular conception. Like most legendary heroes of folk-lore, his character was in keeping with the crude morals of the primitive age that first sounded his praises. The narrative portions of the epic show him to have been sly and unscrupulous, guilty in word and deed of acts which the higher Brahmin conscience would reprove.

But it is in the fuller legendary story of his life as given in the so-called "Hari-vansa," a later supplement to the epic, and also in some of the Puranas of the ninth and tenth centuries of our era, that the character of the popular Krishna appears in its true light. Here we learn that Krishna was one of eight sons of noble birth, whom a Herod-like tyrant was bent on destroying. The infant god was saved from the wicked designs of the king by being secretly substituted for a herdsman's babe. Krishna grew up among the simple country-people, performing prodigies of valor, and engaging in many amorous adventures with the Gopis, the wives and daughters of the herdsmen. Eight of these were his favourites, but one he loved best of all,

Radha. Krishna finally succeeded in killing the king, and brought peace to the kingdom.

Between this deified Hindu Hercules and Our Divine Lord, there is no ground for comparison, one only for contrast. That the idea of incarnate deity should be found in pre-Christian Hindu thought is not so remarkable when we consider that it answers to the yearning of the human heart for union with God. But what is at first sight astonishing is to find in the religious writings subsequent to the "Mahabharata" legendary tales of Krishna that are almost identical with the stories of Christ in the canonical and apocryphal Gospels.

From the birth of Krishna in a stable, and his adoration by shepherds and magi, the leader is led on through a series of events the exact counterparts of those related of Our Divine Lord. Writers hostile to Christianity seized on this chain or resemblances, too close to be mere coincidence, in order to convict the Gospel writers of plagiarism from Hindu originals. But the very opposite resulted. All Indianists of authority are agreed that these Krishna legends are not earlier than the seventh century of the Christian Era, and must have been borrowed from Christian sources.

Later, or Sectarian Hinduism

The steady weakening of Brahmin influence, in consequence of the successive waves of foreign conquest, made it possible for the religious preferences of the huge, heterogeneous population of India to assert themselves more strongly. Both Shivaism and Vishnuism departed more and more strongly from traditional Brahminism, and assumed a decidedly sectarian character towards the older religion and also towards each other. With this weakening of Brahmin influence they absorbed the grosser elements of low-grade popular worship, and became abused by the accretion of immoral rites and groveling superstitions.

While, on the one hand, the practice of asceticism was pushed to its utmost extremes of fanaticism, on the other the doctrine of bhakti was perverted into a system of gross sexual indulgence, for which the amours of Krishna and the Gopis served as the model and sanction. The Brahmin-caste distinctions were broken down, and an equality of all men and women was asserted, at least during the ceremonies of public worship. The Brahmin rites were in great measure replaced by others particular to each cult and held to be all-sufficient for salvation. Everywhere splendid temples arose to Shiva, Vishnu, and his two human avatars; idols and phallic symbols innumerable filled the land; and each rival cult lauded its own special deity as supreme, subordinating all others to it, and looking down with more or less contempt on forms of worship other than its own.

One factor which contributed strongly to the degradation of these sectarian forms of religion was the veneration of the Sakti, or female side, of these deities. Popular theology would not rest until each deity was supplemented with a wife, in whom the active nature of the god was personified. With Brahma was associated an ancient river-goddess, Sarasvati, honoured as the patroness of letters. Vishnu's Sakti was Sri, or Lakshmi, patroness of good fortune. With Shiva the destroyer there was associated the terrible, blood-thirsty, magical goddess Durga, or Kali, formerly delighting in human victims, now appeased with sacrifices of goats and buffaloes. Rama had his consort, Sita, and Krishna his favourite Gopi, Radha. The worship of these Saktis, particularly Shiva's consort Durga-Kali, degenerated into shocking orgies of drunkenness and sexual immorality, which even today are the crying scandal of Hinduism.

Such were the sectarian developments of post-epic times. They found expression in the inferior, quasi-historic Puranas, of the seventh and following centuries, and in the Tantras, which are more modern still, and teach the symbolic magic of Sakti-worship. Neither of these classes of writings is regarded by orthodox Brahmin as canonical.

Of the two hundred million adherents of Hinduism today, only a few hundred thousand can be called orthodox Brahmin worshipers. Shivaism and Vishnuism have overshadowed the older religion like a rank growth of poisonous weeds. In their main outlines, these two great sects have retained the characteristics of the Purana period, but differences of view on minor points have lead to a multiplication of schismatic divisions, especially among Vishnu-worshipers. Both sects, which today are fairly tolerant of each other, have a number of devotional and liturgical practices that are alike in kind, though marked by differences in sectarian belief. Both Shivaite and Vishnuite lay great stress on the frequent recital of the numerous names of their respective supreme gods, and to facilitate this piety, each carries with him, often about his neck, a rosary, varying in material and the number of beads according as it is dedicated to Shiva or Vishnu.

Each sect has an initiation rites, which is conferred upon the young at the age of reason and in which the officiating guru puts a rosary around the neck of the applicant and whispers into his ear the mantra, or sacred motto, the recital of which serves as a profession of faith and is of daily obligation. Another rite common to both is that in which the presiding officer brands on the body of the worshiper with hot metal stamps the sacred symbols of his sect, the trident and the linga of Shiva, or the discus and conch-shell (or lotus) of Vishnu.

But in their highest act of ceremonial worship the two sects differ radically. The Shivaite takes his white stone pebble, the conventional phallic emblem which he always carries with him, and while muttering his mantra, sprinkles it with water and applies to it cooling Bilva leaves. Owing to its simplicity and cheapness, this rite is much in vogue with the ignorant lower classes. The Vishnu rite is less degrading but more childish. It consists of an elaborate and costly worship of the temple image of Vishnu, or more often of Rama, or Krishna. The image is daily awakened, undressed, bathed, decked with rich robes and adorned with necklaces, bracelets, crowns of gold and precious stones, fed with choice kinds of food, honoured with flowers, lights, an incense, and then entertained with vocal and instrumental music, and with dancing by the temple girls of doubtful virtue, consecrated to this service. As Krishna is generally worshipped in the form of a child-image, his diversion consists largely in the swinging of his image, the spinning of tops, and other games dear to the heart of the child.

Shiva, too, has his temples, vying in magnificence with those of Vishnu, but in all these, the holy place is the linga-shrine, and the temple worship consists in the application of water and Bilva leaves to the stone symbol.

The interior walls of these, and of Vishnu temples as well, are covered with shocking representations of sexual passion. and yet, strange to say, these forms of religion, while giving a sanction to the indulgence of the lowest passions, at the same time inspire other devotees to the practice of the severest asceticism. They wander about in lonely silence, naked and filthy, their hair matted from long neglect, their bodies reduced to mere skin and bones by dint of incredible fasts. They will stand motionless for hours under the blazing son, with their emaciated arms uplifted toward heaven. Some go about with face ever turned upwards. Some are known to have kept their fists tightly clenched until their growing nails protruded through the backs of their hands.

Reform Movements

Enlightened Hindus of modern times have made attempts to institute a reform in Hinduism by rejecting all idolatrous and immoral rites, and by setting up a purely monotheistic form of worship. Of these, the earliest and most noted was the so-called Brahma Samaj (Congregation of Brahma), founded in Calcutta in 1828, by the learned Rammohun Roy. He tried to combine a Unitarian form of Christianity with the Brahmin conception of the supreme personal God.

After his death in 1833, differences of view as to the nature of God, the authority of the Vedas, and the obligation of caste-customs caused the society to split up into a number of small congregations. At present there are more than a hundred independent theistic congregations in India. Some, like the Arya Samaj, rest on the sole authority of the Vedas. Others are eclectic, even to the extent of choosing for devotional reading in their public services passages from the Avesta, Koran, and Bible. Few of them are altogether free from the taint of pantheism, and, being more like clubs for intellectual and moral improvement than for ritualistic forms of worship, they make but little progress in the way of conversion. In short, Brahminism cannot succeed in reforming itself.

Its earlier sacred books are steeped in the polytheism out of which it grew, and the pantheistic view of the world, to which it was afterwards committed, has been like a dead weight dragging it hopelessly into the stagnant pool of superstition, pessimism, and immorality. In virtue of its pantheistic attitude, there is no form of religion, high or low, that cannot be tolerated and incorporated into its capacious system.

The indifference of Brahminism to the gross buses of Hinduism is, after all, but a reflex of the indifference of its supreme god. Sin loses most of its hideousness when it can be traced ultimately to the great impersonal Brahma. There is but one form of religion that has any prospect of reforming the religious life of India, and that is the Roman Catholic. For the shadow, pantheistic deity it can set form the One, Eternal, Personal Spirit and creator; for the crude Tri-murti, the sublime Trinity; and for the coarse and degrading avatars of Vishnu, the incarnation of the Son of God. It can replace the idolatrous and immoral Hindu rites with its own imposing liturgy, and substitute the Cross for the abominable linga.

Brahminism, being a natural religion and a privilege of Hindu birth, has never made any concerted attempt at proselytizing in foreign lands. But some years ago steps were taken by a few individuals of England to foist upon English-speaking people a new religious system embodying the pantheistic belief and magical superstition of the Vedanta school of Brahminism.

This new system, known as Theosophy, was to embrace within its fold members of every form of religion, reconciling all differences of creed in the pantheistic view that all deities, high and low, are but transitory emanations of the supreme, incomprehensible Reality, devotion to which was the highest religion. This quasi-cult, which also made pretensions to the exercise of magical powers, soon met the ridicule and obloquy it deserved. It is practically obsolete at the present day.

2

Antiquity of Brahmanism and its Nature

The term religion comes from Latin word consisting of two Latin words, re (back) and ligare (to bind or bring). The absence of religion from the life of a man causes his existence to become like animal existence. All over the world people of all castes, colours, creeds, races and nationality have devised religion in some form or the other to give meaning and purpose to their lives. Hinduism however, is not just a religion.

It is a way of life, a philosophy and a guiding principle. It is the faith primarily followed by the people in the Indian subcontinent. It is also the religion of Nepal, a small Himalayan kingdom bordering India. Of course there are people all over the world who believe in and follow the Hindu religion.

The exact origin of the Hindu religion has been a matter of dispute to date and several theories regarding its origin have been forwarded. However, it is generally believed that the Indus Valley civilisation flourished near the river Indus around 3200 B.C.-1600 B.C. They developed a religion that bore a close relationship to Hinduism. Later, this religion was influenced by the combined religious practices of the southern Dravidians and the Aryan invaders who arrived in the north of India around 1500 BC.

The period from 1500 B.C. to 1400 B.C. goes undocumented. However in the recent times this theory of Aryan invaders is being repeatedly challenged. It is being widely believed that the Indus valley civilization died a natural death. In fact if ever there was a war, it was between people of the same culture and not two different cultures. Edmund Leach a distinguished British anthropologist makes a clear rejection of the Aryan invasion theory and he has termed it a theory born out of European racism

Around 1000 BC, the Vedic scriptures were introduced, providing the first loose framework for the religion. Rig Veda was one of the first Vedas to be written. Hinduism today has a number of holy books, the most important being the four Vedas (divine knowledge), which are the foundation of Hindu philosophy. The Upanishads are contained within the Vedas and delve into the metaphysical nature of the universe and soul. After these are the Great epics Ramayana and Mahabharata. Several texts were also written including the 'Manu smriti' and 'srutis'. It has been through these epics and texts that the essence of Hindu religion unfolds.

The origin of the term Hindu also has historical connotations. The part of the Aryan race that migrated from central Asia, through the mountain passes into India settled first in the districts near the river Sindhu, now called the Indus. The Persians pronounced the word Sindhu as Hindu, and named their Aryan brethren Hindus. Thus Hindu is only a corrupt form of Sindhu. According to Lokmanya Tilak one of the prominent Indian freedom fighters "A Hindu is one who believes that the Vedas contain self-evident and axiomatic truths" The word Hindu is a geographic rather than a religious term. Hindus call their religion Sanatana Dharma - 'Eternal law'.

It is based on the practice of Dharma, the code of life. Since Hinduism has no founder, anyone who practices Dharma can call himself a Hindu. Hinduism lays emphasis on direct Experience rather than on authority. The aim is not intellectual conformity to inherited doctrine, but one of attainment of knowledge. He can question the authority of any scripture, or even the existence of the Divine. Despite being the oldest religion, the truth realized by the seers prove that the Truth and path provided by Hinduism is beyond time. Its concern is with the absolute Truth, not with systems of belief. The absolute

Truth is universal, and forever impersonal. No one has a proprietary claim to it.

There are numerous Gods and Goddesses worshipped by Hindus all over the World. In fact Hinduism perpetrates polytheism. Mark Twain had said, " India has two million gods, and worships them all. In religion all other countries are paupers; India is the only millionaire." However there exist several tenets of this ancient religion that attract people towards it. As Hinduism is a way of life, it offers something for everyone, including the atheist. It has delighted its followers, with its richness, its antiquity and its depth. Hinduism is a religion that is doctrinally less clear cut than say Christianity, politically less determined than Islam. Hinduism is a philosophy that appeals to reason, love, tolerance, harmony, unity and truth. It prompts us to live life to the fullest, to achieve and realize our goals; In fact communalism has never been a feature of Hinduism.

The Rig Veda has declared the Ultimate Reality (God) as:

"Ekam sat vipraha, bahudha vadanti" (Sanskrit)

"Truth is one, the wise call it by various names"

Symbolism in Hinduism is sublime and profound. Each act of Hindu worship reflects some deep spiritual significance. Meditation that has gained immense popularity in the west requires the mind to be fixed on God. If god becomes formless then where does one fix the mind?

Today Hinduism in India to an extent is plagued by fanaticism but still its purity and its true followers uphold relevance. Hinduism has withstood the test of time. Brutal attempts to uproot its existence by the Afghan invaders proved futile as also the subtle attempts by the Christians. Annie Besant leader of Indian freedom movement and member of Indian National Congress said "After a study of some forty years and more of the great religions of the world, I find none so perfect, none so scientific, none so philosophical and no so spiritual that the great religion known by the name of Hinduism. Make no mistake, without Hinduism, India has no future. Hinduism is the soil in to which India's roots are stuck and torn out of that she will inevitably wither as a tree torn out from its place.

Hinduism, a term generally employed to comprehend the social institutions, past and present, of the Hindus who form the great majority of the people of India; as well as the multitudinous crop of their religious beliefs which has grown up, in the course of many centuries, on the foundation of the Brahmanical scriptures. The actual proportion of the total population of India (294 millions) included under the name of "Hindus" has been computed in the census report for 1901 at something like 70% (206 millions); the remaining 30% being made up partly of the followers of foreign creeds, such as Mahommedans, Parsees, Christians and Jews, partly of the votaries of indigenous forms of belief which have at various times separated from the main stock, and developed into independent systems, such as Buddhism, Jainism and Sikhism; and partly of isolated hill and jungle tribes, such as the Santals, Bhils (Bhilla) and Kols, whose crude animistic tendencies have hitherto kept them, either wholly or for the most part, outside the pale of the Brahmanical community.

The name "Hindu" itself is of foreign origin, being derived from the Persians, by whom the river Sindhu was called Hindu, a name subsequently applied to the inhabitants of that frontier district, and gradually extended over the upper and middle reaches of the Gangetic valley, whence this whole tract of country between the Himalaya and the Vindhya mountains, west of Bengal, came to be called by the foreign conquerors "Hindustan," or the abode of the Hindus; whilst the native writers called it "Aryavarta," or the abode of the Aryas.

But whilst, in its more comprehensive acceptation, the term Hinduism would thus range over the entire historical development of Brahmanical India, it is also not infrequently used in a narrower sense, as denoting more especially the modern phase of Indian social and religious institutions - from the earlier centuries of the Christian era down to our own days - as distinguished from the period dominated by the authoritative doctrine of pantheistic belief, formulated by the speculative theologians during the centuries immediately succeeding the

Vedic period (see Brahmanism). In this its more restricted sense the term may thus practically be taken to apply to the later bewildering variety of popular sectarian forms of belief, with its social concomitant, the fully developed caste-system. But, though one may at times find it convenient to speak of "Brahmanism and Hinduism," it must be clearly understood that the distinction implied in the combination of these terms is an extremely vague one, especially from the chronological point of view. The following considerations will probably make this clear.

Connexion with Brahmanism

The characteristic tenet of orthodox Brahmanism consists in the conception of an absolute, all-embracing spirit, the Brahma (neutr.), being the one and only reality, itself unconditioned, and the original cause and ultimate goal of all individual souls (*jiva, i.e.* living things). Coupled with this abstract conception are two other doctrines, *viz.* first, the transmigration of souls (*sainsara*), regarded by Indian thinkers as the necessary complement of a belief in the essential sameness of all the various spiritual units, however contaminated, to a greater or less degree, they may be by their material embodiment; and in their ultimate re-union with the *Paramatman,* or Supreme Self; and second, the assumption of a triple manifestation of the ceaseless working of that Absolute Spirit as a creative, conservative and destructive principle, represented respectively by the divine personalities of Brahma (masc.), Vishnu and Shiva, forming the *Trimurti* or Triad.

As regards this latter, purely exoteric, doctrine, there can be little doubt of its owing its origin to considerations of theological expediency, as being calculated to supply a sufficiently wide formula of belief for general acceptance; and the very fact of this divine triad including the two principal deities of the later sectarian worship, Vishnu and Shiva, goes far to show that these two gods at all events must have been already in those early days favourite objects of popular adoration to an extent sufficient to preclude their being ignored by a diplomatic priesthood bent upon the formulation of a common creed.

Thus, so far from sectarianism being a mere modern development of Brahmanism, it actually goes back to beyond the formulation of the Brahmanical creed. Nay, when, on analysing the functions and attributes of those two divine figures, each of them is found to be but a compound of several previously recognized deitics, sectarian worship may well be traced right up to the Vedic age. That the theory of the triple manifestation of the deity was indeed only a compromise between Brahmanical aspirations and popular worship, probably largely influenced by the traditional sanctity of the number three, is sufficiently clear from the fact that, whilst Brahma, the creator, and at the same time the very embodiment of Brahmanical class pride, has practically remained a mere figurehead in the actual worship of the people, Shiva, on the other hand, so far from being merely the destroyer, is also the unmistakable representative of generative and reproductive power in nature.

In fact, Brahma, having performed his legitimate part in the mundane evolution by his original creation of the universe, has retired into the background, being, as it were, looked upon as *functus officio,* like a venerable figure of a former generation, whence in epic poetry he is commonly styled *pitamaha,* " the grandsire." But despite the artificial character of the *Trimurti,* it has retained to this day at least its theoretical validity in orthodox Hinduism, whilst it has also undoubtedly exercised considerable influence in shaping sectarian belief, in promoting feelings of toleration towards the claims of rival deities; and in a tendency towards identifying divine figures newly sprung into popular favour with one or other of the principal deities, and thus helping to bring into vogue that notion of avatars, or periodical descents or incarnations of the deity, which has become so prominent a feature of the later sectarian belief.

Under more favourable political conditions, the sacerdotal class might perhaps, in course of time, have succeeded in imposing something like an effective common creed on the heterogeneous medley of races and tribes scattered over the peninsula, just as they certainly did succeed in establishing the social prerogative of their own order over the length and breadth of India. They were, however, fated to fall far short of such a consummation; and at all times orthodox Brahmanism has had to wink at, or ignore, all manner of gross superstitions and repulsive practices, along with the popular worship of countless hosts of godlings, demons, spirits and ghosts, and mystic objects and symbols of every description. Indeed, according to a recent account by a close observer of the religious practices prevalent in southern India, fully four-fifths of the people of the Dravidian race, whilst nominally acknowledging the spiritual guidance of the Brahmans, are to this day practically given over to the worship of their nondescript local village deities (*grama-devata*), usually attended by animal sacrifices frequently involving the slaughter, under revolting circumstances, of thousands of victims. Curiously enough these local deities are nearly all of the female, not the male sex.

In the estimation of these people "Shiva and Vishnu may be more dignified beings, but the village deity is regarded as a more present help in trouble, and more intimately concerned with the happiness and prosperity of the villagers. The origin of this form of Hinduism is lost in antiquity, but it is probable that it represents a pre-Aryan religion, more or less modified in various parts of south India by Brahmanical influence. At the same time, many of the deities themselves are of quite recent origin, and it is easy to observe a deity in making even at the present day." 2 It is a significant fact that, whilst in the worship of Shiva and Vishnu, at which no animal sacrifices are offered, the officiating priests are almost invariably Brahmans, this is practically never the case at the popular performance of those "gloomy and weird rites for the propitiation of angry deities, or the driving away of evil spirits, when the pujaris (or ministrants) are drawn from all other castes, even from the Pariahs, the out-caste section of Indian society." As from the point of view of religious belief, so also from that of social organization no clear line of demarcation can be drawn between Brahmanism and Hinduism.

Though it was not till later times that the network of class divisions and subdivisions attained anything like the degree of intricacy which it shows in these latter days, still in its origin the caste-system is undoubtedly coincident with the rise of Brahmanism, and may even be said to be of the very essence of it. The cardinal principle which underlies the system of caste is the preservation of purity of descent, and purity of religious belief and ceremonial usage. Now, that same principle had been operative from the very dawn of the history of Aryanized India.

The social organism of the Aryan tribe did not probably differ essentially from that of most communities at that primitive stage of civilization; whilst the body of the people - the *Vis* (or aggregate of *Vaishyas)—would* be mainly occupied with agricultural and pastoral pursuits, two professional classes - those of the warrior and the priest - had already made good their claim to social distinction. As yet, however, the tribal community would still feel one in race and traditional usage. But 1 "It is, perhaps, by surveying India that we at this day can best represent to ourselves and appreciate the vast external reform worked upon the heathen world by Christianity, as it was organized and executed throughout Europe by the combined authority of the Holy Roman Empire and the Church Apostolic." Sir Alfred C. Lyall, *Asiatic Studies,* i. 2.2 Henry Whitehead, D.D., bishop of Madras, *The Village Deities of Southern India* (Madras, 1907).

The effect of caste is to give all Hindu society a religious basis. "Sir A. C. Lyall, *Brahmanism* when the fair-coloured Aryan immigrants first came in contact with, and drove back or subdued the dark-skinned race that occupied the northern plains - doubtless the ancestors of the modern Dravidian people - the preservation of their racial type and traditionary order of things would naturally become to them a matter of serious concern. In the extreme northwestern districts - the Punjab and Rajputana, judging from the fairly uniform physical features of the present population of these parts - they seem to have been signally successful in their endeavour to preserve their racial purity, probably by being able to clear a sufficiently extensive area of the original occupants for themselves with their wives and children to settle upon. The case was, however, very different in the adjoining valley of the Jumna and Ganges, the sacred *Madhyadesa* or Middle-land of classical India. Here the Aryan immigrants were not allowed to establish themselves without undergoing a considerable admixture of foreign blood.

It must remain uncertain whether it was that the thickly-populated character of the land scarcely admitted of complete occupation, but only of a conquest by an army of fighting men, starting from the Aryanized region - who might, however, subsequently draw women of their own kin after them - or whether, as has been suggested, a second Aryan invasion of India took place at that time through the mountainous tracts of the upper Indus and northern Kashmir, where the nature of the road would render it impracticable for the invading bands to be accompanied by women and children. Be this as it may, the physical appearance of the population of this central region of northern India - Hindustan and Behar - clearly points to an intermixture of the tall, fair-coloured, fine-nosed Aryan with the short-sized, dark-skinned, broad-nosed Dravidian; the latter type becoming more pronounced towards the lower strata of the social order.' Now, it was precisely in this part of India that mainly arose the body of literature which records the gradual rise of the Brahmanical hierarchy and the early development of the castesystem.

The problem that now lay before the successful invaders was how to deal with the indigenous people, probably vastly outnumbering them, without losing their own racial identity. They dealt with them in the way the white race usually deals with the coloured race - they kept them socially apart. The land being appropriated by the conquerors, husbandry, as the most respectable industrial occupation, became the legitimate calling of the Aryan settler, the *Vaishya;* whilst handicrafts, gradually multiplying with advancing civilization and menial service, were assigned to the subject race. The generic name applied to the latter was *Sudra,* originally probably the name of one of the subjected tribes. So far the social development proceeded on lines hardly differing from those with which one is familiar in the history of other nations.

The Indo-Aryans, however, went a step farther. What they did was not only to keep the native race apart from social intercourse with themselves, but to shut them out from all participation in their own higher aims, and especially in their own religious convictions and ceremonial practices. So far from attempting to raise their standard of spiritual life, or even leaving it to ordinary intercourse to gradually bring about a certain community of intellectual culture and religious sentiment, they deliberately set up artificial barriers in order to prevent their own traditional modes of worship from being contaminated with the obnoxious practices of the servile race. The serf, the *Sudra,* was not to worship the gods of the Aryan freemen. The result was the system of four castes (*varna, i.e."* colour "; or *jati,"* gens").

Though the Brahman, who by this time had firmly secured his supremacy over the *kshatriya,* or noble, in matters spiritual as well as in legislative and administrative functions, would naturally be the prime mover in this regulation of the social 4 Thus, in Berar," there is a strong non-Aryan leaven in the dregs of the agricultural class, derived from the primitive races which have gradually melted down into settled life, and thus become fused with the general community, while these same races are still distinct tribes in the wild tracts of hill and jungle." Sir Alfred C. Lyall, *As. St.,* i. 6. order, there seems no reason to believe that the other two upper classes were not equally interested in seeing their hereditary privileges thus perpetuated by divine sanction.

Nothing, indeed, is more remarkable in the whole development of the caste-system than the jealous pride which every caste, from the highest to the lowest, takes in its own peculiar occupation and sphere of life. The distinctive badge of a member of the three upper castes was the sacred triple cord or thread (*sutra) - made* of cotton, hemp or wool, according to the respective caste-with which he was invested at the *upanayana* ceremony, or initiation into the use of the sacred *savitri,* or prayer to the sun (also called *gayatri*), constituting his second birth.

Whilst the Arya was thus a *dvija,* or twice-born, the Sudra remained unregenerate during his lifetime, his consolation being the hope that, on the faithful performance of his duties in this life, he might hereafter be born again into a higher grade of life.

In later times, the strict adherence to caste duties would naturally receive considerable support from the belief in the transmigration of souls, already prevalent before Buddha's time, and from the very general acceptance of the doctrine of *karma* (" deed "), or retribution, according to which a man's present station and manner of life are the result of the sum-total of his actions and thoughts in his former existence; as his actions here will again, by the same automatic process of retribution, determine his status and condition in his next existence.

Though this doctrine is especially insisted upon in Buddhism, and its designation as a specific term (Pali, *Kamma*) may be due to that creed, the notion itself was doubtless already prevalent in pre-Buddhist times. It would even seem to be necessarily and naturally implied in Brahmanical belief in metempsychosis; whilst in the doctrine of Buddha, who admits no soul, the theory of the net result or fruit of a man's actions serving hereafter to form or condition the existence of some new individual who will have no conscious identity with himself, seems of a peculiarly artificial and mystic character.

But, be this as it may," the doctrine of *karma* is certainly one of the firmest beliefs of all classes of Hindus, and the fear that a man shall reap as he has sown is an appreciable element in the average morality... the idea of forgiveness is absolutely wanting; evil done may indeed be outweighed by meritorious deeds so far as to ensure a better existence in the future, but it is not effaced, and must be atoned for "(*Census Report,* i. 364).

In spite, however, of the artificial restrictions placed on the intermarrying of the castes, the mingling of the two races seems to have proceeded at a tolerably rapid rate. Indeed, the paucity of women of the Aryan stock would probably render these mixed unions almost a necessity from the very outset; and the vaunted purity of blood which the caste rules were calculated to perpetuate can scarcely have remained of more than a relative degree even in the case of the Brahman caste.

Certain it is that mixed castes are found referred to at a comparatively early period; and at the time of Buddha - some five or six centuries before the Christian era - the social organization would seem to have presented an appearance not so very unlike that of modern times. It must be confessed, however, that our information regarding the development of the caste-system is far from complete, especially in its earlier stages.

Thus, we are almost entirely left to conjecture on the important point as to the original social organization of the subject race. Though doubtless divided into different tribes scattered over an extensive tract of land, the subjected aborigines were slumped together under the designation of Sudras, whose duty it was to serve the upper classes in all the various departments of manual labour, save those of a downright sordid and degrading character which it was left to *vratyas* or outcasts to perform. How, then, was the distribution of crafts and habitual occupations of all kinds brought about?

Was the process one of spontaneous growth adapting an already existing social organization to a new order of things; or was it originated and perpetuated by regulation from above? Or was it rather that the status and duties of existing offices and trades came to be determined and made hereditary by some such artificial system as that by which the Theodosian Code succeeded for a time in organizing the Roman society in the 5th century of our era ?" It is well known "(says Professor Dill)" that the tendency of the later Empire was to stereotype society, by compelling men to follow the occupation of their fathers, and preventing a free circulation among different callings and grades of life.

The man who brought the grain from Africa to the public stores at Ostia, the baker who made it into loaves for distribution, the butchers who brought pigs from Samnium, Lucania or Bruttium, the purveyors of wine and oil, the men who fed the furnaces of the public baths, were bound to their callings from one generation to another. It was the principle of rural serfdom applied to social functions. Every avenue of escape was closed. A man was bound to his calling not only by his father's but also by his mother's condition. Men were not permitted to marry out of their gild. If the daughter of one of the baker caste married a man not belonging to it, her husband was bound to her father's calling. Not even a dispensation obtained by some means from the imperial chancery, not even the power of the Church could avail to break the chain of servitude."

It can hardly be gainsaid that these artificial arrangements bear a very striking analogy to those of the Indian caste-system; and if these class restrictions were comparatively short-lived on Italian ground, it was not perhaps so much that so strange a plant found there an ethnic soil less congenial to its permanent growth, but because it was not allowed sufficient time to become firmly rooted; for already great political events were impending which within a few decades were to lay the mighty empire in ruins. In° India, on the other hand, the institution of caste - even if artificially contrived and imposed by the Indo-Aryan priest and ruler - had at least ample time allowed it to become firmly established in the social habits, and even in the affections, of the people.

At the same time, one could more easily understand how such a system could have found general acceptance all over the Dravidian region of southern India, with its merest sprinkling of Aryan blood, if it were possible to assume that class arrangements of a similar kind must have already been prevalent amongst the aboriginal tribes prior to the advent of the Aryan. Whether a more intimate acquaintance with the manners and customs of those rude tribes that have hitherto kept themselves comparatively free from Hindu influences may yet throw some light on this question, remains to be seen.

But, by this as it may, the institution of caste, when once established, certainly appears to have gone on steadily developing; and not even the long period of Buddhist ascendancy, with its uncompromising resistance to the Brahman's claim to being the sole arbiter in matters of faith, seems to have had any very appreciable retardant effect upon the progress of the movement. It was not only by the formation of ever new endogamous castes and sub-castes that the system gained in extent and intricacy, but even more so by the constant subdivision of the castes into numerous exogamous groups or sects, themselves often involving gradations of social status important enough to seriously affect the possibility of intermarriage, already hampered by various other restrictions.

Thus a man wishing to marry his son or daughter had to look for a suitable match outside his sect, but within his caste. But whilst for his son he might choose a wife from a lower sept than his own, for his daughter, on the other hand, the law of hypergamy compelled him, if at all possible, to find a husband in a higher sept. This would naturally lead to an excess of women over men in the higher septs, and would render it difficult for a man to get his daughter respectably married without paying a high price for a suitable bridegroom and incurring other heavy marriage expenses.

It can hardly be doubted that this custom has been largely responsible for the crime of female infanticide, formerly so prevalent in India; as it also probably is to some extent for infant marriages, still too common in some parts of India, especially Bengal; and even for the all but universal repugnance to the re-marriage of widows, even when these had been married in early childhood and had never joined their husbands. Yet violations of these rules are jealously watched by the other members of the sept, and are liable - in accordance with the general custom in which communal matters are regulated in India - to be brought before a special council (*panchayat*), originally consisting of five (*pancha*), but now no longer limited to that number, since it is chiefly the greater or less strictness in the observance of caste rules and the orthodox ceremonial generally that determine the status of the sept in the social scale of the caste. Whilst community of occupation was an important factor in the original formation of non-tribal castes, the practical exigencies of life have led to considerable laxity in this respect - not least so in the case of Brahmans who have often had to take to callings which would seem altogether incompatible with the proper spiritual functions of their caste.

Thus," the prejudice against eating cooked food that has been touched by a man of an inferior caste is so strong that, although the Shastras do not prohibit the eating of food cooked by a Kshatriya or Vaishya, yet the Brahmans, in most parts of the country, would not eat such food. For these reasons, every Hindu household - whether Brahman, Kshatriya or Sudra - that can afford to keep a paid cook generally entertains the services of a Brahman for the performance of its *cuisine - the* result being that in the larger towns the very name of Brahman has suffered a strange degradation of late, so as to mean only a cook "(Jogendra Nath Bhattacharya, *Hindu Castes and Sects).* In this caste, however, as in all others, there are certain kinds of occupation to which a member could not turn for a livelihood without incurring serious defilement. In fact, adherence to the traditional ceremonial and respectability of occupation go very much hand-in-hand.

Thus, amongst agricultural castes, those engaged in vegetable-growing or market-gardening are inferior to the genuine peasant or yeoman, such as the Jat and Rajput; whilst of these the Jat who practises widow-marriage ranks below the Rajput who prides himself on his tradition of ceremonial orthodoxy - though racially there seems little, if any, difference between the two; and the Rajput, again, is looked down upon by the Babhan of Behar because he does not, like himself, scruple to handle the plough, instead of invariably employing low-caste men for this manual labour. So also when members of the Baidya, or physician, caste of Bengal, ranging next to that of the Brahman, farm land on tenure," they will on no account hold the plough, or engage in any form of manual labour, and thus necessarily carry on their cultivation by means of hired servants "(H. *H.* Risley, *Census Report).*

The scale of social precedence as recognized by native public opinion is concisely reviewed (ib.) as revealing itself" in the facts that particular castes are supposed to be modern representatives of one or other of the original castes of the theoretical Hindu system; that Brahmans will take water from certain castes; that Brahmans of high standing will serve particular castes; that certain castes, though not served by the best Brahmans, have nevertheless got Brahmans of their own whose rank varies according to circumstances; that certain castes are not served by Brahmans at all but have priests of their own; that the status of certain castes has been raised by their taking to infant-marriage or abandoning the remarriage of widows; that the status of others has been modified by their pursuing some occupations in a special or peculiar way; that some can claim the services of the village barber, the village palanquin-bearer, the village midwife, &c., while others cannot; that some castes may not enter the courtyards of certain temples; that some castes are subject to special taboos, such as that they must not use the village well, or may draw water only with their own vessels, that they must live outside the village or in a separate quarter, that they must leave the road on the approach of a highcaste man and must call out to give warning of their approach."

The first point to observe is the predominance throughout India of the influence of the traditional system of four original castes. In every scheme of grouping the Brahman heads the list. Then come the castes whom popular opinion accepts as the modern representatives of the Kshatriyas; and these are followed by the mercantile groups supposed to be akin to the Vaishyas. When we leave the higher circles of the twice-born, the difficulty of finding a uniform basis of classification becomes apparent. The ancient designation Sudra finds no great favour in modern times, and we can point to no group that is generally recognized as representing it.

The term is used in Bombay, Madras and Bengal to denote a considerable number of castes of moderate respectability, the higher of whom are considered 'clean' Sudras, while the precise status of the lower is a question which lends itself to endless controversy. "In northern and northwestern India, on the other hand," the grade next below the twice-born rank is occupied by a number of castes from whose hands Brahmans and members of the higher castes will take water and certain kinds of sweetmeats. Below these again is rather an indeterminate group from whom water is taken by some of the higher castes, not by others.

Further down, where the test of water no longer applies, the status of the caste depends on the nature of its occupation and its habits in respect of diet. There are castes whose touch defiles the twice-born, but who do not commit the crowning enormity of eating beef. In western and southern India the idea that the social state of a caste depends on whether Brahmans will take water and sweetmeats from its members is unknown, for the higher castes will as a rule take water only from persons of their own caste and sub-caste. In Madras especially the idea of ceremonial pollution by the proximity of an unclean caste has been developed with much elaboration.

Thus the table of social precedence attached to the Cochin report shows that while a Nayar can pollute a man of a higher caste only by touching him, people of the Kammalan group, including masons, blacksmiths, carpenters and workers in leather, pollute at a distance of 24 ft., toddy-drawers at 36 ft., Pulayan or Cheruman cultivators at 48 ft., while in the case of the Paraiyan (Pariahs) who eat beef the range of pollution is no less than 64 ft. "In this bewildering maze of social grades and class distinctions, the Brahman, as will have been seen, continues to hold the dominant position, being respected and even worshipped by all the others."

The more orthodox Sudras carry their veneration for the priestly class to such a degree that they will not cross the shadow of a Brahman, and it is not unusual for them to be under a vow not to eat any food in the morning, before drinking *Bipracharanamrita, i.e.* water in which the toe of a Brahman has been dipped. On the other hand, the pride of the Brahmans is such that they do not bow to even the images of the gods worshipped in a Sudra's house by Brahman priests "(Jog. Nath Bh.). There are, however, not a few classes of Brahmans who, for various reasons, have become degraded from their high station, and formed separate castes with whom respectable Brahmans refuse to intermarry and consort. Chief amongst these are the Brahmans who minister for" unclean "Sudras and lower castes, including the makers and dealers in spirituous liquors; as well as those who officiate at the great public shrines or places of pilgrimage where they might be liable to accept forbidden gifts, and, as a matter of fact, often amass considerable wealth; and those who officiate as paid priests at cremations and funeral rites, when the wearing apparel and bedding of the deceased are not unfrequently claimed by them as their perquisites. As regards the other two" twice-born "castes, several modern groups do indeed claim to be their direct descendants, and in vindication of their title make it a point to perform the *upanayana* ceremony and to wear the sacred thread.

But though the Brahmans, too, will often acquiesce in the reasonableness of such claims, it is probably only as a matter of policy that they do so, whilst in reality they regard the other two higher castes as having long since disappeared and been merged by miscegenation in the Sudra mass. Hence, in the later classical Sanskrit literature, the term *dvija,* or twice-born, is used simply as a synonym for a Brahman. As regards the numerous groups included under the term of Sudras, the distinction between" clean "and" unclean "Sudras is of especial importance for the upper classes, inasmuch as only the former - of whom nine distinct castes are usually recognized - are as a rule considered fit for employment in household service.

The picture thus presented by Hindu society - as made up of a confused congeries of social groups of the most varied standing, each held together and kept separate from others by a traditional body of ceremonial rules and by the notion of social gradations being due to a divinely instituted order of things - finds something like a counterpart in the religious life of the people. As in the social sphere, so also in the sphere of religious belief, we find the whole scale of types represented from the lowest to the highest; and here as there, we meet with the same failure of welding the confused mass into a well-ordered whole. In their theory of a triple manifestation of an impersonal deity, the Brahmanical theologians, as we have seen, had indeed elaborated a doctrine which might have seemed to form a reasonable, authoritative creed for *logy* a community already strongly imbued with pantheistic notions; yet, at best, that creed could only appeal to the sympathies of a comparatively limited portion of the people.

Indeed, the sacerdotal class themselves had made its universal acceptance an impossibility, seeing that their laws, by which the relations of the classes were to be regulated, aimed at permanently excluding the entire body of aboriginal tribes from the religious life of their Aryan masters. They were to be left for all time coming to their own traditional idolatrous notions and practices. However, the two races could not, in the nature of things, be permanently kept separate from each other. Indeed, even prior to the definite establishment of the caste-system, the mingling of the lower race with the upper classes, especially with the aristocratic landowners and still more so with the yeomanry, had probably been going on to such an extent as to have resulted in two fairly well-defined intermediate types of colour between the priestly order and the servile race and to have facilitated the ultimate division into four" colours "(*varna*).

In course of time the process of intermingling, as we have seen, assumed such proportions that the priestly class, in their pride of blood, felt naturally tempted to recognize, as of old, only two" colours, "the Aryan Brahman and the non-Aryan Sudra. Under these conditions the religious practices of the lower race could hardly have failed in the long run to tell seriously upon the spiritual life of the lay body of the Brahmanical community. To what extent this may have been the case, our limited knowledge of the early phases of the sectarian worship of the people does not enable us to determine.

But, on the other hand, the same process of racial intermixture also tended to gradually draw the lower race more or less under the influence of the Brahmanical forms of worship, and thus contributed towards the shaping of the religious system of modern Hinduism. The grossly idolatrous practices, however, still so largely prevalent in the Dravidian South, show how superficial, after all, that influence has been in those parts of India where the admixture of Aryan blood has been so slight as to have practically had no effect on the racial characteristics of the people.

These present-day practices, and the attitude of the Brahman towards them, help at all events to explain the aversion with which the strange rites of the subjected tribes were looked upon by the worshippers of the Vedic pantheon. At the same time, in judging the apparently inhuman way in which the Sudras were treated in the caste rules, one has always to bear in mind the fact that the belief in metempsychosis was already universal at the time, and seemed to afford the only rational explanation of the apparent injustice involved in the unequal distribution of the good things in this world; and that, if the Sudra was strictly excluded from the religious rites and beliefs of the superior classes, this exclusion in no way involved the question of his ultimate emancipation and his union with the Infinite Spirit, which were as certain in his case as in that of any other sentient being. What it did make impossible for him was to attain that union immediately on the cessation of his present life, as he would first have to pass through higher and purer stages of mundane existence before reaching that goal; but in this respect he only shared the lot of all but a very few of the saintliest in the higher spheres of life, since the ordinary twice-born would be liable to sink, after his present life, to grades yet lower than that of the Sudra.

To what extent the changes, which the religious belief of the Aryan classes underwent in post-Vedic times, may have been due to aboriginal influences is a question not easily answered, though the later creeds offer only too many features in which one might feel inclined to suspect influences of that kind. The literary documents, both in Sanskrit and Pali, dating from about the time of Buddha onwards - particularly the two epic poems, the *Mahabharata* and *Ramayana - still* show us in the main the *personnel* of the old pantheon; but the character of the gods has changed; they have become anthropomorphized and almost purely mythological figures. A number of the chief gods, sometimes four, but generally eight of them, now appear as *lokapalas* or world-guardians, having definite quarters or intermediate quarters of the compass assigned to them as their special domains.

One of them, Kubera, the god of wealth, is a new figure; whilst another, Varuna, the most spiritual and ethical of Vedic deities - the king of the gods and the universe; the nightly, star-spangled firmament - has become the Indian Neptune, the god of waters. Indra, their chief, is virtually a kind of superior raja, residing in *svarga,* and as such is on visiting terms with earthly kings, driving about in mid-air with his charioteer Matali. As might happen to any earth-lord, Indra is actually defeated in battle by the son of the demon-king of Lanka (Ceylon), and kept there a prisoner till ransomed by Brahma and the gods conferring immortality on his conqueror. A quaint figure in the pantheon of the heroic age is Hanuman, the deified chief of monkeys - probably meant to represent the aboriginal tribes of southern India - whose wonderful exploits as Rama's ally on the expedition to Lanka Indian audiences will never weary of hearing recounted.

The Gandharvas figure already in the Veda, either as a single divinity, or as a class of genii, conceived of as the bodyguard of Soma and as connected with the moon. In the later Vedic times they are represented as being fond of and dangerous to, women; the Apsaras, apparently originally water-nymphs, being closely associated with them. In the heroic age the Gandharvas have become the heavenly minstrels plying their art at Indra's court, with the Apsaras as their wives or mistresses. These fair damsels play, however, yet another part, and one far from complimentary to the dignity of the gods. In the epics considerable merit is attached to a life of seclusion and ascetic practices by means of which man is considered capable of acquiring supernatural powers equal or even superior to those of the gods - a notion perhaps not unnaturally springing from the pantheistic conception.

Now, in cases of danger being threatened to their own ascendancy by such practices, the gods as a rule proceed to employ the usually successful expedient of despatching some lovely nymph to lure the saintly men back to worldly pleasures. Seeing that the epic poems, as repeated by professional reciters, either in their original Sanskrit text, or in their vernacular versions, as well as dramatic compositions based on them, form to this day the chief source of intellectual enjoyment for most Hindus, the legendary matter contained in these heroic poems, however marvellous and incredible it may appear, still enters largely into the religious convictions of the people." These popular recitals from the Ramayana are done into Gujarati in easy, flowing narrative verse... by Premanand, the sweetest of our bards. They are read out by an intelligent Brahman to a mixed audience of all classes and both sexes. It has a perceptible influence on the Hindu character. I believe the remarkable freedom from infidelity which is to be seen in most Hindu families, in spite of their strange gregarious habits, can be traced to that influence; and little wonder "(B. M. Malabari, *Gujarat and the Gujaratis).* Hence also the universal reverence paid to serpents (*raga*) since those early days; though whether it simply arose from the superstitious dread inspired by the insidious reptile so fatal to man in India, or whether the verbal coincidence with the name of the once-powerful non-Aryan tribe of Nagas had something to do with it must remain doubtful. Indian myth represents them as a race of demons sprung from Kadru, the wife of the sage Kasyapa, with a jewel in their heads which gives them their sparkling look; and inhabiting one of the seven beautiful worlds below the earth (and above the hells), where they are ruled over by three chiefs or kings, Sesha, Vasuki and Takshaka; their fair daughters often entering into matrimonial alliances with men, like the mermaids of western legend.

In addition to such essentially mythological conceptions, we meet in the religious life of this period with an element of more serious aspect in the two gods, on one or other of whom the religious fervour of the large majority of Hindus has ever since concentrated itself, *viz.* Vishnu and Shiva. Both these divine figures have grown out of Vedic conceptions - the genial Vishnu mainly out of a not very prominent solar deity of the same name; whilst the stern Shiva, *i.e.* the kind or gracious one - doubtless a euphemistic name-has his prototype in the old fierce storm-god Rudra, the" Roarer, "with certain additional features derived from other deities, especially Pushan, the guardian of flocks and bestower of prosperity, worked up therewith.

The exact process of the evolution of the two deities and their advance in popular favour are still somewhat obscure. In the epic poems which may be assumed to have taken their final shape in the early centuries before and after the Christian era, their popular character, so strikingly illustrated by their inclusion in the Brahmanical triad, appears in full force; whilst their cult is likewise attested by the coins and inscriptions of the early centuries of our era. The coordination of the two gods in the Trimurti does not by any means exclude a certain rivalry between them; but, on the contrary, a supreme position as the true embodiment of the Divine Spirit is claimed for each of them by their respective votaries, without, however, an honourable, if subordinate, place being refused to the rival deity, wherever the latter, as is not infrequently the case, is not actually represented as merely another form of the favoured god. Whilst at times a truly monotheistic fervour manifests itself in the adoration of these two gods, the polytheistic instincts of the people did not fail to extend the pantheon by groups of new deities in connexion with them.

Two of such new gods actually pass as the sons of Shiva and his consort Parvati, *viz.* Skandalso called Kumara (the youth), Karttikeya, or Subrahmanya (in the south)-the six-headed war-lord of the gods; and Ganese, the lord (or leader) of Shiva's troupes of attendants, being at the same time the elephant-headed, paunch-bellied god of wisdom; whilst a third, Kama (Kamadeva) or Kandarpa, the god of love, gets his popular epithet of Ananga," the bodiless, "from his having once, in frolicsome play, tried the power of his arrows upon Shiva, whilst engaged in austere practices, when a single glance from the third (forehead) eye of the angry god reduced the mischievous urchin to ashes. For his chief attendant, the great god (Mahadeva, Mahesvara) has already with him the" holy "Nandi-presumably, though his shape is not specified, identical in form as in name with Shiva's sacred bull of later times, the appropriate symbol of the god's reproductive power. But, in this repect, we also meet in the epics with the first clear evidence of what in after time became the prominent feature of the worship of Shiva and his consort all over India, *viz.* the feature represented by the *linga,* or phallic symbol.

As regards Vishnu, the epic poems, including the supplement to the Mahabharata, the Harivamsa, supply practically the entire framework of legendary matter on which the later Vaishnava creeds are based. The theory of Avataras which makes the deity - also variously called Narayana, Purushottama, or Vasudeva - periodically assume some material form in order to rescue the world from some great calamity, is fully developed; the ten universally recognized" descents "being enumerated in the larger poem. Though Shiva, too, assumes various forms, the incarnation theory is peculiarly characteristic of Vaishnavism; and the fact that the principal hero of the Ramayana (Rama), and one of the prominent warriors of the Mahabharata (Krishna) become in this way identified with the supreme god, and remain to this day the chief objects of the adoration of Vaishnava sectaries, naturally imparts to these creeds a human interest and sympathetic aspect which is wholly wanting in the worship of Shiva. It is, however, unfortunately but too true that in some of these creeds the devotional ardour has developed features of a highly objectionable character.

Even granting the reasonableness of the triple manifestation of the Divine Spirit, how is one to reconcile all these idolatrous practices, this worship of countless gods and godlings, demons and spirits indwelling in every imaginable object round about us, with the pantheistic doctrine of the *Ekam Advitiyam,"* the One without a Second "? The Indian theosophist would doubtless have little difficulty in answering that question. For him there is only the One Absolute Being, the one reality that is all in all; whilst all the phenomenal existences and occurrences that crowd upon our senses are nothing more than an illusion of the individual soul estranged for a time from its divine source - an illusion only to be dispelled in the end by the soul's fuller knowledge of its own true nature and its being one with the eternal fountain of blissful being.

But to the man of ordinary understanding, unused to the rarefied atmosphere of abstract thought, this conception of a transcendental, impersonal Spirit and the unreality of the phenomenal world can have no meaning: what he requires is a deity that stands in intimate relation to things material and to all that affects man's life. Hence the exoteric theory of manifestations of the Supreme Spirit; and that not only the manifestations implied in the triad of gods representing the cardinal processes of mundane existence - creation, preservation, and destruction or regeneration - but even such as would tend to supply a rational explanation for superstitious imaginings of every kind. For" the Indian philosophy does not ignore or hold aloof from the religion of the masses: it underlies, supports and interprets their polytheism. This may be accounted the keystone of the fabric of Brahmanism, which accepts and even encourages the rudest forms of idolatry, explaining everything by giving it a higher meaning. It treats all the worships as outward, visible signs of some spiritual truth, and is ready to show how each particular image or rite is the symbol of some aspect of universal divinity. The Hindus, like the pagans of antiquity, adore natural objects and forces - a mountain, a river or an animal.

The Brahman holds all nature to be the vesture or cloak of indwelling, divine energy, which inspires everything that produces awe or passes man's understanding "(Sir Alfred C. Lyall, *Brahminism).* During the early centuries of our era, whilst Buddhism, where countenanced by the political rulers, was still holding its own by the side of Brahmanism, sectarian belief in the Hindu gods seems to have made steady progress. The caste system, always calculated to favour unity of religious practice within its social groups, must naturally have contributed to the advance of sectarianism. Even greater was the support it received later on from the Puranas, a class of poetical works of a partly legendary, partly discursive and controversial character, mainly composed in the interest of special deities, of which eighteen principal (*maha-purana*) and as many secondary ones (*upa-purana*) are recognized, the oldest of which may go back to about the 4th century of our era.

It was probably also during this period that the female element was first definitely admitted to a prominent place amongst the divine objects of sectarian worship, in the shape of the wives of the principal gods viewed as their *shakti,* or female energy, theoretically identified with the *Maya,* or cosmic Illusion, of the idealistic Vedanta, and the *Prakriti,* or plastic matter, of the materialistic Sankhya philosophy, as the primary source of mundane things. The connubial relations of the deities may thus be considered" to typify the mystical union of the two eternal principles, spirit and matter, for the production and reproduction of the universe. "But whilst this privilege of divine worship was claimed for the consorts of all the gods, it is principally to Shiva's consort, in one or other of her numerous forms, that adoration on an extensive scale came to be offered by a special sect of votaries, the *Saktas.* In the midst of these conflicting tendencies, an attempt was made, about the latter part of the 8th century, by the distinguished Malabar theologian and philosopher Shankara Acharya to restore the Brahmanical creed to ?' something like its pristine purity, and thus once more to bring about a uniform system of orthodox Hindu belief. Though himself, like most Brahmans, apparently by predilection a follower of Shiva, his aim was the revival of the doctrine of the Brahma as the one self-existent Being and the sole cause of the universe; coupled with the recognition of the practical worship of the orthodox pantheon, especially the gods of the Trimurti, as manifestations of the supreme deity.

The practical result of his labours was the foundation of a new sect, the *Smartas, i.e.* adherents of the *smriti* or tradition, which has a numerous following amongst southern Brahmans, and, whilst professing Shankara's doctrines, is usually classed as one of the Shaiva sects, its members adopting the horizontal sectarial mark peculiar to Shaivas, consisting in their case of a triple line, the *tripundra,* prepared from the ashes of burnt cow-dung and painted on the forehead. Shankara also founded four Maths, or convents, for Brahmans; the chief one being that of Sringeri in Mysore, the spiritual head (*Guru*) of which wields considerable power, even that of excommunication, over the Shaivas of southern India. In northern India, the professed followers of Shankara are mainly limited to certain classes of mendicants and ascetics, although the tenets of this great Vedanta teacher may be said virtually to constitute the creed of intelligent Brahmans generally.

Whilst Shankara's chief title to fame rests on his philosophical works, as the upholder of the strict monistic theory of Vedanta, he doubtless played an important part in the partial remodelling of the Hindu system of belief at a time when Buddhism was rapidly losing ground in India. Not that there is any evidence of Buddhists ever having been actually persecuted by the Brahmans, or still less of Shankara himself ever having done so; but the traditional belief in some personal god, as the principal representative of an invisible, all-pervading deity, would doubtless appeal more directly to the minds and hearts of the people than the colourless ethical system promulgated by the Sakya saint. Nor do Buddhist places of worship appear as a rule to have been destroyed by Hindu sectaries, but they seem rather to have been taken over by them for their own religious uses; at any rate there are to this day not a few Hindu shrines, especially in Bengal, dedicated to Dharmaraj," the prince of righteousness, "as the Buddha is commonly styled.

That the tenets and practices of so characteristic a faith as Buddhism, so long prevalent in India, cannot but have left their marks on Hindu life and belief may readily be assumed, though it is not so easy to lay one's finger on the precise features that might seem to betray such an influence. If the general tenderness towards animals, based on the principle of *ahimsa,* or inflicting no injury on sentient beings, be due to Buddhist teaching, that influence must have made itself felt at a comparatively early period, seeing that sentiments of a similar nature are repeatedly urged in the Code of Manu. Thus, in v. 46-48," He who does not willingly cause the pain of confinement and death to living beings, but desires the good of all, obtains endless bliss. He who injures no creature obtains without effort what he thinks of, what he strives for, and what he fixes his mind on.

Flesh-meat cannot be procured without injury to animals, and the slaughter of animals is not conducive to heavenly bliss: from flesh-meat, therefore, let man abstain. "Moreover, in view of the fact that Jainism, which originated about the same time as Buddhism, inculcates the same principle, even to an extravagant degree, it seems by no means improbable that the spirit of kindliness towards living beings generally was already widely diffused among the people when these new doctrines were promulgated. To the same tendency doubtless is due the gradual decline and ultimate discontinuance of animal sacrifices by all sects except the extreme branch of Shakti-worshippers.

In this respect, the veneration shown to serpents and monkeys has, however, to be viewed in a somewhat different light, as having a mythical background; whilst quite a special significance attaches to the sacred character assigned to the cow by all classes of Hindus, even those who are not prepared to admit the claim of the Brahman to the exalted position of the earthly god usually conceded to him.

In the Veda no tendency shows itself as yet towards rendering divine honour to the cow; and though the importance assigned her in an agricultural community is easily understood, still the exact process of her deification and her identification with the mother earth in the time of Manu and the epics requires further elucidation. An idealized type of the useful quadruped - likewise often identified with the earth - presents itself in the mythical Cow of Plenty, or" wish-cow "(Kamadhenu, or Kamadugha, *i.e.* wish-milker), already appearing in the Atharvaveda, and in epic times assigned to Indra, or identified with Surabhi," the fragrant, "the sacred cow of the sage Vashistha. Possibly the growth of the legend of Krishna - his being reared at Gokula (cow-station); his tender relations to the *gopis,* or cowherdesses, of Vrindavana; his epithets *Gopala,"* the cowherd, "and *Govinda,"* cow-finder, "actually explained as" recoverer of the earth "in the great epic, and the *go-loka,* or" cow-world, "assigned to him as his heavenly abode - may have some connexion with the sacred character ascribed to the cow from early times.

Since the time of Shankara, or for more than a thousand years, the gods Vishnu and Shiva, or *Hari* and *Hara* as they are also commonly called - with their wives, especially that of the latter god - have shared between them the practical worship of the vast majority of Hindus. But, though the people have thus been divided between two different religious camps, sectarian animosity has upon the whole kept within reasonable limits. In fact, the respectable Hindu, whilst owning special allegiance to one of the two gods as his *ishta devata* (favourite deity), will not withhold his tribute of adoration from the other gods of the pantheon. The high-caste Brahman will probably keep at his home asalagram stone, the favourite symbol of

Vishnu, as well as the characteristic emblems of Shiva and his consort, to both of which he will do reverence in the morning; and when he visits some holy place of pilgrimage, he will not fail to pay his homage at both the Shaiva and the Vaishnava shrines there.

Indeed," sectarian bigotry and exclusiveness are to be found chiefly among the professional leaders of the modern brotherhoods and their low-caste followers, who are taught to believe that theirs are the only true gods, and that the rest do not deserve any reverence whatever "(Jog. Nath). The same spirit of toleration shows itself in the celebration of the numerous religious festivals. Whilst some of these - *e.g.* the *Sankranti* (called *Pongal, i.e.* "boiled rice," in the south), which marks the entrance of the sun into the sign of Capricorn and the beginning of its northward course (*uttarayana*) on the 1st day of the month Magha (*c.* Jan. 12); the *Ganesha-chaturthi,* or 4th day of the light fortnight of Bhadra (August - September), considered the birthday of Ganesha, the god of wisdom; and the *Holi,* the Indian Saturnalia in the month of Phalguna (February to March) - have nothing of a sectarian tendency about them; others again, which are of a distinctly sectarian character - such as the *Krishna janmashtami,* the birthday of Krishna on the 8th day of the dark half of Bhadra, or (in the south) of Sravana (July-August), the *Durgapuja* and the *Dipavali,* or lamp feast, celebrating Krishna's victory over the demon Narakasura, on the last two days of Asvina (September-October) - are likewise observed and heartily joined in by the whole community irrespective of sect. Widely different, however, as is the character of the two leading gods are also the modes of worship practised by their votaries.

Shiva has at all times been the favourite god of the Brahmans, and his worship is accordingly more widely extended than that of his rival, especially in southern India. Indeed there is hardly a village in India which cannot boast of a shrine dedicated to Shiva, and containing the emblem of his reproductive power; for almost the only form in which the" Great God "is adored is the *Linga,* consisting usually of an upright cylindrical block of marble or other stone, mostly resting on a circular perforated slab. The mystic nature of these emblems seems, however, to be but little understood by the common people; and, as H. H. Wilson remarks," notwithstanding the acknowledged purport of this worship, it is but justice to state that it is unattended in Upper India by any indecent or indelicate ceremonies, and it requires a rather lively imagination to trace any resemblance in its symbols to the objects they are supposed to represent.

"In spite, however, of its wide diffusion, and the vast number of shrines dedicated to it, the worship of Shiva has never assumed a really popular character, especially in northern India, being attended with scarcely any solemnity or display of emotional spirit. The temple, which usually stands in the middle of a court, is as a rule a building of very moderate dimensions, consisting either of a single square chamber, surmounted by a pyramidal structure, or of a chamber for the linga and a small vestibule. The worshipper, having first circumambulated the shrine as often as he pleases, keeping it at his right-hand side, steps up to the threshold of the sanctum, and presents his offering of flowers or fruit, which the officiating priest receives; he then prostrates himself, or merely lifts his hands - joined so as to leave a hollow space between the palms - to his forehead, muttering a short prayer, and takes his departure.

Amongst the many thousands of Lingas, twelve are usually regarded as of especial sanctity, one of which, that of Somnath in Gujarat, where Shiva is worshipped as" the lord of Soma, "was, however, shattered by Mahmud of Ghazni; whilst another, representing Shiva as *Visvesvara,* or" Lord of the Universe, "is the chief object of adoration at Benares, the great centre of Shiva-worship. The Shaivas of southern India, on the other hand, single out as peculiarly sacred five of their temples which are supposed to enshrine as many characteristic aspects (linga) of the god in the form of the five elements, the most holy of these being the shrine of Chidambaram (*i.e.*" thoughtether ") in S. Arcot, supposed to contain the ether-linga. According to Pandit S. M. Natesa (*Hindu Feasts, Fasts and Ceremonies),*" the several forms of the god Shiva in these sacred shrines are considered to be the bodies or casements of the soul whose ' Shiva is said to have first appeared in the beginning of the present age as Sveta, the White, for the purpose of benefiting the Brahmans, and he is invariably painted white; whilst Vishnu, when pictured, is always of a dark-blue colour.

Natural bases are the five elements - earth, water, fire, air and ether. The apprehension of God in the last of these five as ether is, according to the Shaiva school of philosophy, the highest form of worship, for it is not the worship of God in a tangible form, but the worship of what, to ordinary minds, is vacuum, which nevertheless leads to the attainment of a knowledge of the all-pervading without physical accessories in the shape of any linga, which is, after all, an emblem. That this is the case at Chidambaram is known to every Hindu, for if he ever asks the priests to show him the God in the temple he is pointed to an empty space in the holy of holies, which has been termed the Akasa, or ether-linga. But, however congenial this refined symbolism may be to the worshipper of a speculative turn of mind, it is difficult to see how it could ever satisfy the religious wants of the common man little given to abstract conceptions of this kind.

From early times, detachment from the world and the practice of austerities have been regarded in India as peculiarly conducive to a spirit of godliness, and ultimately to a state of ecstatic communion with the deity. On these grounds it was actually laid down as a rule for a man solicitous for his spiritual welfare to pass the last two of the four stages ((*anima*) of his life in such condítions of renunciation and self-restraint. Though there is hardly a sect which has not contributed its share to the element of religious mendicancy and asceticism so prevalent in India, it is in connexion with the Shiva-cult that these tendencies have been most extensively cultivated. Indeed, the personality of the stern God himself exhibits this feature in a very marked degree, whence the term *maḥayogi* or" great ascetic "is often applied to him.

Of Shaiva mendicant and ascetic orders, the members of which are considered more or less followers of Shankara Acharya, the following may be mentioned: (I) *Dandis,* or staff-bearers, who carry a wand with a piece of red cloth, containing the sacred cord, attached to it, and also wear one or more pieces of cloth of the same colour. They worship Shiva in his form of Bhairava, the "terrible." A sub-section of this order are the Dandi Dasnamis, or Dandi of ten names, so called from their assuming one of the names of Shankara's four disciples, and six of their pupils. (2) *Yogis* (or popularly, Jogis), *i.e.* adherents of the Yoga philosophy and the system of ascetic practices enjoined by it with the view of mental abstraction and the supposed attainment of superhuman powers - practices which, when not merely pretended, but rigidly carried out, are only too apt to produce vacuity of mind and wild fits of frenzy. In these degenerate days their supernatural powers consist chiefly in conjuring, sooth-saying, and feats of jugglery, by which they seldom fail in imposing upon a credulous public. (3) *Sannyasis,* devotees who" renounce "earthly concerns, an order not confined either to the Brahmanical caste or to the Shaiva persuasion. Those of the latter are in the habit of smearing their bodies with ashes, and wearing a tiger-skin and a necklace or rosary of *rudraksha* berries (Elaeocarpus Ganitrus, lit." Rudra's eye"), sacred to Shiva, and allowing their hair to grow till it becomes matted and filthy. (4) *Parama-hamsas, i.e.* "supreme geese (or swans)," a term applied to the world-soul with which they claim to be identical. This is the highest order of asceticism, members of which are supposed to be solely engaged in meditating on the Brahma, and to be" equally indifferent to pleasure or pain, insensible of heat or cold, and incapable of satiety or want. Some of them go about naked, but the majority are clad like the Dandis. (5) *Aghora Panthis,* a vile and disreputable class of mendicants, now rarely met with. Their filthy habits and disgusting practices of gross promiscuous feeding, even to the extent of eating offal and dead men's flesh, look almost like a direct repudiation of the strict Brahmanical code of ceremonial purity and cleanliness, and of the rules regulating the matter and manner of eating and drinking; and they certainly make them objects of loathing and terror wherever they are seen.

On the general effect of the manner of life led by *Sadhus* or" holy men, "a recent observer (J. C. Oman, *Mystics, Ascetics and Saints of India,* p. 273) remarks:" *Sadlzuism,* whether perpetuating the peculiar idea of the efficiency of austerities for the acquisition of far-reaching powers over natural phenomena, or bearing its testimony to the belief in the indispensableness of detachment from the world as a preparation for the ineffable joy of ecstatic communion with the Divine Being, has undoubtedly tended to keep before men's eyes, as the highest ideal, a life of purity, self-restraint, and contempt of the world and human affairs. It has also necessarily maintained amongst the laity a sense of the righteous claims of the poor upon the charity of the more affluent members of the community.

Moreover, *sadhuism,* by the multiplicity of the independent sects which have arisen in India, has engendered and favoured a spirit of tolerance which cannot escape the notice of the most superficial observer. "An independent Shaiva sect, or, indeed, the only strictly Shaiva sect, are the *Vira Shaivas,* more commonly called *Lingayats* (popularly Lingaits) or *Lingavats,* from their practice of wearing on their person a phallic emblem of Shiva, made of copper or silver, and usually enclosed in a case suspended from the neck by a string. Apparently from the movable nature of their badge, their *Gurus* are called *Jangamas* (" movable "). This sect counts numerous adherents in southern India; the Census Report of 1901 recording nearly a million and a half, including some 70 or 80 different, mostly endogamous, castes. The reputed founder, or rather reformer, of the sect was Basava (or Basaba), a Brahman of the Belgaum district who seems to have lived in the 11th or 12th century.

According to the Basava-purana he early in life renounced his caste and went to reside at Kalyana, then the capital of the Chalukya kingdom, and later on at Sangamesvara near Ratnagiri, where he was initiated into the Vira Shaiva faith which he subsequently made it his life's work to propagate. His doctrine, which may be said to constitute a kind of reaction against the severe sacerdotalism of Shankara, has spread over all classes of the southern community, most of the priests of Shaiva temples there being adherents of it; whilst in northern India its votaries are only occasionally met with, and then mostly as mendicants, leading about a neatly caparisoned bull as representing Shiva's sacred bull *Nandi.* Though the Lingayats still show a certain animosity towards the Brahmans, and in the Census lists are accordingly classes as an independent group beside the Hindus, still they can hardly be excluded from the Hindu community, and are sure sooner or later to find their -way back to the Brahmanical fold.

Vishnu, whilst less popular with Brahmans than his rival, has from early times proved to the lay mind a more attractive object of adoration on account of the genial and, so to speak, romantic character of his mythical personality. It is not, however, so much the original figure of the god himself that enlists the sympathies of his adherents as the additional elements it has received through the theory of periodical" descents "(*avatara*) or incarnations applied to this deity. Whilst the Shaiva philosophers do not approve of the notion of incarnations, as being derogatory to the dignity of the deity, the Brahmans have nevertheless thought fit to adopt it as apparently a convenient expedient for bringing certain tendencies of popular worship within the pale of their system, and probably also for counteracting the Buddhist doctrines; and for this purpose Vishnu would obviously offer himself as the most attractive figure in the Brahmanical trinity.

Whether the incarnation theory started from the original solar nature of the god suggestive of regular visits to the world of men, or in what other way it may have originated, must remain doubtful. Certain, however, it is that at least one of his Avatars is clearly based on the Vedic conception of the sun-god, *viz.* that of the dwarf who claims as much ground as he can cover by three steps, and then gains the whole universe by his three mighty strides. Of the ten or more Avatars, assumed by different authorities, only two have entered to any considerable extent into the religious worship of the people, *viz.* those of *Rama* (or Ramachandra) and *Krishna,* the favourite heroes of epic romance.

That these two figures would appeal far more strongly to the hearts and feelings of the people, especially the warlike Kshatriyas, 1 than the austere Shiva is only what might have been expected; and, indeed, since the time of the epics their cult seems never to have lacked numerous adherents. But, on the other hand, the essentially human nature of these two gods 1 As in the case of Shiva's traditional white complexion, it may not be without significance, from a racial point of view, that Vishnu, Rama and Krishna have various darker shades of colour attributed to them, *viz.* blue, hyacinthine, and dark azure or dark brown respectively. The names of the two heroes meaning simply" black "or" dark, "the blue tint may originally have belonged to Vishnu, who is also called *pitavasas,* dressed in yellow garment, *i.e.* the colours of sky and sun combined would naturally tend to modify the character of the relations between worshipper and worshipped, and to impart to the modes and forms of adoration features of a more popular and more human kind.

And accordingly it is exactly in connexion with these two incarnations of Vishnu, especially that of Krishna, that a new spirit was infused into the religious life of the people by the sentiment of fervent devotion to the deity, as it found expression in certain portions of the epic poems, especially the *Bhagavadgita,* and in the *Bhagavatapurana* (as against the more orthodox Vaishnava works of this class such as the Vishnupurana), and was formulated into a regular doctrine of faith in the *Sandilya-sutra,* and ultimately translated into practice by the Vaishnava reformers.

The first successful Vaishnava reaction against Shankara's reconstructed creed was led by Ramanuja, a southern Brahman of the 12th century. His followers, the Ramanujas, or Sri-Vaishnavas as they are usually called, worship Y Y, P Vishnu (Narayana) with his consort Sri or Lakshmi (the goddess of beauty and fortune), or their incarnations Rama with Sita and Krishna with Rukmini. Ramanuja's doctrine, which is especially directed against the Linga-worship, is essentially based on the tenets of an old Vaishnava sect, the Bhagavatas or Pancharatras, who worshipped the Supreme Being under the name of Vasudeva (subsequently identified with Krishna, as the son of Vasudeva, who indeed is credited by some scholars with the foundation of that monotheistic creed). The sectarial mark of the Ramanujas resembles a capital U (or, in the case of another division, a Y), painted with a white clay called gopichandana; between the hair and the root of the nose, with a red or yellow vertical stroke (representing the female element) between the two white lines. They also usually wear, like all Vaishnavas, a necklace of *tulasi,* or basil wood, and a rosary of seeds of the same shrub or of the lotus. Their most important shrines are those of Srirangam near Trichinopoly, Mailkote in Mysore, Dwarka (the city of Krishna) on the Kathiawar coast, and Jagannath in Orissa; all of them decorated with Vishnu's emblems, the tulasi plant and salagram stone.

The Ramanuja Brahmans are most punctilious in the preparation of their food and in regard to the privacy of their meals, before taking which they have to bathe and put on woollen or silk garments. Whilst Shankara's mendicant followers were prohibited to touch fire and had to subsist entirely on the charity of Brahman householders, Ramanuja, on the contrary, not only allowed his followers to use fire, but strictly forbade their eating any food cooked, or even seen, by a stranger.

On the speculative side, Ramanuja also met Shankara's strictly monistic theory by another recognizing Vishnu as identical with Brahma as the Supreme Spirit animating the material world as well as the individual souls which have become estranged from God through unbelief, and can only attain again conscious union with him through devotion or love (*bhakti).* His tenets are expounded in various works, especially in his commentaries on the Vedantasutras and the Bhagavadgita.

The followers of Ramanuja have split into two sects, a northern one, recognizing the Vedas as their chief authority, and a southern one, basing their tenets on the Nalayir, a Tamil work of the Upanishad order. In point of doctrine, they differ in their view of the relation between God Vishnu and the human soul; whilst the former sect define it by the ape theory, which makes the soul cling to God as the young ape does to its mother, the latter explain it by the *cat* theory, by which Vishnu himself seizes and rescues the souls as the mother cat does her young ones.

Madhya Acharya, another distinguished Vedanta teacher and founder of a Vaishnava sect, born in Kanara in A.D. 1199, was less intolerant of the Linga cult than Ramanuja, but seems rather to have aimed at a reconciliation of the Shaiva and Vaishnava forms of worship. The *Madhvas* or *Madhvacharis* favour Krishna and his consort as their special objects of adoration, whilst images of Shiva, Parvati, and their son Ganesha are, however, likewise admitted and worshipped in some of their temples, the most important of which is at Udipi in South Kanara, with eight monasteries connected with it.

This shrine contains an image of Krishna which is said to have been rescued from the wreck of a ship which brought it from Dwarka, where it was supposed to have been set up of old by no other than Krishna's friend Arjuna, one of the five Pandava princes. Followers of the Madhya creed are but rarely met with in Upper India. Their sectarial mark is like the U of the Sri Vaishnavas, except that their central line is black instead of red or yellow. Madhva - who after his initiation assumed the name Anandatirtha - composed numerous Sanskrit works, including commentaries on the Brahma sutras (*i.e.* the Vedanta aphorisms), the Gita, the Rigveda and many Upanishads. His philosophical theory was a dualistic one, postulating distinctness of nature for the divine and the human soul, and hence independent existence, instead of absorption, after the completion of mundane existence.

The Ramanandis or Ramavats (popularly Ramats) are a numerous northern sect of similar tenets to those of the Ramanujas. Indeed its founder, Ramananda, who probably flourished in the latter part of the 14th century, according to the traditional account, was originally a Sri Vaishnava monk, and, having come under the suspicion of laxity in observing the strict rules of food during his peregrinations, and been ordered by his superior (Mahant) to take his meals apart from his brethren, left the monastery in a huff and set up a schismatic math of his own at Benares. The sectarial mark of his sect differs but slightly from that of the parent stock. The distinctive features of their creed consist in their making Rama and Sita, either singly or conjointly, the chief objects of their adoration, instead of Vishnu and Lakshmi, and their attaching little or no importance to the observance of privacy in the cooking and eating of their food. Their mendicant members, usually known as Vairagis, are, like thc general body of the sect, drawn from all castes without distinction. Thus, the founder's twelve chief disciples include, besides Brahmans, a weaver, a currier, a Rajput, a Jat and a barber - for, they argue, seeing that Bhagavan, the Holy One (Vishnu), became incarnate even in animal form, a Bhakta (believer) may be born even in the lowest of castes. Ramananda's teaching was thus of a distinctly levelling and popular character; and, in accordance therewith, the Bhakta-mala and other authoritative writings of the sect are composed, not in Sanskrit, but in the popular dialects. A follower of this creed was the distinguished poet Tulsidas, the composer of the beautiful Hindi version of the Ramayana and other works which" exercise more influence upon the great body of Hindu population than the whole voluminous series of Sanskrit composition "(H. H. Wilson).

The traditional list of Ramananda's immediate disciples includes the name of Kabir, the weaver, a remarkable man who would accordingly have lived in the latter part of the 15th century, and who is claimed by both Hindus and Moslems as having been born within their fold. The story goes that, having been deeply impressed by Ramananda's teaching, he sought to attach himself to him; and, one day at Benares, in stepping down the ghat at daybreak to bathe in the Ganges, and putting himself in the way of the teacher, the latter, having inadvertently struck him with his foot, uttered his customary exclamation" Ram Ram, "which, being also the initiatory formula of the sect, was claimed by Kabir as such, making him Ramananda's disciple.

Be this as it may, Kabir's own reformatory activity lay in the direction of a compromise between the Hindu and the Muhammadan creeds, the religious practices of both of which he criticized with equal severity. His followers, the Kabir Panthis (" those following Kabir's path "), though neither worshipping the gods of the pantheon, nor observing the rites and ceremonial of the Hindus, are nevertheless in close touch with the Vaishnava sects, especially the Ramavats, and generally worship Rama as the supreme deity, when they do not rather address their homage, in hymns and otherwise, to the founder of their creed himself. Whilst very numerous, particularly amongst the low-caste population, in western, central and northern India, resident adherents of Kabir's doctrine are rare in Bengal and the south; although there is hardly a town in India where strolling beggars may not be found singing songs of Kabir in the original or as translated into the local dialects." The mendicants of this creed, however, never actually solicit alms; and, indeed, "the quakerlike spirit of the sect, their abhorrence of all violence, their regard for truth and the inobtrusiveness of their opinions render them very inoffensive members of the state" (H. H. Wilson). The doctrines of Kabir are taught, mostly in the form of dialogues, in numerous Hindi works, composed by his disciples and adherents, who, however, usually profess to give the teacher's own words.

The peculiar conciliatory tendencies of Kabir were carried on with even greater zeal from the latter part of the 15th century by one of his followers, Nanak Shah, the promulgator of the creed of the *Nanak Shahis* or *Sikhs* - *i.e.* (Sanskr.) *sishya,* disciples, whose guru, or teacher, he called himself - a peaceful sect at first until, in consequence of Muhammadan persecution, a martial spirit was infused into it by the tenth, and last, guru, Govinda Shah, changing it into a political organization. Whilst originally more akin in its principles to the Moslem faith, the sect seems latterly to have shown tendencies towards drifting back to the Hindu pale.

Of Ramananda's disciples and successors several others, besides Kabir, have established schismatic divisions of their own, which do not, however, offer any very marked differences of creed. The most important of these, the Dadu Panthi sect, founded by Dadu about the year 1600, has a numerous following in Ajmir and Marwar, one section of whom, the Nagas, engage largely in military service, whilst the others are either householders or mendicants. The followers of this creed wear no distinctive sectarial mark or badge, except a skull-cap; nor do they worship any visible image of any deity, the repetition (*japa*) of the name of Rama being the only kind of adoration practised by them.

Although the Vaishnava sects hitherto noticed, in their adoration of Vishnu and his incarnations, Krishna and Ramachandra, usually associate with these gods their *Brot* wives, as their *shaktis,* or female energies, the sexual element is, as a rule, only just allowed sufficient scope to enhance the emotional character of the rites of worship. In some of the later Vaishnava creeds, on the other hand, this element is far from being kept within the bounds of moderation and decency.

The favourite object of adoration with adherents of these sects is Krishna with his mate - but not the devoted friend and counsellor of the Pandavas and deified hero of epic song, nor the ruler of Dwarka and wedded lord of Rukmini, but the juvenile Krishna, Govinda or Bala Gopala, "the cowherd lad," the foster son of the cowherd Nanda of Gokula, taken up with his amorous sports with the *Gopis,* or wives of the cowherds of Vrindavana (Brindaban, near Mathura on the Yamuna), especially his favourite mistress Radha or Radhika. This episode in the legendary life of Krishna has every appearance of being a later accretion.

After barely a few allusions to it in the epics, it bursts forth full-blown in the Harivansa, the Vishnu-purana, the Narada-Pancharatra and the Bhagavata-purana, the tenth canto of which, dealing with the life of Krishna, has become, through vernacular versions, especially the Hindi *Prem-sagar,* or "ocean of love," a favourite romance all over India, and has doubtless helped largely to popularize the cult of Krishna.

Strange to say, however, no mention is as yet made by any of these works of Krishna's favourite Radha; it is only in another Purana - though scarcely deserving that designation - that she makes her appearance, *viz.* in the Brahma-vaivarta, in which Krishna's amours in Nanda's cow-station are dwelt upon in fulsome and wearisome detail; whilst the poet Jayadeva, in the 12th century, made her love for the gay and inconstant boy the theme of his beautiful, if highly voluptuous, lyrical drama, *Gita-govinda.*

The earliest of the sects which associate Radha with Krishna in their worship is that of the Nimavats, founded by Nimbaditya or Nimbarka (*i.e.* "the sun of the Nimba tree"), a teacher of uncertain date, said to have been a Telugu Brahman who subsequently established himself at Mathura (Muttra) on the Yamuna, where the headquarters of his sect have remained ever since. The Mahant of their monastery at Dhruva Kshetra near Mathura, who claims direct descent from Nimbarka, is said to place the foundation of that establishment as far back as the 5th century-doubtless an exaggerated claim; but if Jayadeva, as is alleged, and seems by no means improbable, was really a follower of Nimbarka, this teacher must have flourished, at latest, in the early part of the 12th century.

He is indeed taken by some authorities to be identical with the mathematician Bhaskara Acharya, who is known to 'have completed his chief work in A.D. 1150. It is worthy of remark, in this respect, that - in accordance with Ramanuja's and Nimbarka's philosophical theories - Jayadeva's presentation of Krishna's fickle love for Radha is usually interpreted in a mystical sense, as allegorically depicting the human soul's striving, through love, for reunion with God, and its ultimate attainment, after many backslidings, of the longed-for goal. As the chief authority of their tenets, the Nimavats recognize the Bhagavata-purana; though several works, ascribed to Nimbarka - partly of a devotional character and partly expository of Vedanta topics - are still extant, Adherents of this sect are fairly numerous in northern India, their frontal mark consisting of the usual two perpendicular white lines, with, however, a circular black spot between them.

Of greater importance than the sect just noticed, because of their far larger following, are the two sects founded early in the 16th century by Vallabha (Ballabha) Acharya and Chaitanya. In the forms of worship favoured by votaries of these creeds the emotional and erotic elements are allowed yet freer scope than in those that preceded them; and, as an effective auxiliary to these tendencies, the use of the vernacular dialects in prayers and hymns of praise takes an important part in the religious service. The Vallabhacharis, or, as they are usually called, from the title of their spiritual heads, the Gokulastha Gosains, *i.e.* " the cow-lords (*gosvamin*) residing in Gokula," are very numerous in western and central India. Vallabha, the son of a Telinga Brahman, after extensive journeyings all over India, settled at Gokula near Mathura, and set up a shrine with an image of Krishna Gopala. About the year 1673, in consequence of the fanatical persecutions of the Mogul emperor, this image was transferred to Nathdvara in Udaipur (Mewar), where the shrine of Srinatha ("the lord of Sri," *i.e.* Vishnu) continues to be the chief centre of worship for adherents of this creed; whilst seven other images, transferred from Mathura at the same time, are located at different places in Rajputana. Vallabha himself went subsequently to reside at Benares, where he died.

In the doctrine of this Vaishnava prophet, the adualistic theory of Shankara is resorted to as justifying a joyful and voluptuous cult of the deity. For, if the human soul is identical with God, the practice of austerities must be discarded as directed against God, and it is rather by a free indulgence of the natural appetites and the pleasures of life that man's love for God will best be shown. The followers of his creed, amongst whom there are many wealthy merchants and bankers, direct their worship chiefly to Gopal Lal, the boyish Krishna of Vrindavana, whose image is sedulously attended like a revered living person eight times a day - from its early rising from its couch up to its retiring to repose at night. The sectarial mark of the adherents consists of two red perpendicular lines, meeting in a semicircle at the root of the nose, and having a round red spot painted between them.

Their principal doctrinal authority is the Bhagavata-purana, as commented upon by Vallabha himself, who was also the author of several other Sanskrit works highly esteemed by his followers. In this sect, children are solemnly admitted to full membership at the early age of four, and even two, years of age, when a rosary, or necklace, of 108 beads of basil (tulsi) wood is passed round their necks, and they are taught the use of the octo-syllabic formula *Sri-Krishnah saranam mama,* " Holy Krishna is my refuge." Another special feature of this sect is that their spiritual heads, the Gosains, also called Maharajas, so far from submitting themselves to self-discipline and austere practices, adorn themselves in splendid garments, and allow themselves to be habitually regaled by their adherents with choice kinds of food; and being regarded as the living representatives of the "lord of the Gopis" himself, they claim and receive in their own persons all acts of attachment and worship due to the deity, even, it is alleged, to the extent of complete self-surrender. In the final judgment of the famous libel case of the Bombay Maharajas, before the Supreme Court of Bombay, in January 1862, these improprieties were severely commented upon; and though so unsparing a critic of Indian sects as Jogendra Nath seems not to believe in actual immoral practices on the part of the Maharajas, still he admits that "the corrupting influence of a religion, that can make its female votaries address amorous songs to their spiritual guides, must be very great."

A modern offshoot of Vallabha's creed, formed with the avowed object of purging it of its objectionable features, was started, in the early years of the 19th century, by Sahajananda, a Brahman of the Oudh country, who subsequently assumed the name of Swami Narayana. Having entered on his missionary labours at Ahmedabad, and afterwards removed to Jetalpur, where he had a meeting with Bishop Heber, he subsequently settled at the village of Wartal, to the northwest of Baroda, and erected a temple to Lakshmi Narayana, which, with another at Ahmedabad, forms the two chief centres of the sect, each being presided over by a Maharaja. Their worship is addressed to Narayana, *i.e.* Vishnu, as the Supreme Being, together with Lakshmi, as well as to Krishna and Radha.

The sect is said to be gaining ground in Gujarat. Chaitanya, the founder of the great Vaishnava sect of Bengal, was the son of a high-caste Brahman of Nadiya, the famous Bengal seat of Sanskrit learning, where he was born in 1485, two years after the birth of Martin Luther, the German reformer. Having married in due time, and a second time after the death of his first wife, he lived as a "householder" (*grihastha*) till the age of 24, when he renounced his family ties and set out as a religious mendicant (*vairagin*), visiting during the next six years the principal places of pilgrimage in northern India, and preaching with remarkable success his doctrine of Bhakti, or passionate devotion to Krishna, as the Supreme Deity. He subsequently made over to his principal disciples the task of consolidating his community, and passed the last twelve years of his life at Puri in Orissa, the great centre of the worship of Vishnu as Jagannath, or "lord of the world," which he remodelled in accordance with his doctrine, causing the mystic songs of Jayadeva to be recited before the images in the morning and evening as part of the daily service; and, in fact, as in the other Vaishnava creeds, seeking to humanize divine adoration by bringing it into accord with the experience of human love.

To this end, music, dancing, singing-parties (*sankirtan*), theatricals - in short anything calculated to produce the desired impression - would prove welcome to him. His doctrine of Bhakti distinguishes five grades of devotional feeling in the *Bhaktas,* or faithful adherents: *viz.* (*santi)* calm contemplation of the deity; (*dasya*) active servitude; (*sakhya)* friendship or personal regard; (*vatsalya*) tender affection as between parents and children; (*madhurya*) love or passionate attachment, like that which the Gopis felt for Krishna. Chaitanya also seems to have done much to promote the celebration on an imposing scale of the great Puri festival of the Ratha-yatra, or "car-procession," in the month of Ashadha, when, amidst multitudes of pilgrims, the image of Krishna, together with those of his brother Balram and his sister Subhadra, is drawn along, in a huge car, by the devotees.

Just as this festival was, and continues to be, attended by people from all parts of India, without distinction of caste or sex, so also were all classes, even Mahommedans, admitted by Chaitanya as members of his sect. Whilst numerous observances are recommended as more or less meritorious, the ordinary form of worship is a very simple one, consisting as it does mainly of the constant repetition of names of Krishna, or Krishna and Radha, which of itself is considered sufficient to ensure future bliss. The partaking of flesh food and spirituous liquor is strictly prohibited. By the followers of this sect, also, an extravagant degree of reverence is habitually paid to their *gurus* or spiritual heads. Indeed, Chaitanya himself, as well as his immediate disciples, have come to be regarded as complete or partial incarnations of the deity to whom adoration is due, as to Krishna himself; and their modern successors, the Gosains, share to the fullest extent in the devout attentions of the worshippers. Chaitanya's movement, being chiefly directed against the vile practices of the Saktas, then very prevalent in Bengal, was doubtless prompted by the best and purest of intentions; but his own doctrine of divine, though all too human, love was, like that of Vallabha, by no means free from corruptive tendencies, - yet, how far these tendencies have worked their way, who would say?

On this point, Dr. W. W. Hunter - who is of opinion that "the death of the reformer marks the beginning of the spiritual decline of Vishnu-worship," observes (*Orissa, i. III),* " The most deplorable corruption of Vishnu-worship at the present day is that which has covered the temple walls with indecent sculptures, and filled its innermost sanctuaries with licentious rites"... yet... "it is difficult for a person not a Hindu to pronounce upon the real extent of the evil. None but a Hindu can enter any of the larger temples, and none but a Hindu priest really knows the truth about their inner mysteries"; whilst the well-known native scholar Babu Rajendralal Mitra points out (*Antiquities of Orissa,* i. III) that "such as they are, these sculptures date from centuries before the birth of Chaitanya, and cannot, therefore, be attributed to his doctrines or to his followers.

As a Hindu by birth, and a Vaishnava by family religion, I have had the freest access to the innermost sanctuaries and to the most secret of scriptures. I have studied the subject most extensively, and have had opportunities of judging which no European can have, and I have no hesitation in saying that, 'the mystic songs' of Jayadeva and the 'ocean of love' notwithstanding, there is nothing in the rituals of Jagannath which can be called licentious." Whilst in Chaitanya's creed, Krishna, in his relations to Radha, remains at least theoretically the chief partner, an almost inevitable step was taken by some minor sects in attaching the greater importance to the female element, and making Krishna's love for his mistress the guiding sentiment of their faith. Of these sects, it will suffice to mention that of the Radha-Vallabhis, started in the latter part of the 16th century, who worship Krishna as Radhavallabha, "the darling of Radha." The doctrines and practices of these sects clearly verge upon those obtaining in the third principal division of Indian sectarians which will now be considered.

The Saktas, as we have seen, are worshippers of the *shakti,* or the female principle as a primary factor in the creation and reproduction of the universe. And as each of the principal gods is supposed to have associated with him his own particular *shakti,* as an indispensable complement enabling him to properly perform his cosmic functions, adherents of this persuasion might be expected to be recruited from all sects. To a certain extent this is indeed the case; but though Vaishnavism, and especially the Krishna creed, with its luxuriant growth of erotic legends, might have seemed peculiarly favourable to a development in this direction, it is practically only in connexion with the Shaiva system that an independent cult of the female principle has been developed; whilst in other sects - and, indeed, in the ordinary Shaiva cult as well - such worship, even where it is at all prominent, is combined with, and subordinated to, that of the male principle.

What has made this cult attach itself more especially to the Shaiva creed is doubtless the character of Shiva as the type of reproductive power, in addition to his function as destroyer which, as we shall see, is likewise reflected in some of the forms of his Shakti. The theory of the god and his Shakti as cosmic principles is perhaps already foreshadowed in the Vedic couple of Heaven and Earth, whilst in the speculative treatises of the later Vedic period, as well as in the post-Vedic Brahmanical writings, the assumption of the self-existent being dividing himself into a male and a female half usually forms the starting-point of cosmic evolution.' In the later Shaiva mythology this theory finds its artistic representation in Shiva's androgynous form of Ardha-narisa, or "halfwoman-lord," typifying the union of the male and female energies; the male half in this form of the deity occupying the right-hand, and the female the left-hand side.

In accordance with this type of productive energy, the Saktas divide themselves into two distinct groups, according to whether they attach the greater importance to the male or to the female principle; *viz.* the *Dakshinacharis,* or "right-hand-observers" (also called *Dakshina-margis,* or followers "of the right-hand path"), and the *Vamacharis,* or "left-hand-observers" (or *Vama-margis,* followers "of the left path"). Though some of the Puranas, the chief repositories of sectarian doctrines, enter largely into Shakta topics, it is only in the numerous Tantras that these are fully and systematically developed. In these works, almost invariably composed in the form of a colloquy, Shiva, as a rule, in answer to questions asked by his consort Parvati, unfolds the mysteries of this occult creed.

The principal seat of Shakta worship is the northeastern part of India - Bengal, Assam and Bihar. The great majority of its adherents profess to follow the right-hand practice; and apart from the implied purport and the emblems of the cult, their mode of adoration does not seem to offer any very objectionable features. And even amongst the adherents of the left-hand mode of worship, many of these are said to follow it as a matter of family tradition rather than of religious conviction, and to practise it in a sober and temperate manner; whilst only an extreme section-the so-called *Kaulas* or *Kulinas,* who appeal to a spurious Upanishad, the Kaulopanishad, as the divine authority of their tenets - persist in carrying on the mystic and licentious rites taught in many of the Tantras. But strict secrecy being enjoined in the performance of these rites, it is not easy to check any statements made on this point. The Shakta cult is, however, known to be especially prevalent - though apparently not in a very extreme form - amongst members of the very respectable Kayastha or writer caste of Bengal, and as these are largely employed as clerks and accountants in Upper India, there is reason to fear that their vicious practices are gradually being disseminated through them.

The divine object of the adoration of the Saktas, then, is Shiva's wife - the *Devi* (goddess), *Mahadevi* (great goddess), or

Jagan-mata (mother of the world) - in one or other of her numerous forms, benign or terrible. The forms in which she is worshipped in Bengal are of the latter category, *viz. Durga,* " the unapproachable," and *Kali,* " the black one," or, as some take it, the wife of *Kala,* " time," or death the great dissolver, *viz.* Shiva. In honour of the former, the *Durga-puja* is celebrated 'This notion not improbably took its origin in the mystic cosmogonic hymn, Rigv. x. 129, where it is said that - "that one (existent, neutr.) breathed breathless by (or with) its *svadha* (inherent power, or nature), beyond that there was nothing whatever... that one live (germ) which was enclosed in the void was generated by the power of heat (or fervour); desire then first came upon it, which was the first seed of the mind... fertilizing forces there were, *svadha* below, *prayati* (will) above." during ten days at the time of the autumnal equinox, in commemoration of her victory over the buffalo-headed demon Mahishasura; when the image of the ten-armed goddess, holding a weapon in each hand, is worshipped for nine days, and cast into the water on the tenth day, called the Dusshera, whence the festival itself is commonly called Dasara in western India.

Kali, on the other hand, the most terrible of the goddess's forms, has a special service performed to her, at the *Kali-puja,* during the darkest night of the succeeding month; when she is represented as a naked black woman, four-armed, wearing a garland of heads of giants slain by her, and a string of skulls round her neck, dancing on the breast of her husband (Mahakala), with gaping mouth and protruding tongue; and when she has to be propitiated by the slaughter of goats, sheep and buffaloes.

On other occasions also Vamacharis commonly offer animal sacrifices, usually one or more kids; the head of the victim, which has to be severed by a single stroke, being always placed in front of the image of the goddess as a blood-offering (*bali*), with an earthen lamp fed with ghee burning above it, whilst the flesh is cooked and served to the guests attending the ceremony, except that of buffaloes, which is given to the low-caste musicians who perform during the service. Even some adherents of this class have, however, discontinued animal sacrifices, and use certain kinds of fruit, such as cocoanuts or pumpkins, instead.

The use of wine, which at one time was very common on these occasions, seems also to have become much more restricted; and only members of the extreme section would still seem to adhere to the practice of the so-called five *m's* prescribed by some of the Tantras, *viz. mainsa* (flesh), *matsya* (fish), *madya* (wine), *maithuna* (sexual union), and *mudra* (mystical finger signs) - probably the most degrading cult ever practised under the pretext of religious worship.

In connexion with the principal object of this cult, Tantric theory has devised an elaborate system of female figures representing either special forms and personifications or attendants of the "Great Goddess." They are generally arranged in groups, the most important of which are the *Mahavidyas* (great sciences), the 8 (or 9) *Mataras* (mothers) or *Mahamataras* (great mothers), consisting of the wives of the principal gods; the 8 *Nayikas* or mistresses; and different classes of sorceresses and ogresses, called *Yoginis, Dakinis* and *Sakinis.* A special feature of the Shakti cult is the use of obscure Vedic *mantras,* often changed so as to be quite meaningless and on that very account deemed the more efficacious for the acquisition of superhuman powers; as well as of mystic letters and syllables called *bija* (germ), of magic circles (*chakra*) and diagrams (*yantra*), and of amulets of various materials inscribed with formulae of fancied mysterious import.

This survey of the Indian sects will have shown how little the character of their divine objects of worship is calculated to exert that elevating and spiritualizing influence, so characteristic of true religious devotion. In all but a few of the minor groups religious fervour is only too apt to degenerate into that very state of sexual excitation which devotional exercises should surely tend to repress. If the worship of Shiva, despite the purport of his chief symbol, seems on the whole less liable to produce these undesirable effects than that of the rival deity, it is doubt-less due partly to the real nature of that emblem being little realized by the common people, and partly to the somewhat repellent character of the "great god," more favourable to evoking feelings of awe and terror than a spirit of fervid devotion. All the more are, however, the gross stimulants, connected with the adoration of his consort, calculated to work up the carnal instincts of the devotees to an extreme degree of sensual frenzy.

In the Vaishnava camp, on the other hand, the cult of Krishna, and more especially that of the youthful Krishna, can scarcely fail to exert an influence which, if of a subtler and more insinuating, is not on that account of a less demoralizing kind. Indeed, it would be hard to find anything less consonant with godliness and divine perfection than the pranks of this juvenile god; and if poets and thinkers try to explain them away by dint of allegorical interpretation, the plain man will not for all their refinements take these amusing adventures any the less *au pied de la lettre.* No fault, in this respect, can assuredly be found with the legendary Rama, a very paragon of knightly honour and virtue, even as his consort Sita is the very model of a noble and faithful wife; and yet this cult has perhaps retained even more of the character of mere hero-worship than that of Krishna.

Since by the universally accepted doctrine of *karman* (deed) or *karmavipaka* (" the maturing of deeds") man himself - either in his present, or some future, existence - enjoys the fruit of, or has to atone for, his former good and bad actions, there could hardly be room in Hindu pantheism for a belief in the remission of sin by divine grace or vicarious substitution. And accordingly the "descents" or incarnations of the deity have for their object, not so much the spiritual regeneration of man as the deliverance of the world from some material calamity threatening to overwhelm it.

The generally recognized principal Avatars do not, however, by any means constitute the only occasions of a direct intercession of the deity in worldly affairs, but - in the same way as to this day the eclipses of the sun and moon are ascribed by the ordinary Hindu to these luminaries being temporarily swallowed by the dragon *Rahu* (or *Graha,* " the seizer") - so any uncommon occurrence would be apt to be set down as a special manifestation of divine power; and any man credited with exceptional merit or achievement, or even remarkable for some strange incident connected with his life or death, might ultimately come to be looked upon as a veritable incarnation of the deity, capable of influencing the destinies of man, and might become an object of local adoration or superstitious awe and propitiatory rites to multitudes of people.

That the transmigration theory, which makes the spirit of the departed hover about for a time in quest of a new corporeal abode, would naturally lend itself to superstitious notions of this kind can scarcely be doubted. Of peculiar importance in this respect is the worship of the *Pitris* (" fathers") or deceased ancestors, as entering largely into the everyday life and family relations of the Hindus. At stated intervals to offer reverential homage and oblations of food to the forefathers up to the third degree is one of the most sacred duties the devout Hindu has to discharge.

The periodical performance of the commemorative rite of obsequies called *Sraddha - i.e.* an oblation "made in faith" (*sraddha,* Lat. *credo) - is* the duty and privilege of the eldest son of the deceased, or, failing him, of the nearest relative who thereby establishes his right as next of kin in respect of inheritance; and those other relatives who have the right to take part in the ceremony are called *sapinda, i.e.* sharing in the *pindas* (or balls of cooked rice, constituting along with libations of water the usual offering to the Manes) - such relationship being held a bar to intermarriage. The first *Sraddha* takes place as soon as possible after the *antyeshti* (" final offering") or funeral ceremony proper, usually spread over ten days; being afterwards repeated once a month for a year, and subsequently at every anniversary and otherwise voluntarily on special occasions.

Moreover, a simple libation of water should be offered to the Fathers twice daily at the morning and evening devotion called *sandhya* ("twilight"). It is doubtless a sense of filial obligation coupled with sentiments of piety and reverence that gave rise to this practice of offering gifts of food and drink to the deceased ancestors. Hence also frequent allusion is made by poets to the anxious care caused to the Fathers by the possibility of the living head of the family being afflicted with failure of offspring; this dire prospect compelling them to use but sparingly their little store of provisions, in case the supply should shortly cease altogether. At the same time one also meets with frank avowals of a superstitious fear lest any irregularity in the performance of the obsequial rites should cause the Fathers to haunt their old home and trouble the peace of their undutiful descendant, or even prematurely draw him after them to the Pitri-loka or world of the Fathers, supposed to be located in the southern region.

Terminating as it usually does with the feeding and feeding of a greater or less number of Brahmans and the feasting of members of the performers' own caste, the Sraddha, especially its first performance, is often a matter of very considerable expense; and more than ordinary benefit to the deceased is supposed to accrue from it when it takes place at a spot of recognized sanctity, such as one of the great places of pilgrimage like Prayaga (Allahabad, where the three sacred rivers, Ganga, Yamuna and Saraswati, meet), Mathura, and especially Gaya and Kashi (Benares).

But indeed the *tirthayatra,* or pilgrimage to holy bathing-places, is in itself considered an act of piety conferring religious merit in proportion to the time and trouble expended upon it. The number of such places is legion and is constantly increasing. The banks of the great rivers such as the Ganga (Ganges), the Yamuna (Jumna), the Narbada, the Krishna (Kistna), are studded with them, and the water of these rivers is supposed to be imbued with the essence of sanctity capable of cleansing the pious bather of all sin and moral taint. To follow the entire course of one of the sacred rivers from the mouth to the source on one side and back again on the other in the sun-wise (pradakshina) direction - that is, always keeping the stream on one's right-hand side-is held to be a highly meritorious undertaking which it requires years to carry through.

No wonder that water from these rivers, especially the Ganges, is sent and taken in bottles to all parts of India to be used on occasion as healing medicine or for sacramental purposes. In Vedic times, at the *Rajasuya,* or inauguration of a king, some water from the holy river Saraswati was mixed with the sprinkling water used for consecrating the king. Hence also sick persons are frequently conveyed long distances to a sacred river to heal them of their maladies; and for a dying man to breathe his last at the side of the Ganges is devoutly believed to be the surest way of securing for him salvation and eternal bliss.

Such probably was the belief of the ordinary Hindu two thousand years ago, and such it remains to this day. In the light of facts such as these, who could venture to say what the future of Hinduism is likely to be ? Is the regeneration of India to be brought about by the modern theistic movements, such as the Brahma-samaj and Arya-samaj, as so close and sympathetic an observer of Hindu life and thought as Sir A. Lyall seems to think ? "The Hindu mind," he remarks, "is essentially speculative and transcendental; it will never consent to be shut up in the prison of sensual experience, for it has grasped and holds firmly the central idea that all things are manifestations of some power outside phenomena.

And the tendency of contemporary religious discussion in India, so far as it can be followed from a distance, is towards an ethical reform on the old foundations, towards searching for some method of reconciling their Vedic theology with the practices of religion taken as a rule of conduct and a system of moral government.

One can already discern a movement in various quarters towards a recognition of impersonal theism, and towards fixing the teaching of the philosophical schools upon some definitely authorized system of faith and morals, which may satisfy a rising ethical standard, and may thus permanently embody that tendency to substitute spiritual devotion for external forms and caste rules which is the characteristic of the sects that have from time to time dissented from orthodox Brahminism."

3

Historical Vedic Religion

The religion of the Vedic period (also known as Vedism or Vedic Brahmanism or, in a context of Indian antiquity, simply Brahmanism) is the historical predecessor of Hinduism and the other Indian religions. Its liturgy is reflected in the Mantra portion of the four Vedas. The religious practices centered on a clergy administering sacrificial rites. A small fraction of conservative Shrautins continue this tradition today within contemporary Hinduism.

Texts dating to the Vedic period, composed in Vedic Sanskrit, are mainly the four Vedic Samhitas, but the Brahmanas, and some of the older Upanishads (BAU, ChU, JUB) are also considered Vedic. The Vedas record the liturgy connected with the rituals and sacrifices performed by the purohitas. According to traditional views, the hymns of the Rigveda and other Vedic hymns were divinely revealed to the rishis, who were considered "hearers" (*shruti* means "what is heard"), rather than "authors". However, the Rigvedic hymns clearly speak about composing new hymns by individual authors who were in competition with their colleagues.

The mode of worship was worship of the elements like fire and rivers, worship of heroic gods like Indra (quite similar to the Greek religion), chanting of hymns and performance of sacrifices. The priests helped the common man in performing rituals. People prayed for abundance of children, rain, cattle (wealth), long life and an afterlife in the heavenly world of the ancestors. This mode of worship has been preserved even today in Hinduism, which involve recitations from the Vedas by a purohit (priest), for prosperity, wealth and general well-being. Elements of Vedic religion reach back into Proto-Indo-Iranian times. The Vedic period is held to have ended around 500 BC, Vedic religion gradually metamorphosizing into the historical Indian religions, among them the Vedanta school of Hinduism and Buddhism, the former further evolving into Puranic Hinduism, the latter diversifying into Chinese and Japanese schools.

Rituals

Specific rituals and sacrifices of the Vedic religion include:

- The Soma cult described in the Rigveda, descended from a common Indo-Iranian practice.
- Fire rituals, also a common Indo-Iranian practice, cf. Zoroastrianism:
    - o The Agnihotra or oblation to Agni, a sun charm,
    - o The Agnicayana, the sophisticated ritual of piling the fire altar.
    - o The Agnistoma or Soma sacrifice
- The Ashvamedha or horse sacrifice
- The Purushamedha, or sacrifice of a man, imitating that of the the cosmic Purusha, cf. Purusha Sukta
- The rituals described in the Atharvaveda concerned with medicine and healing practises, as well as black and white magic.

The Ashvamedha (horse sacrifice) has parallels in the 2nd millennium BC Sintashta and Andronovo culture, in India allegedly continued until the 4th and even the 18th century CE (Jaya Singh at Jaipur). The practice of vegetarianism may already have arisen in late Vedic times. Although in the Rigveda, the cow's description as *aghnya* (that which should not be killed) may refer to poetry, it is certain to be reflective of the social practice as were other practices like rituals and deity worship. The overall metamorphosis into contemporary vegeteranism is seen as early as the late Brahmanas and Upanishads and may have continued under the influence of the nascent Vedanta reform and possibly Buddhism, which began as a reform-movement of the Vedic religion.

The Hindu rites of cremation were developed during the Vedic period; while they are attested from early times in the Cemetery H culture, there is a late Rigvedic reference in RV 10.15.14, invoking forefathers "both cremated (*agnidagdha-*) and uncremated (*anagnidagdha-*)".

Pantheon

The Vedic pantheon, similar to its Greek or Germanic counterparts, comprises clans of anthropomorphic deities as well as deified natural phenomena, and like the Germanic Vanir and Aesir it knows two classes of gods, Devas and Asuras. The Asuras (Mitra, Varuna, Aryaman, Bhaga, Amsa, etc.) are deities of cosmic and social order, from the universe and kingdoms down to the individual. The Rigveda is a collection of hymns to various deities, most notably heroic Indra, Agni the sacrificial fire and messenger of the gods, and Soma, the deified sacred drink of the Indo-Iranians. Also prominent is Varuna (often paired with Mitra) and the group of "all-gods", the Vishvadevas.

Monistic Tendencies

Already the Rigveda, in its youngest books (books 1 and 10) contains hymns for monistic thought, that however need to be interpreted in the context of the individual hymn. Often quoted are pada 1.164.46c,

ekam sad vipra bahudha vadanti

"To what is One, sages give many a title" (trans. Griffith)

and hymns 10.129 and 10.130, dealing with a creator deity, especially verse 10.129.7:

iyam viscmi yata ababhuva /
yadi va dadhe yadi va na /
ya asya adhyakca parame vyoman /
sa aega veda yadi va na veda /

"He, the first origin of this creation, whether he formed it all or did not form it, / Whose eye controls this world in highest heaven, he verily knows it, or perhaps he knows not." (trans. Griffith)

Ekam sat in 1.164.46c means "One Being" or "One Truth". Such concepts received greater emphasis in classical Hinduism, from the time of Adi Shankara at the latest, and they receive emphasis in contemporary Hinduism from pantheistic sects like Arya Samaj.

Post-Vedic Religions

Vedic religion gradually diversified into the Hindu paths of Yoga and Vedanta, a religious path considering itself the 'essence' of the Vedas. The Vedic pantheon was interpreted as a unitary view of the universe with God seen as immanent and transcendent in the forms of Ishvara (God's Personal Feature), Paramatma (God's localised feature) and Brahman (God's Impersonal Energies). There are also conservative schools which continue portions of the historical Vedic religion largely unchanged until today (see shrauta, Nambudiri).

Religions that have continued from the Vedic religion :

- Shramana traditions (*nastika*):
    - o Jainism, from the 6th century BC
    - o Buddhism, from ca. 500 BC; declined in India over the 8th to 12th centuries in favour of Pauranic Hinduism.
- Hinduism is an umbrella term for *astika* traditions in India (see History of Hinduism)
    - o Puranas, Sanskrit epics
    - o the classical schools of Hindu philosophy, of which only Vedanta is extant.
    - o Shaivism
    - o Vaishnavism
    - o Bhakti
    - o Shrauta traditions, maintaining much of the original form of the Vedic religion.

Shramana

A sharmana is a wandering monk in certain ascetic traditions of ancient India, including Jainism, Buddhism, and

Ajivika religion (now extinct). Famous sharmana include religious leaders Mahavira and Gautama Buddha.

Traditionally, a sharmana is one who performs acts of mortification or austerity. According to typical sharmana worldviews, a being is himself responsible for his own deeds. Salvation, therefore, can be achieved by anybody irrespective of caste, creed, colour or culture (in contradistinction to certain historical caste-based traditions). The cycle of rebirth (*samsara*) to which every individual is subject is viewed as the cause and substratum of misery. The goal of every person is to evolve a way to escape from the cycle of rebirth, namely by discounting ritual as a means of an emancipation and establishing from the misery of samsara, through pious religious activities.

Etymology

The Sanskrit word sharmana is derived from the Sanskrit verbal root *shram* "to exert, effort, labour or to perform austerity". Shramana thus means "one who strives" in Sanskrit.

A traditional Sanskrit definition is uramati tapasyatiti shramana ("a shramana is he who exerts himself and performs religious austerities"). One of the earliest uses of the word is in Taittiriya Aranyaka (2-7-1) with the meaning of 'performer of austerities'.

Buddhist commentaries associate the word's etymology with the quieting (*samita*) of evil (*papa*) as in the following phrase from the Dhammapada, verse 265: samitatta papanak samana ti pavuccati ("someone who has pacified evil is called 'samana'").

Various forms of the word became known throughout Central and East Asia, largely through the spread of Buddhism in that area. According to a still disputed etymology, the word *shaman*, used by the Tungus people for their religious practitioners, may be borrowed from a local variant of the word sharmana.

Historicity of Shraman Culture

Lord Parshwanathji 23rd Jineshwar was born in kashi (varanasi) in 19th century BC. His parents were King Aswasena, the ruler of kashi & Vamdevi mataji.

Lord Mahavir was the senior contemporary of Gautama Buddha, the founder of Buddhism. In Buddhist books Lord Mahavir is always described as nigantha Nataputta (Nirgrantha Jnatrputra), *i.e.*, the naked ascetic of the Jnätr clan. Further, in the Buddhist literature Jainism is referred to as an ancient religion. There are ample references in Buddhist books to the Jain naked ascetics, to the worship of Arhats in Jain chaityas or temples and to the chaturyäma dharma (*i.e.* fourfold religion) of 23rd Tirthankar Parsvanath.

Moreover, the Buddhist literature refers to the Jain tradition of Tirthankars and specifically mentions the names of Jain Tirthankars/Arhats/Arihants like Rishabhdev(First Tirthankar), Padmaprabh, Chandraprabh, Puspdant, Vimalnath, Dharmanath and Neminath. The Buddhist book Manorathapurani, mentions the names of many lay men and women as followers of the Parsvanath (23rd jain tirthankar)tradition and among them is the name of Vappa, the uncle of Gautama Buddha. In fact it is mentioned in the Buddhist literature that Gautama Buddha himself practiced penance according to the Jain way before he propounded his new religion. Ashraman culture also Known as Arhat Culture preceded Vedic religion and culture in India,term shraman culture constitues 24 jain tirthankars / gods/ jinas/ arhats whereby shraman culuture was started by first tirthankar Rishabhdevji/ Adinathji.

Aryans were too influenced by 23rd tirthankar parswanathji. Lord Mahavir & Lord Gautam Buddha were both heirs to lord parshwanathjis legacy. During The time of Lord Mahavira & Lord Buddha, there were many shraman monks who belonged an order, samgha, founded by Lord parshwanathji. They eventually joined Lord Mahavirs order or Lord Buddhas order. Jainism & Buddhism both belong to shramana tradition. Unlike Buddhism, which traces its origin to lord Buddha, The jain shramana tradition is represented in its legendary glory by 24 jinas/tirthankars, the first of whom was Lord Rishabha/ adinathji & last 24th lord Mahavira. Hence shraman culture today constitutes to Jainism & Buddhism.

Jainism traces its roots to a succession of 24 Jinas ("those who overcome", or conqueror).The first Jina (Lord Rishabdev) lived 8.4 million years ago who founded Jainism for this era. The most recent and last Jina was Vardhamana (a.k.a. Mahavira, "The Great Hero") He was born in 550 BC) and misrepresented most often as founder of jainism He attained enlightenment after 13 years of deprivation. Each Jina has "conquered love and hate, pleasure and pain, attachment and aversion, and has thereby freed `his' soul from the karmas obscuring knowledge, perception, truth, and ability..."

Jainism was name given to Shraman Culture by Britishers which was Orginal Source of Religion which existed in Indus Valley from which branched out Brahminism & Buddhism. Today All Vedic (Hinduism name given by Britishers), Jainism & Buddhism followers live in harmony with each other respecting each others faith though in Past Both Jainism & Buddhism suffered agressive attacks from Vedic from 7th to 10 century approx. as claimed by few unbiased researchers.

Sramana Movement

Several sramana movements are known to have existed in the 5th century BC. These were people who strove for an alternate path to achieve salvation, alternate to the Vedic rituals, while renouncing the household life. In addition, sharmana typically engaged in three types of activities: austerities, meditation, and associated theories (or views). As spiritual authorities, sharmana at times were at variance with traditional brahmanical authority and often recruited members from Brahmin circles themselves such as Chanakya and Sariputra.

The Views of Six Samana *in the Pali Canon*

Question: "Is it possible to point out the fruit of thecontemplative life, visible in the here and now?"– *from the Samannaphala Sutta*

Samana	*View (ditthi)*
Punanakassapa	Amoralism: denies any reward orpunishment for either good or bad deeds.
Makkhali Gosala	Fatalism: we are powerless;suffering is pre-destined.

Contd..

Samana	***View (ditthi)***
Ajitakesakambali	Materialism:with death, all is annihilated.
Pakudha Kaccayana	Eternalism: Matter, pleasure, pain andthe soul are eternal and do not interact.
Niganmha Nataputta	Restraint: be endowed with, cleansed byand suffused with the avoidance of all evil.
SanjayaBelammhaputta	Agnosticism: "I don't think so. I don't think inthat way or otherwise. I don't think not or not not."

Mahavira, the 24th *Jina,* and Gautama Buddha were leaders of their *sharmana* orders. According to Jain literature and the Buddhist Pali Canon, there were other *sharmana* leaders at that time. For instance, in the Mahaparinibbana Sutta (DN 16), a sharmana named Subhadda mentions:

"those ascetics [*samana*] and Brahmins who have orders and followings, who are teachers, well-known and famous as founders of schools, and popularly regarded as saints, like PuraGa Kassapa, Makkhali Gosala, Ajita Kesakambali, Pakudha Kaccayana, Sanjaya Belammhaputta and the Niganmha Nataputta...."

Niganmha Nataputta (Pali; Skt.: Nirgrantha Jnataputra) refers to Mahavira. In regards to the other Pali-Canon-identified teachers, Jaina literature mentions Purana Kassapa, Makkhali Gosala and Sanjaya Belatthiputta. (The Pali Canon is the only source for Ajita Kesakambali and Pakudha Kaccayana.)

Gautama the Buddha regarded rigorous asceticism extreme and not leading to enlightenment and did not institute such methods, and thus adapted the "middle way," while the followers of Mahavira continued to practice asceticism. Devadatta, the cousin of Gautama, caused a split in the Buddhist *sangha* by demanding more rigorous practices.

The *sharmana* ideal of wandering also began to change early in Buddhism, when the *bhikcu* started living in monasteries (Pali, Skt. *vihara*) at first during the rainy season, but eventually permanently. In mediaeval Jainism also, the tradition of wandering nearly became extinct, but was revived in the 19th century. Similar reforms have also regularly occurred in Buddhism.

Sramana in Western Literature

Various references to sharmanas, with the name more or less distorted, have been handed down in Western literature about India.

Nicolaus of Damascus (c.10 CE)

Nicolaus of Damascus is famous for his account of an embassy sent by an Indian king "named Pandion (Pandyan kingdom) or, according to others, Porus" to Caesar Augustus around 13 CE. He met with the embassy at Antioch. The embassy was bearing a diplomatic letter in Greek, and one of its members was a "Sarmano" who burnt himself alive in Athens to demonstrate his faith. The event made a sensation and was quoted by Strabo and Dio Cassius. A tomb was made to the "Sarmano", still visible in the time of Plutarch, which bore the mention "(Zarmanochçgas indos apo Bargosçs – The *sramana* master from Barygaza in India).

Clement of Alexandria (150-211)

Clement of Alexandria makes several mentions of the Sramanas, both in the context of the Bactrians and the Indians:

"Thus philosophy, a thing of the highest utility, flourished in antiquity among the barbarians, shedding its light over the nations. And afterwards it came to Greece. First in its ranks were the prophets of the Egyptians; and the Chaldeans among the Assyrians; and the Druids among the Gauls; and the Samanaeans among the Bactrians; and the philosophers of the Celts; and the Magi of the Persians, who foretold the Saviour's birth, and came into the land of Judaea guided by a star. The Indian gymnosophists are also in the number, and the other barbarian philosophers. And of these there are two classes, some of them called Sarmanae and Brahmanae.Clement of Alexandria, "Exhortation to the Heathen".

To Clement of Alexandria, "Bactrians" apparently means "Oriental Greek", as in a passage of the Stromata:

"It was after many successive periods of years that men worshipped images of human shape, this practice being introduced by Artaxerxes, the son of Darius, and father of Ochus, who first set up the image of Aphrodite Anaitis at Babylon and Susa; and Ecbatana set the example of worshipping it to the Persians; the Bactrians, to Damascus and Sardis." The Stromata, or Miscellanies, Book I, Clement of Alexandria.

Porphyry (233-305)

Porphyry extensively describes the habits of the Sramanas (whom he calls Samanaeans) in his "On abstinence from animal food" Book IV. He says his information was obtained from "the Babylonian Bardesanes, who lived in the times of our fathers, and was familiar with those Indians who, together with Damadamis, were sent to Caesar":

"For the polity of the Indians being distributed into many parts, there is one tribe among them of men divinely wise, whom the Greeks are accustomed to call Gymnosophists. But of these there are two sects, over one of which the Brahmins preside, but over the other the Samanaeans. The race of the Brahmins, however, receive divine wisdom of this kind by succession, in the same manner as the priesthood. But the Samanaeans are elected, and consist of those who wish to possess divine knowledge." Porphyry, "On abstinence from animal food," Book IV.

"All the Brahmins originate from one stock; for all of them are derived from one father and one mother. But the Samanaeans are not the offspring of one family, being, as we have said, collected from every nation of Indians..." Porphyry, "On abstinence from animal food," Book IV.

On entering the order:

"The Samanaeans are, as we have said, elected. When, however, any one is desirous of being enrolled in their order, he proceeds to the rulers of the city; but abandons the city or village that he inhabited, and the wealth and all the other property that he possessed. Having likewise the superfluities of his body cut off, he receives a garment, and departs to the Samanaeans, but does not return

either to his wife or children, if he happens to have any, nor does he pay any attention to them, or think that they at all pertain to him. And, with respect to his children indeed, the king provides what is necessary for them, and the relatives provide for the wife. And such is the life of the Samanaeans. But they live out of the city, and spend the whole day in conversation pertaining to divinity. They have also houses and temples, built by the king". Porphyry, "On abstinence from animal food," Book IV.

On life and death:

"They are so disposed with respect to death, that they unwillingly endure the whole time of the present life, as a certain servitude to nature, and therefore they hasten to liberate their souls from the bodies [with which they are connected]. Hence, frequently, when they are seen to be well, and are neither oppressed, nor driven to desperation by any evil, they depart from life." Porphyry, "On abstinence from animal food", Book IV.

Sramana in Contemporary Western Culture

German novelist Hermann Hesse, long interested in Eastern, especially Indian, spirituality, wrote *Siddhartha*, in which the main character becomes a Samana upon leaving his home (where he was a Brahmin).

Brahmin

The term Brahmin denotes both a member of the priestly class in the Hindu *varna* system, and a member of a caste in the caste system of Hindu society.

The Sanskrit word BrahmaGa denotes priestly class (varGa) and caste (tribe). The Sanskrit terms Brahman and Brahman ("belonging to Brahman") are also used. The English word *brahmin* is an anglicised form of Sanskrit word *brahmana*.

Brahmins are also called Vipra "inspired", or Dvija "twice-born". In 1931 (the last Indian census to record caste), Brahmins accounted for 4.32% of the total population. Brahmins even in Uttar Pradesh, where they were most numerous, constituted just 9% of the recorded population. In Tamil Nadu they formed less than 3% and in Andhra Pradesh, less than 2%.

History

The history of the Brahmin community in India begins with the Vedic religion, also known as Brahminism or Sanatana Dharma, in ancient India. The Vedas are the primary source of knowledge for brahmin practices. All the sampradayas of Brahmins take inspiration from the Vedas. According to Brahmin tradition, it is believed that Vedas are *apauruceya* (not written by either humans or god) and *anadi* (beginning-less), but are revealed truths of eternal validity. Accordig to Rigveda, Mandala 10 (or chapter / adhyaya 8), brahmins were *situated* ("asita")in the mouth of Puruca at the beginning of Creation (in Purucasukta, which occurs in YV.32 also).

The Vedas are considered *shruti* (*that which is heard*, signifying the oral tradition). The "Brahmanas" "Manusmiriti", not the Vedas, are the primary source of knowledge for all Brahmin traditions, both orthodox and heterodox. All religions of Brahmins and all traditions, in one way or other, take inspiration from the Vedas. Traditional Brahmin accepts Vedas as apaurusheyam (not man-made), but revealed truths and of eternal validity or relevance and hence the Vedas are considered Srutis that which have been heard and are the paramount source of Brahmin traditions and is believed to be divine. These Srutis include not only the four Vedas (the Rigveda, the Yajurveda, the Samaveda and the Atharvaveda), but also their respective Brahmanas.

Brahmin Communities

Brahmins are a very diverse community. Major Brahmin castes in the Indian Continent include Babboor Kamme Brahmins, Chitpavana Brahmins, Daivajna Brahmins, Deshastha Brahmins, Dhima Brahmins; Gouda Saraswat Brahmins, Havyaka Brahmins, Hoysala Karnataka Brahmins, Iyers, Kandavara Brahmins, Karade Brahmins, Karhada Brahmins, Kayastha Brahmins, Khandelwal Brahmins, Kota Brahmins, Konkanastha Brahmins, Koteshwara Brahmins, Nagar Brahmins, Namboothiri Brahmins, Niyogi Brahmins,

Padia Brahmins, Rajapur Saraswat Brahmins, Saklapuri Brahmins, Sanketi Brahmins, Saraswat Brahmins, Shivalli Brahmins, Smarta Brahmins, Sthanika Brahmins, Thenkalai Iyengars, Tuluva Brahmins, Vadagalai Iyengars, Vaidiki Brahmins and Vaishnava Brahmins. According to the Rev. M.A. Sherring, there were some 2,000 Brahmin groups.

These Brahmin castes are broadly divided into two regional groups: Pancha-Gauda Brahmins and Pancha-Dravida Brahmins as per the shloka,

Translation: Karnataka, Telugu (Andhra), Dravida (Tamil and Kerala), Maharashtra and Gujarat are Five Southern (Panch Dravida). Saraswata, Kanyakubja, Gauda, Utkala, Maithili are Five Northern (Pancha Gauda). This classification occurs in Rajatarangini of Kalhana and is mentioned by Jogendra Nath Bhattacharya in "Hindu Castes and Sects."

Pancha Dravida Brahmins

Panch Dravida (the five classes of Southern India): 1) Andhra, 2) Dravida (Tamil and Kerala), 3) Karnataka, 4) Maharashtra and Konkon, and 5) Gujarat.

In Andhra Pradesh, Brahmins are broadly classified into 2 groups: Vaidika (meaning educated in vedas and performing religious vocations) and Niyogi (performing only secular vocation), which are further divided into several sub-castes. However, majority of Brahmins, both Vaidika and Niyogi, perform only secular professions.

In Kerala, Brahmins are classified into three groups: Namboothiris, Pottis and Pushpakas. (Pushpakas are commonly clubbed with Ampalavasi community). The major priestly activities are performed by Namboothiris while the other temple related activities known as Kazhakam are performed by Pushpaka Brahmins and other Ampalavasis. Sri Adi Shankara was born in Kalady, a village in Kerala, to a Namboothiri Brahmin couple, Shivaguru and Aryamba and lived for thirty-two years. The Namboothiri Brahmins, Potti Brahmins and Pushpaka Brahmins in Kerala follow the Philosophies of Sri Adi Sankaracharya. The Brahmins migrated to Kerala from Tamil Nadu are known as Pattar in Kerala. They possess almost same status of Potti Brahmins in Kerala. In Tamil Nadu, Brahmins belong to 2 major groups: Iyer including dikshitar, shastri, sharma and gurukkal of Smarthas, the followers of Sri Adi Shankaracharya, Sri-Vaishnavas (Iyengars), who are the followers of Sri Ramanujacharya's vision.

In Karnataka, Brahmins belong to 3 major groups: Smarthas, the followers of Sri Adi Shankaracharya, Madhvas (or Vaishnavas) who are the followers of Sri Madhvacharya, and Sri-Vaishnavas (Iyengars), who are the followers of Sri Ramanujacharya and Srimathe Vedanta Desika.

In Maharashtra, Brahmins are classified into four groups: Chitpavan Konkanastha Brahmins, Deshastha Brahmin and Karhade Brahmin, Devrukhe. As the name indicates, Kokanastha Brahmin are from Konkan area. Deshastha Brahmin are from other plains region of Maharashtra. Karhade Brahmins are perhaps from Karhatak, and an ancient region in India that included present day south Maharashtra and northern Karnataka, Devrukhe Brihamins are from Devrukh near Ratnagiri.

Pancha Gauda Brahmins

Panch Gaur (the five classes of Northern India): 1) Saraswata, 2) Kanyakubja, 3) Gaua brahmins, 4) Utkala Brahmin, and 5) Maithil Brahmin. In addition, for the purpose of giving an account of Northern Brahmins each of the provinces must be considered separately, such as, North Western Provinces and Pakistan, Gandhar, Punjab, Kashmir, Sindh, Rajputana, Kurukshetra, Oudh, Central India, Trihoot, Bihar, Orissa, Bengal, Assam etc.

In Bihar, majority of Brahmins are Bhumihar Brahmins and Maithil Brahmins.

In Haryana, the brahmin classified in mainly Dahima/ Dayama/Dahima brahmin, Gaud brahmin, Khandelwal brahmin.

In Punjab, they are classified as Saraswat Brahmins.

In Rajasthan, the Brahmins are classified in mainly Dahima/ Dayama/Dahima brahmin, Gaud Brahmin, Sri Gaud Brahmin, Khandelwal Brahmin, Gujar-Gaud Brahmins.

Gotras and Pravaras

In general, gotra denotes all persons who trace descent in an unbroken male line from a common male ancestor. Panini defines gotra for grammatical purposes as ' apatyam pautraprabh*rti gotram' (IV. 1. 162), which means 'the word gotra denotes the progeny (of a sage) beginning with the son's son. When a person says ' I am Kashypasa-gotra' he means that he traces his descent from the ancient sage Kashyapa by unbroken male descent. According to the Baudhayanas'rauta-sutra Viuvamitra, Jamadagni, Bharadvaja, Gautama, Atri, Vasishtha, Kashyapa and Agastya are 8 sages; the progeny of these eight sages is declared to be gotras. This enumeration of eight primary gotras seems to have been known to Panini. The offspring (apatya) of these eight are gotras and others than these are called ' gotravayava '.

The gotras are arranged in groups, *e.g.* there are according to the Asvalayana-srautasutra four subdivisions of the Vasishtha gana, *viz.* Upamanyu, Parashara, Kundina and Vasishtha (other than the first three). Each of these four again has numerous sub-sections, each being called gotra. So the arrangement is first into ganas, then into pakshas, then into individual gotras. The first has survived in the Bhrigu and Angirasa gana. According to Baud, the principal eight gotras were divided into pakshas. The pravara of Upamanyu is Vasishtha, Bharadvasu, Indrapramada; the pravara of the Parashara gotra is Vasishtha, Shaktya, Parasharya; the pravara of the Kundina gotra is Vasishtha, Maitravaruna, Kaundinya and the pravara of Vasishthas other than these three is simply Vasishtha. It is therefore that some define pravara as the group of sages that distinguishes the founder (lit. the starter) of one gotra from another.

There are two kinds of pravaras, 1) sishya-prasishya-rishi-parampara, and 2) putrparampara. Gotrapravaras can be ekarsheya, dwarsheya, triarsheya, pancharsheya, saptarsheya, and up to 19 rishis. Kashyapasa gotra has at least two distinct pravaras in Andhra Pradesh: one with three sages (triarsheya pravara) and the other with seven sages (saptarsheya pravara). This pravara may be either sishya-prasishya-rishi-parampara or putraparampara. When it is sishya-prasishya-rishi-parampara marriage is not acceptable if half or more than half of the rishis are same in both bride and bridegroom gotras. If it is putraparampara, marriage is totally unacceptable even if one rishi matches.

Sects and Rishis

Due to the diversity in religious and cultural traditions and practices, and the Vedic schools which they belong to, Brahmins are further divided into various subcastes. During the sutra period, roughly between 1000 BC to 200 BC, Brahmins became divided into various Shakhas (branches), based on the adoption of different Vedas and different rescension Vedas. Sects for different denominations of the same branch of the Vedas were formed, under the leadership of distinguished teachers among Brahmins. There are several Brahmin law givers such as Angirasa, Apasthambha, Atri, Brihaspati, Boudhayana, Daksha, Gautam, Harita, Katyayana, Likhita, Manu, Parasara, Samvarta, Shankha, Shatatapa, Ushanasa, Vashishta, Vishnu, Vyasa, Yajnavalkya and Yama. These twenty-one rishis were the propounders of Smritis. The oldest among these smritis are Apastamba, Baudhayana, Gautama, and Vasishta Sutras.

Descendants from Rishis

From the Vedic Rishis, many Indians and non-Indians claim descent who are not from the Brahmin caste. For example the Dash and Nagas are said to be the descendants of Kashyapa Muni, the Gotamas (including Lord Buddha apart from the Gautam Brahmins are said to descendants of Gautama Muni. It is also believed that Buddha was a descendant of the Vedic Angirasa Muni. The backward-caste Matangs claim to descend from Matang Muni,

It is said that an educated person of their caste, named Deben Babu, came to this region from Calcutta about 50 or 60 years ago, and called a convention of all people of that caste at Navaran in Jessore district. At the convention, Deben Babu told them that they were actually the descendants of the ancient Rishis and Munis (sages) who wrote the Vedas and the Puranas, but that they had fallen in Society as a result of their lowly occupation. He called upon them to abandon their dirty occupation and adopt the surname or caste name Rishi.

The Kani tribe of South India claim to descend from Agastya Muni. The Gondhali, Kanet, Bhot, Lohar, Dagi, and Hessis claim to be from Renuka Devi. Many Jats clans claim to descend from Dadhichi Rishi while the Dudi Jats claim to be in the linear of Duda Rishi.

Practices

Brahmins adhere to the principles of Brahmanism or Sanatana Dharma or Hinduism, such as acceptance of the Vedas with reverence, adherence to the position that the means or ways to salvation and realization of the ultimate truth are diverse, that God is one, but has innumerable names and forms to chant and worship due to our varied perceptions, cultures and languages. Brahmins believe in *Sarvejanassukhinobhavactu-* Let the entire society be happy and prosperous and *Vasudhaiva kumucbakac*—the whole world is one family. Most Brahmins practice vegetarianism or lacto-vegetarianism. However, some may follow veganism or ovo-lacto-vegetarianism or pescetarianism. In addition, many prominent communists and atheists in India are of Brahmin origin.

Traditional Duties

The six duties of Brahmin are given as per the Sloka

adhyapanam adhyayanam
yajanam yajanam tatha
danam pratigraham caiva
brahmananamakalpayat

Teaching, study (*svadhyaya*), performing Yajna, make performing Yajna, accept Daana, and give Daana are the six duties of a Brahmin.

samodamastapah saucham
kshanthirarjavamevaca
jnanam vijnanamastikyam
brahmakarma svabhavajam

In the ancient times the priests were expected to have control of their emotions, control of senses, purity, truthfulness, tolerance, simplicity, renounce material wealth and have sustenance from other community, belief in God, and studying and teaching of sacred scriptures.

The daily routine includes performing

- Snana (bathing),
- Sandhyavandana,
- Japa,
- Puja,
- Aupasana and
- Agnihotra.

The last two named Yajnas are performed in only a few households today. Brahmacharis perform Agnikaryam instead of Agnihotra or Aupasana. The other rituals followed include Amavasya tarpanam and Shraddha.

Samskaras

Brahmins also perform sixteen major Samskaras (rites) during the course of their lifetime.

- In the pre-natal stage,
    - o Garbhadharana (conception),
    - o Pumsavana (rite for consecrating a male child in the womb) and
    - o Simantonnayana (rite for parting the hair of a pregnant woman) are performed.
- During infancy,
    - o Jatakarma (birth ceremony),
    - o Namakarana (naming ceremony),
    - o Nishkarmana (first outing),
    - o Annaprasana (first feeding solid food),
    - o Choodakarana (first tonsure) and
    - o Karnavedha (ear piercing) are performed.
- During childhood and adolescence of the child,
    - o Vidhyarambha (starting of education),

- Upanayanam (thread ceremony-initiation),
- Vedarambha (starting of the study of the Vedas),
- Keshanta or Godana (first shaving of the beard) and
- Samavartanam or Snaana (ending of studentship) are performed.

• During adulthood,

- Vivaha (marriage)
- Nisheka (first sexual intercourse, 4 days after marriage) and
- Antyesti (funeral rites) are the main ceremonies.

Sampradayas

The three sampradayas (traditions) of Brahmins, especially in South India are the Smarta sampradaya, the Srivaishnava sampradaya and the Madhva sampradaya.

Vaishnavism

Srivaishnava sampradaya and the Madhva sampradaya are the two major Vaishnavite sects. From these two were influenced several other Vaishnavite sects such as the Ramananda Sampraday, and Ramdassi Sampraday. The founder of the Sri Vaishnava Sampraday was Ramanuja while Madhava was the founder of the Madhav Sampraday. The Pushtimarg Sampraday, founded by Vallabh Acharya is yet another sect influenced by the other two major Vaishnavite sect.

Vaishnavism included many sect such as the Swaminarayan Sampraday.

There are many members of the Swaminarayan Sampraday founded by Bhagwan Swaminarayan, born as Ghanshyam Pande a Vaishnavite Brahmin of present-day Uttar Pradesh. He later settled in Gujarat, wherein the highest density of sampraday members live. This is a Vaishnavite sect. This sect was founded in the latter part of the 18th century.

There is also the Varkari Sampraday, which worships Sri Krishna as "Vithal". The word "Varkari" means *travelers* because members of this sect travel from their home towns on a pilgrimage to Pandharpur, almost always on foot! Important saints of this movement were the Brahmins Dnyaneshwar, [[Muktabai] as well as several non-Brahmin icons.

There is also the Mahanubhava sampraday founded by King Cakradhara, known popularly to members as Sri Chakradhar Swami, in the 12th century. The members of this sect worship Lord Vishnu in His five forms; Lord Krishna, Lord Sri Dattatreya, Lord Sri Chakrapani, Lord Sri Govindaprabhu, and Lord Cakradhara (the founder Himself).

Shaivism

Arumuka Navalar, the defender of Shaivism in Sri Lanka against the missionary activity. The Shaiva Brahmins have important icons such as Adi Shankara of Tamil Nadu, Basava Swami of Karnataka, and Raja Bhojdeva Paramar of Gujarat.

Other Sects

There are additional sampradayas as well which are not as widely followed as the rest. The Mahima Dharma or "Satya Mahima Alekha Dharma" was founded by the Brahmin Mukanda Das of present-day Orissa, popularly know by followers as Mahima Swami according to the *Bhima Bhoi* text. He was born in the last part of 18th century in Baudh ex-state as a son of Ananta Mishra. He was Brahmin by caste as mentioned in Mahima Vinod of *Bhima Bhoi* in Vol.11. This sampradaya is similar to Vaishnavism. Although the members of this sect do not worship Lord Vishnu as their Ishta-Deva, they believe that the Srimad Bhagavatam is sacred. The founder of this sect was a Vaishnavite before founding the new order. This sampradaya was founded in the latter part of the 18th century.

There is also the Avadhoot Panth, wherein Lord Dattertaya and his forms such as Narasimha Saraswati and Sai Baba of Shirdi are worshiped. Lord Dattatreya is worshiped by many as the Hindu trinity-Brahma, Vishnu and Shiva in one divine entity. Many even worship Dattatreya as an avatar of Vishnu or of Shiva.

Brahmins Taking up Other Duties

Brahmins in history have taken on many professions-from being preists, ascetics and scholars to becoming warriors and even businesspeople. Brahmins with the qualities of Kshatriyas are known as 'Brahmkshatriyas'. An example is the avatara Parshurama who destroyed the entire Haiheyas 21 times. Not only did Sage Parashurama have warrior skills but they were so powerful that He could even fight without the use of any weapons and trained others to fight without weapons. The Pallavas were an example of Brahmakshatiryas as that is what they called themselves. King Lalitaditya Muktapida of Kashmir ruled all of India and even Central Asia according to many historians.

Today are is the caste Brahmakhatris, who are a clan of the Khatris. Brahmins with the qualities of a Vaisya or merchant are known as 'Brahmvyasya'.

Brahmins in Buddhism

Brahmins feature extensively in Buddhist canonical texts *i.e.* the Tripitaka, and are found among the chief disciples of the Buddha. The Brahmana Varga (section on Brahmins) contained in the Dharmapada lists down the Buddha's views on Brahmins

Brahmin Bhikshus

- Abhaya Raja (built Mahabouddha temple with his descendants in Patan, Nepal in year 1604)
- Asvaghosa (wrote the 'Buddhacharita' and is considered along with Nagarjuna to have founded the Mahayana). His philosophy was favoured in the court of King Kanishka.
- Atapa
- Bakula
- Bhitka (Buddha's fifth successor)
- Cuda Panthaka
- Dignaga
- Gopaka

- Guhyashila
- Harita (wrote the "Harita Dharmasutra")
- Humkara
- Jnanadharma
- Kacanna
- Kamashila (Kashmiri Pandit)
- Kalika
- Kumarajiva (was imprisoned in China for spreading Buddhism)
- Kanaka (Yamantaka Tantra)
- Kukuraja
- Manjushri (The mentor of Asoka)
- Padma (woman)
- Palden Dekyong
- Pingala-Koccha (preached to the Buddha the Culasaropama Sutta, after which he became a dedicated student of the Buddha)
- Radhasvami (another mentor of Asoka)
- Majnushrimitra
- Nagasena
- Narpola (student of Tipola)
- Sahara (master of Tipola)
- Sariputra
- Shantideva
- Shantarakshita (Kashmiri Pandit)
- Subha
- Subhadra
- Subrahman (coming father of Bodhisattva Maitreya)
- Tipola (Mahasiddha, from modern-day Bangladesh)
- Vakkali
- Vanavasi

Brahmin Bodhisattvas

Aryadeva (successor of Nagarjuna) Asangha (from Hinayana

sect and Peshwar city founded the Yogacarya and established the Classical age of Buddhism)

- Bodhidharma (royalty of Pallava, from Kanchi) that went to China
- Brahmadatta
- Nagarjuna (founded the Shunyata concept and considered along with Asvaghosa to have founded the Mahayana)
- Kusanda Buddha
- Konagamana Buddha
- Kasyapsa Buddha
- Kshitagarbha
- Maitreya (Bodhisattva to come)
- Parmasambhava (founder of Vajrayana Buddhism)

Scriptures Dedicated to Brahmin Bhikkus

Because of the aim of the Brahmins, and the Buddha following on their path, several Buddhist texts have been dedicated to them.

- Annatara Brahmana Sutta: To a Brahmin
- Annatra Sutta: To a certain Brahman (SN XII.46)
- Brahmana Sutta 1: To Unnabha the Brahman
- Cankii Sutta: To the Brahmin Cankii
- Esukaari Sutta: To the Brahmin Esukari
- Janussoni Brahmana Sutta: To the Brahmin Janussoni
- Ganakamoggallaanasuttam B: To the Brahmin Ganakamoggallaana
- Paccha-bhumika Sutta: To Brahmins of the Western Land (SN XLII.6)
- Saleyyaka Sutta A: The Brahmins of Sela
- Saleyyaka Sutta B: The Brahmans of Salahar"

In Kingdoms

There have been Brahmin Buddhists too in Buddhist kingdoms.

- In Cambodia (Sanskrit Kambhoja) there is an edict saying that King Jayavarman and his son Rudravarman build a monument in dedication of Lord Buddha and appointed a Brahmin to protect it.
- In Sri Lanka, Maha Adigar was the first Buddhist emperor of Sri Lanka, converting many to Buddhism.
- In 120 BC, the Indo-Greek King Milinda converted to Buddhism under sage Nagasena.
- The Shunga Dynasty is thought by neo-Buddhists as an anti-Buddhist dynasty but the Shungas themselves built a stupa dedicated to the Buddha at Baharut.

Brahmins in Jainism

- The founder of the new Jain religion was the Tirthankara or Jina Mahavira but his first convert was Indrabhuti (aka Gautamswami) the Brahmin, who headed a group of other Brahmins and converted them to Jainism. He was from the village Gobbar (also called Govarya) near Rajgriha.
- Sajjambhava was another born from Rajgriha and was elected the head of the Jain temple. He is famous for his composition of the "Dasavaikalika Sutra."
- Acharya Vidyanand is a Brahmin of the Dhigambar Jain sect and compiled in the Sanskrit language, "Ashta Shahastri" with eight thousand verses.
- Acharya Shushil Kumar, known better to Jains as "Guruji", was born a Vaidik in the Shakarpur village of the Haryana province. At the age of 15, he took Diksha (became a sanyassin) into the Sthanakvasi, a Swhetambara sub-sect.
- There is also a story about a wealthy Brahmin named Dhangiri in the town of Tumbhivan, who, when heard the sermons of the Jain Acharya Sinhgiri, while he regularly listened to but later lost his interest in wealth and decided to take the Diksha.
- Umasvati was a composer who was so loved by Jains that he is considered by the Dhigambar sect to be a

Dhigambar member and the Svetambara sect to be a Svetambara member.

In Kingdoms

- The Jain Acharya Bhadrabahu of Pundravardhana is said to be the preceptor of Chandragupta Maurya of the Mauryan dynasty, grandfather of Ashoka the Buddhist ruler.
- A copperplate grant from the Gupta period found in the vincity of Somapura mentioned a Brahmin donating land to a Jain vihara at Vatagohali.
- A Brahmin general by the name of Vasudeva in the army of Kamadeva in the Vijayaditya dynasty had built a temple to Lord Parshvanath.
- The Kadamba kings of Palasika were Jain Brahmins who supported Jainism and gave land grants and erected many temples and hence, patronised Jainism. This supports the view that Jainism entered South India through the West and perhaps from Ujjayini itself.
- King Mrigesavarman of the Kadamba dynasty of palasika further went on to give grants to Yapaniyas, Nigranthas and Kurchakas.
- The Brahmin Haribhadra was a pupil of Jinabhadra (or Jinabhata) and Jinadatta and later received the title of "Suri" (an honourable epithet of learning Jain monks.)

Brahmin Icons of Sikhism

Sikhism recognized the three main bhagats before the life of Guru Nanak; they are Bhagat Ramananda, Bhagat Surdas, Bhagat Jayadeva. Many of the other icons of Sikhism are disciple of Brahmins such as Bhagat Kabir, Bhagat Dhanna, Bhagat Ravidas, Bhaga Pipa, Bhagat Sain. The writings and sayings of these icons are preserved in the Sikh text, the Sri Guru Granth Sahib. Many writers of the Guru Granth Sahib are of the Bhatt surname. The Sikh composed Mathura Bhatt's fourteen verses are seven each in praise of Guru Ram Das and Guru Arjan.

There are also several Mohyals (Brahmin warriors) in the Sikh community.

Contributions to Modern India

Brahmins have immensely contributed to the making of modern India and to the world in fields such as literature, science and technology, politics, culture, and religion.

Brahmins played an extraordinary role in the spread of knowledge and vitalizing the Indian society for millennia. Recently, in the freedom movement and national revitalization movements they proved their merit by playing their traditional role as usual. Brahmin tribe's contribution in fighting against the British imperialism was immense. One can give innumerable examples of Brahmin contributions.

Their role and participation was great in various legislative bodies. During the Indian independence movement, many Brahmins, including Mangal Pandey, Chandrashekar Azad, Balgangadhar Tilak, Gopal Krishna Gokhale, Vinayak Damodar Savarkar, C. Rajagopalachari, Swami Sahajanand Saraswati, Basawon Singh (Sinha), Yogendra Shukla, and Sheel Bhadra Yajee, to name just a few, were at the forefront of the struggle for freedom. Jawaharlal Nehru, a Brahmin, was the first Prime Minister of India.

Other Brahmins who later attained this position are Morarji Desai, P.V. Narasimha Rao and Atal Behari Vajpayee.

Among the great Brahmin scholars and writers are Nobel laureates Rabindranath Tagore and V. S. Naipaul and others like Mahapandit Rahul Sankrityayan, Subramanya Bharathy, Ramdhari Singh 'Dinkar', Suryakant Tripathi Nirala, Sarat Chandra Chattopadhyay and Bankim Chandra Chatterjee.

Great Brahmin scientists include Nobel Laureate Sir C.V.Raman and Subrahmanyan Chandrasekhar, and great Brahmin mathematicians include Srinivasa Ramanujan and C. P. Ramanujam.

Srauta

Srauta traditions are conservative ritualistic traditions of historical Vedic religion in Hinduism, based on the body of shruti literature. They persist in a few places in India today although constituting a clear minority within Hinduism. *shrauta* is a vrddhi derivation of *shruti*, just like *Smarta* is the vrddhi derivation of *Smrti*.

Classification

Presently alive shrauta tradions are:

- Rig veda: Ashvalayana and Sankhayana
- Sama veda: Jaiminiya, Kauthuma, Ranayaniya
- Krishna Yajurveda:Baudhayana, Manava, Bharadvaja, Apastamba and Hiranyakesin
- Shukla Yajurveda: Katyayana
- Atharva Veda: Kaushitaki and Vaitana

Practices

The shrauta tradition as per the Vedas lays more emphasis on practice of the Dharma rather than having a set of beliefs. This is a distinguishing feature in Dharmic religions as well as pagan religions and is unlike the case in Abrahamic religions. The daily practices of the shrauta tradition mainly consist of Yajnas.

The Yajnas are divided into two categories, namely: nitya-karma and kaamya karma. *Nitya-karma* refers to those Yajnas that have to be performed daily or as per occasions. *Kaamya-karma* refers to those Yajnas performed with a particular purpose such as getting a child (*e.g.* Putrakameshti).

Yajnas

The Vedas describe 400 Yajnas. The Vedas give a scheme of Pancha Mahayajnas (Five Great Yajnas, see Taittiriya Aranyaka 2.10) namely:

- Devayajna-consists of offering *ahutis* to *devas*
- Pitruyajna-consists of offering Libations to ancestors or pitrus
- Bhutayajna-consists of offering *bali* or foodstuffs to all creatures
- Manushyayajna-consists of feeding guests
- Brahmayajna-consists of chanting Vedas, namely Rigveda, Yajurveda, Samaveda but not the Atharvaveda.

Pantheon

The pantheon in the shrauta tradition consist of various gods and goddesses, known as Devas. The associated theology may, however, not be typical of what is associated with the English term 'god'. Interpretations may go more towards identification with psychological or natural forces, an approach sometimes described as soft polytheism. For instance, the deva Agni has one aspect as the flame. But this flame symbolises the psychological power associated with Agni namely the power of will. Agni can be called God-will, while similarly Indra is the God-mind;Sarasvati is the Power of Inspiration, not merely of learning. But as stated above, the focus of Shrauta is not on theology but rather on ritual practice.

Since Shrauta focuses on conservative Vedic rituals, the pantheon corresponds to the Rigvedic deities more to that of mainstream (Puranic) Hinduism, among the most prominent deities being Agni and Indra, Soma, Savitar, and with goddesses such as Vac or Sarasvati (c.f. Chamakam 6):

Oral Tradition

The word shrauta is derived from the word shruti meaning that which is heard. The shrauta tradition of handing the Vedas down the generations consisted in solely of oral tradition from the Guru (teacher) to the Shishya (student). Vedic scholars have made use of manuscripts in order to teach the Vedas to their students at least since the Middle Ages, and of printed books since the advent of Western philology in British India, but the use of writing has always been clearly secondary to the commitment of the texts to memory.

Methods of Chanting

The oral tradition of the Vedas consists of several ways of chanting the Vedas. Mainly, the students are first taught the Samhita Paatha. Here, paatha means a way of chanting. The other methods of chanting include: "vakya", "pada", "karma", "jata", "mala", "sikha", "rekha", "dhvaja","danda", "ratha", "ghana". Some Vedic scholars are called "ghanapaathins". It means they have learnt the chanting of the scripture up to the advanced stage called "ghana". "Paathin" means one who has learnt the "paatha". Ghanapaathins chant the ghana by intoning a few words of a mantra in different ways, back and forth. The sonority natural to Vedic chanting is enhanced in ghana. Similarly, in the other methods of chanting like karma, jata, sikha, mala, and so on the intonation is nothing less than stately. *The chief purpose of such methods is to ensure that even not even a syllable of a mantra is altered to the slightest extent.* The words are braided together, so to speak, and recited back and forth.

Present Situation of Shrauta Tradition

Today the shrauta tradition most prominent in Southern India, with communities in Tamil Nadu, Kerala, Karnataka, Andhra Pradesh, but also in Uttar Pradesh, Maharashtra and other states; the best known of these groups are the Nambudiri of Kerala, whose traditions were notably documented by Frits Staal. The Smarta tradition of Hinduism is more prevalent in the country. The Smarta and Shrauta traditions are not mutually exclusive; some Smartas continue to practise the Vedic rituals.

The Aupasana is performed in many houses. However the shrauta tradition emphasises also on Agnihotra (whose performer is called Agnihotri).

Prominent Shrauti Scholars and Communities

- The Nambuduris of Kerala are the most famous shrautis in India.
- The other prominent shrautis include smartas in Mattur, Sringeri, Holenarsipur and other places in Karnataka
- The village Sengalipuram in Tamil Nadu is also famous for producing great shrauti scholars like Sengalipuram Anantarama Dikhshitar
- Warangal and Guntur in Andhra Pradesh have produced many shrauti scholars
- Dr. Jayanta Kumar Dirghangi is a shrauti agnihotri living in Memphis, Texas in the United States

Recent Srauta Yaagas

Some recent shrauta Yaagas that took place are:

- Atiraatra-in Kerala
- Agnistoma-in Kerala
- Nakshratreshti-in Karnataka
- Arunaketuka Yaaga-in Kalahasti, Andhra Pradesh

Vedic Priesthood

Priests of the Vedic religion were officiants of the *yajna* service. As persons trained for the ritual and proficient in its practice, they were called [tvij ("regularly-sacrificing"). As members of a social class, they were generically known as vipra ("sage") or kavi ("seer").

Tvij

Specialization of roles attended the elaboration and development of the ritual corpus over time, such that eventually a full complement of sixteen *[tvija*s became customary for the major ceremonials, comprising four chief priests and their assistants:

- The hot[, reciter of verses for invocations and litanies. These verses, either singly (*[ca*), or in strophes (triples called *t[ca* or pairs called *pragatha*), or as entire hymns (*sukta*), were drawn from the *[gveda*. As each phase of the ritual required an invocation, the *hot[* had a natural leading or presiding role.
- The adhvaryu, in charge of the physical details of the sacrifice (in particular an *adhvara*, a term for the Somayajna). According to Monier-Williams, the *adhvaryu* "had to measure the ground, to build the altar, to prepare the sacrificial vessels, to fetch wood and water, to light the fire, to bring the animal and immolate it", among other duties. Each action was accompanied by supplicative or benedictive formulas (*yajus*), drawn from the *yajurveda*. Over time, the role of the *adhvaryu* grew in importance, and many verses of the *[gveda* were incorporated, either intact or adapted, into the texts of the *yajurveda*.

- The udgat[, chanter of hymns, set to melodies (*saman*), drawn from the *samaveda*. This was a specialized role in the major soma sacrifices, praise of the invigorating properties of *soma pavamana*, the freshly pressed juice of the soma plant, being a characteristic function of the *udgat[*.
- The brahman, superintendent of the entire performance, and responsible for correcting mistakes by means of supplementary invocations.

In the chronologically late systematic expositions of the *shrauta sutras*, the assistants were artificially classified into four groups of three and associated with the four chief priests:

- With the *hot[*:
  - o the *maitravaruna*
  - o the *acchavaka*
  - o the *gravastut* (praising the Soma stones)
- With the *udgat[*:
  - o the *prastot[* (who chants the Prastaṿa)
  - o the *pratihart[* ("averter")
  - o the *subrahmanya*
- With the *adhvaryu*:
  - o the *pratiprasthat[*
  - o the *necm[*
  - o the *unnet[* (who pours the Soma juice into the receptacles)
- With the *brahman*:
  - o the *brahmanacchamsin*
  - o the *agnidh* (priest who kindles the sacred fire)
  - o the *pot[* ("purifier")

This did not reflect their ritual roles correctly, as the formal assistants of the *brahman* were actually assistants of the *hot[* and the *adhvaryu*.

A similar attempt at symmetry, as well as a play for preeminence, was in the claim advanced by partisans that the Atharvaveda was the province of the *brahman*: thusly, a fourth and presumably superior *veda* for the fourth and seniormost chief priest. This theoretical fancy had no basis in fact or likelihood, as the Atharvaveda made no contribution to the liturgy of the solemn high rituals. In practice, the *brahman* function was usually performed by a bahv[ca ("one who has many verses", *i.e.* a Rgvedin), suggesting a historical split of the duties of the *hot[* in the development of the *brahman* as a distinct role.

The older references uniformly indicate the *hot[* as the presiding priest, with perhaps only the *adhvaryu* as his assistant in the earliest times. The phrase "seven hotars" is found more than once in the Rgveda. RV.2.1.2 enumerates them as the *hot[*, *pot[*, *necm[*, *agnidh*, *prashast[* (meaning the *maitravaruna*), *adhvaryu* and *brahman* (meaning the *brahmanacchamsin*). The rgvedic Brahmanas, Aitareya and Kausitaki, specify seven *hotraka*s to recite *shastra*s (litanies): *hot[*, *brahmanacchamsin*, *maitravaruna*, *pot[*, *necm[*, *agnidh* and *acchavaka*. They also carry a legend to explain the origin of the offices of the *subrahmanya* and the *gravastut*.

Purohita

The requirements of the fully developed ritual were rigorous enough that only professional priests could perform them adequately. Thus, whereas in the earliest times, the true sacrificer, or intended beneficiary of the rite, might have been a direct participant, in Vedic times he was only a sponsor, the *yajamana*, with the *hot[* or *brahman* taking his stead in the ritual. In this seconding lay the origins of the growing importance of the purohita (literally, "one who is placed in front"), a term originally for a domestic chaplain, especially of a prince. It was not unusual for a *purohita* to be the *hot[* or *brahman* at a sacrifice for his master, besides conducting other more domestic (*g[hya*) rituals for him also. In latter days, with the disappearance of vedic ritual practice, *purohita* has become a generic term for "priest".

Philological comparisons

- Comparison with the sacred texts of Zoroastrianism, a distinct religion with the same origins, shows the antiquity of terms for priests such as *atharvan* (cognate to Avestan *athravan*) "fire-priest" and *hotar* (Av. *zaotar*) "invoker, sacrificer". While *hotar/zaotar* is well understood, there is no consensus on the etymology of *atharvan/athravan*. It has often been connected with Avestan atar-"fire" (not attested in Vedic), but, according to Boyce (1982:16), such connections may "have been prompted by what is probably a mistaken assumption of the importance of fire in the ancient Indo-Iranian religion". The compound *atharvangiras* of *atharvan* and *angiras*, either two eponymous rishis or family names, is the original name of the Atharvaveda as known to the other vedic practitioners.

- The division of priestly functions among the Hotar, the Udgatar and the Adhvaryu is directly comparable to the Celtic priesthood as reported by Strabo, with the Druids as high priests, the Bards doing the chanting and the Vates performing the actual sacrifice.

Shakha

The Sanskrit term shakha (IAST *uakha*), literally "branch" (as of a tree) or "arm", is used to refer either to a school of the Vedas, or to the traditional texts followed by a school. Monier-Williams defines it as "a branch or school of the Veda, each adhering to its own traditional text and interpretation)". That is, a shakha is a theological school that specializes in learning certain Vedic texts chosen from the extensive Vedic corpus.

The related term *caraGa*, which in general means "conduct of life" or "behaviour", is also used to refer to a school or branch of any of the Vedas. Monier-Williams says that "although the words *caraGa* and *uakha* are sometimes used synonymously, yet *caraGa* properly applies to the sect or collection of persons united in one school, and *uakha* to the traditional text followed, as in the phrase *uakham adhite*, he recites a particular version of the Veda."

An individual follower of a particular school or recension is called a "follower" (*uakhin*). This term is also used in Hindu philosophy to refer to an adherent of a particular orthodox system. The schools have different points of view on some things, which are described as "difference of (Vedic) school" (*uakhabheda%*).

In traditional Hinduism affiliation with a specific school is an important aspect of class identity. By the end of the Rig Vedic period the term BramaGa had come to be applied to all members of the priestly class, but there were subdivisions within this order based both on caste and on the shakha (branch) with which they were affiliated. A BramaGa who changed his own school of the Vedas would be called "a traitor to his *uakha*" (*uakharaca*).

Summary of Schools

A Vedic text may have a number of theological schools associated with it. For each school, adherents would learn a specific Vedic SaChita (one of the "four Vedas" properly so-called), as well as its associated Brahmana, Aranyakas, Shrautasutras, Grhyasutras and Upanishads.

Only a small number of recensions have survived. Shaunaka's *CaraGa-vyuha* is a traditional source of information about the shakhas for each Veda, giving lists of the numbers of recensions that were believed to have once existed as well as those still extant at the time the work was compiled.

Rig

- *Monier:* Williams says that shaunaka's *CaraGa-vyuha* lists five shakhas for the Rig Veda, the Uakala, Backala, Auvalayana, UaEkhayana, and Mag ukayana, but that only one, the Uakala, is now extant.
- Uncited notes:
- The Rigveda is known in the Shakala-shakha only (with surviving Bashkala fragments),
- The Bashkala recension of the Rigveda has the Khilani which are not present in the Shakala text.
- *Rigveda:* The *Shakala* has the Aitareya-Brahmana, The Bashkala has the Kausitaki-Brahmana.

Yajur

- *Monier:* Williams says that shaunaka's *CaraGa-vyuha* lists forty-two or forty-four out of eighty-six shakhas for the Yajur Veda, but that only five of these are now extant, with a sixth partially extant.
- Uncited notes:
- For the Yajur Veda the five (partially in six) shakhas are the (Vajasaneyi Madhandina, Kanva; Taittiriya, Maitrayani, Caraka-Katha, Kapisthala-Katha).
- Yajurveda: The Yajurvedin shakhas are divided in "White" and "Black" schools. The White recensions have separate Brahmanas, while the Black ones have their Brahmanas interspersed between the Mantras.
- *White Yajurveda: vajasaneyi madhyandina* (VSM), *vajasaneyi kanva* (VSK): Shatapatha Brahmana (ShBM, ShBK)
- *Black Yajurveda: taittiriya saChita* (TS) with an additional Brahmana, Taittiriya Brahmana (TB), *maitrayani saChita* (MS), *caraka-katha saChita* (KS), *kapicmhala-katha saChita* (KapS).

Sama

- *Monier:* Williams says that shaunaka's *CaraGa-vyuha* lists twelve shakhas for the Sama Veda out of a thousand that are said to have once existed, but that of these only one or perhaps two are still extant.
- Uncited notes:
- The two Samaveda recensions are the Jaiminiya and Kauthuma.
- *Samaveda:* The Kauthuma shakha has the PB, SadvB, the Jaiminiya shakha has the Jaiminiya Brahmana.

Atharva

- Apte says there are nine shakhas and five kalpas for the Atharvaveda.
- *Monier:* Williams says that only one shakha of an original nine is now extant for the Atharvaveda.

- Uncited notes:
- The Shaunaka is the only shakha of the Atharvaveda for which both printed texts and an active oral tradition are known to still exist.
- For the Atharvaveda, both the Shaunakiya and the Paippalada traditions contain textual corruption, and the original text of the Atharvaveda may only be approximated from comparison between the two.
- The Paippalada tradition was discontinued, and its text is known only from manuscripts collected since the 19th century.
- No Brahmana is known for the Shaunaka shakha.
- The Paippalada is possibly associated with the Gopatha Brahmana.

Nastika

Astika and Nastika are technical terms in Hinduism used to classify philosophical schools and persons, according to whether they accept the authority of the Vedas as supreme revealed scriptures, or not. By this definition, Nyaya, Vaisheshika, Samkhya, Yoga, Purva Mimamsa and Vedanta are classified as *astika* schools; while Charvaka, Jainism and Buddhism are considered *nastika* schools.

In non-technical usage, the term *astika* is sometimes loosely translated as "theist" while *nastika* is translated as "atheist". However this interpretation is distinct from the use of the term in Hindu philosophy. Notably even among the *astika* schools, *samkhya* and the early *mimamsa* school do not accept a God (see Atheism in Hinduism) while accepting the authority of the Vedas; they thus are "atheistic *astika* schools".

The different usages of these terms are explained by Chatterjee and Datta as follows:

> *In modern Indian languages, 'astika' and 'nastika' generally mean 'theist' and 'atheist', respectively. But in Sanskrit philosophical literature, 'astika' means 'one who believes in the authority of the Vedas' or 'one who believes in life after death'. ('nastika' means the opposite*

of these). The word is used here in the first sense. In the second sense, even the Jaina and Bauddha schools are 'astika', as they believe in life after death. The six orthodox schools are 'astika', and the Carvaka is 'nastika' in both the senses.

Etymology

Astika (IAST:astika) is a Sanskrit adjective (and noun) that is derived from *asti* ("it is or exists") meaning "believing" or "pious"; or "one who believes in the existence (of God, of another world, etc.)." *Nastika* (*na* (not) + *astika*) is its negative, literally meaning "not believing" or "not pious". As used in Indian philosophy *nastika* refers to belief in Vedic authority, not belief or lack of belief in theism. As N. N. Bhattacharyya writes:

The followers of Tantra are often branded as Nastika by the upholders of the Vedic tradition. The term Nastika does not denote an atheist. It is applied only to those who do not believe in the Vedas.

The SaEkhyas and Mimansakas do not believe in God, buth they believe in the Vedas and hence they are not Nastikas. The Buddhists, Jains, and Carvakas do not believe in the Vedas; hence they are Nastikas.

Classification of Schools

Many Indian intellectual traditions were codified during the medieval period into a standard list of six orthodox systems, the shaddarshanas (*°addarshana*), all of which cite Vedic authority as their source:

- Nyaya, the school of logic
- Vaisheshika, the atomist school
- Samkhya, the enumeration school
- Yoga, the school of Patanjali (which assumes the metaphysics of Samkhya)
- Purva Mimamsa (or simply Mimamsa), the tradition of Vedic exegesis, and
- Vedanta (also called Uttara Mimamsa), the Upanishadic tradition.

These are often coupled into three groups for both historical and conceptual reasons: Nyaya-Vaishesika, Samkhya-Yoga, and Mimamsa-Vedanta.

The three main heterodox schools of Indian philosophy do not base their beliefs on Vedic authority:

- Buddhism
- Jainism
- Carvaka

The use of the term *nastika* to describe Buddhism and Jainism in India is explained by Gavin Flood as follows:

At an early period, during the formation of the Upani°ads and the rise of Buddhism and Jainism, we must envisage a common heritage of meditation and mental discipline practiced by renouncers with varying affiliations to non-orthodox (Veda-rejecting) and orthodox (Veda-accepting) traditions.... These schools [such as Buddhism and Jainism] are understandably regarded as heterodox (*nastika*) by orthodox (*astika*) Brahmanism.

The Tantric traditions in Hinduism, have both *astika* and *nastika* lines; as Banerji writes in "*Tantra in Bengal*":

Tantras are... also divided as *astika* or Vedic and *nastika* or non-Vedic. In accordance with the predominance of the deity the *astika* works are again divided as Uakta, Uaiva, Saura, Ganapatya and Vaicnava.

Mimamsa

Mimamsa is the name of an astika ("orthodox") school of Hindu philosophy whose primary enquiry is into the nature of dharma based on close hermeneutics of the Vedas. Its core tenets are ritualism (orthopraxy), anti-asceticism and anti-mysticism. The central aim of the school is elucidation of the nature of *dharma*, understood as a set ritual obligations and prerogatives to be performed properly. The nature of dharma isn't accessible to reason or observation, and must be inferred from the authority of the revelation contained in the Vedas, which are considered eternal, authorless (*apaurusheyatva*), and infallible.

Overview

Mimamsa is more accurately known as Purva Mimansa "prior inquiry" since it investigates the "earlier" (*purva*) portions of the Vedas, while *Uttara Mimansa* ("posterior or higher inquiry") is the opposing school of Purva Mimamsa. This division is based on the notion of a dichotomy of the Vedic texts into a *karma-kanda*, including the Samhitas and Brahmanas and the *jnana-kanda* of the Upanishads.

The foundational text for the Mimamsa school is the Purva Mimamsa Sutras of Jaimini (ca. 3rd to 1st century BC). A major commentary was composed by Uabara in ca. the 5th or 6th century. The school reaches its height with Kumarila Bhatta and Prabhakara(fl. ca. 700 CE). Both Kumarila Bhatta and Prabhakara (along with one Murari) have written extensive commentaries on Uabara's Mimamsasutrabhashyam. The school for some time in the Early Middle Ages exerted near-dominant influence on learned Hindu thought, and is credited as a major force contributing to the decline of Buddhism in India, but it has fallen into decline in the High Middle Ages and today is all but eclipsed by Vedanta. Mimamsa is still the only one of the six orthodox darshanas besides Vedanta to survive into contemporary Hinduism. There are two surviving traditions, the *Bhattas* and the *Prabhakaras*, following Bhatta and Prabhakara, respectively.

Literature of Mimamsa

The *Mimansa Sutra* of Jaimini (c. 3rd century BC) has summed up the general rules of *nyaya* for Vedic interpretation. The text has 12 chapters, of which the first chapter is of philosophical value. The commentaries on the *Mimansa Sutra* by Bhartmitra, Bhavadasa, Hari and Upavarca are no more extant. shabara (c. 1st century BC) is the first commentator of the *Mimansa Sutra*, whose work is available to us. His *bhacya* is the basis of all later works of *Mimansa*. Kumarila Bhamma (7th century CE), the founder of the first school of the *Mimansa* commented on both the *Sutra* and its *Uabara Bhacya*. His treatise consists of 3 parts, the *Ulokavarttika*, the *Tantravarttika* and the *lupmika*.

Manana Mishra (8th century CE) was a follower of Kumarila, who wrote *Vidhiviveka* and *Mimansanukramani. There are several commentaries on the works of Kumarila. Sucarita Mishra wrote a* Kauika *(commentary) on the* Ulokavarttika. *Someshvara Bhatta wrote* Nyayasudha, *also known as* Ranaka, *a commentary on the* Tantravarttika. *Parthasarathi Miura wrote* Nyayaratnakara *(1300 CE), another commentary on the* Ulokavarttika. *He also wrote* Uastradipika, *an independent work on the* Mimansa and *Tantraratna. Venkama Dikcita's* Varttikabharanya *is a commentary on the* lupmika. Prabhakara (8th century CE), the originator of the second school of the *Mimansa* wrote his commentary *Behati* on the *Uabara Bhacya.* Ualikanatha's *Zjuvimala* (9th century CE) is a commentary on the *Behati.* His *Prakaranapancika is an independent work of this school and the* Parishicma *is a brief explanation of the* Uabara Bhacya. *Bhavanatha's* Nyayaviveka *deals with the views of this school in details. The founder of the third school of the* Mimansa *was* Murari, *whose works have not reached us. Apadeva (17th century CE) wrote an elementary work on the* Mimansa, *known as* Mimansanyayaprakaua *or* Apadevi. Arthasa Agraha *of Laugakci Bhaskara is based on the* Apadevi. *Vedanta Deuika's* Ueuvara Mimansa *was an attempt to combine the views of the* Mimansa *and the* Vedanta *schools.*

Dharma and Atheism

Dharma as understood by Mimamsa can be loosely translated into English as "virtue", "morality" or "duty". The Mimamsa school traces the source of the knowledge of dharma neither to sense-experience nor inference, but to verbal cognition (*i.e.* knowledge of words and meanings). In this respect it is related to the Nyaya school.

The Mimamsa school held dharma to be equivalent to following the prescriptions of the Samhitas and their Brahmana commentaries relating the correct performance of Vedic rituals. Seen in this light, Mimamsa is essentially ritualist (orthopraxy), placing great weight on the performance of Karma or action as enjoined by the Vedas. In this sense, it is a counter-movement to the mysticism of Vedanta, rejecting or de-emphasizing moksha or salvation. To a certain extent, Mimamsa is atheist, placing all importance in proper practice as opposed to belief, rejecting a creator God as well as any scriptures on dharma outside of the Vedic tradition, yet accepting svarga or heaven awaiting the person who has acted righteously in his or her life. In its rejection of belief in a God, it is related to the nastika Carvaka school.

Kalpa (Vedanga)

Tradition does not single out any special work as the Vedanga in this branch of Vedic science; but the sacrificial practice gave rise to a large number of systematic sutras for the several classes of priests. The most important of these works have come down to us, and they occupy by far the most prominent place among the literary productions of the sutra-period. The Kalpa-sutras, or rules of ceremonial, are of two kinds: (1) the *Shrautasutra*s, which are based on the *shruti*, and teach the performance of the great sacrifices, requiring three sacrificial fires; and (2) the *Smrtasutra*s, or rules based on the *smrti* or tradition. The latter class again includes two kinds of treatises: (1) the *Grhyasutra*s, or domestic rules, treating of ordinary family rites, such as marriage, birth, namegiving, etc., connected with simple offerings in the domestic fire; and (2) the *Dharmasutra*s, which treat of customs and temporal duties, and are supposed to have formed the chief sources of the later law-books. Besides, the Shrauta-sutras of the Yajurveda have usually attached to them a set of so-called *Shulva-sutras*, *i.e.* rules of the cord, which treat of the measurement by means of cords, and the construction, of different kinds of altars required for sacrifices. These treatises are of special interest as supplying important information regarding the earliest geometrical operations in India. Along with the Sutras may be classed a large number of supplementary treatises, usually called *Parishishta*, on various subjects connected with the sacred texts and Vedic religion generally.

Shrauta Sutras

The Shrautasutras (*urautasutra*) form a part of the corpus of Sanskrit Sutra literature. Their topic is the interpretation of the shruti corpus and instructions relating to 'kalpa, *the correct performance of ritual sacrifice. The bulk of the Shrautasutras are roughly contemporary to the Grhya corpus of domestic sutras, their language being late Vedic Sanskrit, dating maybe to roughly the 6th century BC (the century predating Panini).*

Veda	***Shrautasutra***
Rigveda	Auvalayana Urautasutra Sankhayana Urautasutra
Samaveda	Latyayana Urautasutra Drahayana Urautasutra Jaiminiya shrautasutra
Krisna Yajurveda	Baudhayana Urautasutra Manava Urautasutra Bharadvaja Urautasutra Apastamba Urautasutra Hiranyakeshi shrautasutra Varaha Urautasutra Vaikhanasa Urautasutra
shukla Yajurveda	Katyayana Urautasutra
Atharvaveda	Vaitana Urautasutra

Grhya Sutras

The Grhya Sutras "domestic sutras" are a category of Sanskrit texts in the tradition of the Brahmanas, commenting on Vedic ritual. Their language is late Vedic Sanskrit, and they date to around roughly 500 BC, contemporary with the Shrautasutras. They are named after Vedic shakhas.

Veda	***Grihyasutra***
Rigveda	Ashvalayana Grhyasutra Kausitaki-Grhyasutra Uankhayana Grihyasutra
Samaveda	Gobhila Grhyasutra Khadira Grhyasutra (Drahyayana-Grhyasutra) Jaiminiya-Grhyasutra Kauthuma-Grhyasutra
Krisna Yajurveda	Baudhayana-Grhyasutra Hiranyakeshi-Grhyasutra (Satyasadha-Grhyasutra) Manava-Grhyasutra Bharadvaja-Grhyasutra Apastamba-Grhyasutra Agniveshya-Grhyasutra Vaikhanasa-Grhyasutra Kathaka-Grhyasutra (Laugaksi-Grhyasutra)Varaha-GrhyasutraVadhula-Grhyasutra

	Kapisthala-Katha Grhyasutra (unpublished)
shukla Yajurveda	Katyayana Grhyasutra (different from Paraskara-Grhyasutra) Paraskara-Grhyasutra
Atharvaveda	Kaushika Grhyasutra

Dharma Sutras

The Dharmasutras are Sanskrit texts dealing with law and rituals. They include the four surviving written works of the ancient Indian tradition on the subject of dharma, or the rules of behaviour recognized by a community. Unlike the later *Dharmashastra*, the dharmasutras are composed in prose. The oldest Dharmasutra is generally believed to have been that of Apastamba, followed by the dharmasutras of Gautama, Baudhayana, and Vasishtha. It is difficult to determine exact dates for these texts, but the dates between 500-300 BC have been suggested for the oldest Dharmasutras. Later Dharmasutras include those of Kasyapa, Brhaspati, and Ushanas.

Veda	*Dharmasutra*
Rigveda	Vasishtha Dharmasutra
Samaveda	Gautama Dharmasutra
Krisna Yajurveda	Baudhayana Dharmasutra Apastamba Dharmasutra

Shulba Sutras

The shulbasutra dealing with altar geometry are notably part of the Shrauta Sutras.

Veda	*Shulbasutra*
Krisna Yajurveda	Baudhayana Uulbasutra Manava Uulbasutra Apastamba Uulbasutra
shukla Yajurveda	Katyayana Uulbasutra

Anti-Brahminism

Anti-Brahminism, also spelled as Anti-Brahmanism, is discrimination, hostility or prejudice directed at the Hindu Brahmin caste, as opposed to Anti-Hinduism which rejects

Hinduism as a whole. Anti-Brahmanism has been associated with Indian reformers Phule and Periyar, Neo-Buddhism, Islamic political movements and Christian missionaries.

Examples of Anti-Brahmanism

In Islamic Extresism: In the book, *Diwan-i-Salman* by Khawajah Masud bin Sa'd bin Salman wrote of the Battle of Jalandhar (Punjab):

> *"The narrative of any battles eclipses the stories of Rustam and Isfandiyar...By morning meal, not one soldier, not one Brahmin remained unkilled or uncaptured. Their heads were levelled with the ground with falming fire..Thou has secured the victory to the country and to religion, for amongst the Hindus this achievement will be remembered till the day of resurrection."*

In Mughal times Sheikh Ahmad (Mujaddid) of Sirhind wrote a letter to Mirza Darab:

> *"Hindu Brahmans and Greek philosophers have spent a lot of time on religion. Since their efforts were not according to the Shariyat of the prophet, they were all fools. They will remain devoid of salvation."*

Further, for the destruction of Mahaviraha (Odantapura), Bihar in 1198 there was a massive slaughter of Buddhist monks. The story was retold in 1243 by the Persian historian Minhaz in his book, *Tabaquat-i-Nasiri* is recorded:

> *"Most of the inhabitants of the place were Brahmanas with shaven heads (monks). They were put to death. Large numbers of books were found there, and when the Mahammadans saw them, they called for some person to explain the contents. But all of the men were killed. It was discovered that the whole 41 fort and city was a place for study (madrasa): in the Hindi language the word Bihar (i.e. Vihara) means a college."*

In media

- The "Secret Circular of the Brahmin Samaj of Balaghat, a document widely disseminated by the missionaries, specially among the dalits and tribals.

- The anti-Hindu website Dalistan (now defunct), included an extensive set of documents promoting anti-Brahmin, anti-Hindu and separationist ideas. They have been widely promoted and quoted by anti-Hindu interests.

In Indian States

In Maharashtra: The anti-brahmin hate group Sambhaji Brigade attacked Bhandarkar Oriental Research Institute of Maharashtra in January 2004, claiming that the Institute had defamed Shivaji. Later the Sambhaji Brigade issued statements reflecting anti-Brahmin sentiments.

There certainly neo-Buddhists who decide to blame Buddhisms downfall on the Brahmans while ignorantly trying to deny or trying to hide from history the contributions made by the Brahmins to Buddhism. To name a few, the Bodhisattva Nagarjuna, Bodhisattva Aryasangha, and Bodhisattva Kshitagarbha.

It is said that before The Buddha Himself, there were also other Buddhas and in those time periods Lord Buddha was Brahmin Suruci, Brahmin Atideva, Brahmin Ajita and there are more past Brahmin lives of The Buddha. Brahmins have significantly helped in spread the Buddha Dharma. In Tibet it was Bodhisattva Padmasambhava, in central Asia it was Kumarajiva, in mainland China it was Bodhisattva Bodhidharma and in Japan it was Nagasena.

In Tamil Nadu: Tamil Nadu is home to one of the oldest anti-Brahmin movements in India. Historically, lower-castes were not allowed into temples and schools in Tamil Nadu.

The self-respect movement founded by Periyar espoused rationalism and atheism, and although Periyar had Brahmin colleagues, the movement had currents of anti-Brahminism. Tamil Brahmins (Iyers and Iyengars) were frequently held responsible by followers of Periyar for direct or indirect oppression of lower-caste people; this contributed to several clashes and a gradual migration of the upper castes. Later, in regards to a DK member's attempt to assassinate Rajagopalachari, Periyar "expressed his abhorrence of violence as a means of settling political differences".

The legacy of the anti-Brahmanism in the self-respect movement was taken over by the later Dravidan parties. Eventually, the virulent anti-Brahmanism subsided somewhat with the replacement of the DMK party by the AIADMK. Now the AIADMK is led by the Brahmin Jayalalitha or "Amma" (*mother*, as her followers call her), which is a pole in the eye of the anti-Brahmin. Dear brahmin friends, your mother jayalalitha became a pole on your own eye by arresting your holy guru sankaracharya!

4

Brahmin Religious Tradition

Silent adorations to *Sachidananda Para-Brahman,* Who is the silent Witness of all minds, Who is the Indweller in all beings, Who has projected this world for His own *Lila* or sport, Who is the support for this world, body and mind and all movements, and Who is the foundation for all societies and their activities.

Purpose of Religion

The word Religion comes from the Latin word *religio* which consists of two words, *viz.*, *re* (back) and *ligare* (to bring or bind). That which binds the soul back to God is religion. Religion shows the way for the attainment of God-realisation.

Religion satisfies the deep inward craving in man who is not always content with leading merely an animal existence and wants spiritual consolation, solace and peace. Man cannot live by bread alone. A time comes in the life of many of us when mere worldly prosperity does not satisfy us and we hanker after something more. In the case of many more, trials and tribulations of life turn their attention to spiritual solace.

Distinguishing Features of Hinduism

A Revealed Religion: Hinduism is the religion of the Hindus, a name given to the Universal Religion which hailed supreme in India. It is the oldest of all living religions. This is not founded by any prophet. Buddhism, Christianity and Mohammedanism owe their origin to the prophets. Their dates are fixed. But no such date can be fixed for Hinduism. Hinduism is not born of the teachings of particular prophets. It is not based on a set of dogmas preached by a particular set of teachers. It is free from religious fanaticism.

Hinduism is also known by the names *Sanatana-Dharma* and *Vaidika-Dharma*.

Sanatana-Dharma means eternal religion. Hinduism is as old as the world itself. Hinduism is the mother of all religions. Hindu scriptures are the oldest in the world, Sanatana-Dharma is so called, not only because it is eternal, but also because it is protected by God and because it can make us eternal.

Vaidika-Dharma means the religion of the Vedas. The Vedas are the foundational scriptures of Hinduism. The ancient Rishis and sages of India have expressed their intuitive spiritual experiences *(Aparoksha-Anubhuti)* in the Upanishads. These experiences are direct and infallible. Hinduism regards the spiritual experiences of the Rishis of yore as its authority. The priceless truths that have been discovered by the Hindu Rishis and sages through millennia constitute the glory of Hinduism. Therefore, Hinduism is a revealed religion.

A Religion of Freedom: Hinduism, unlike other religions, does not dogmatically assert that the final emancipation is possible only through its means and not through any other. It is only a means to an end and all means which will ultimately lead to the end are equally approved.

Hinduism allows absolute freedom to the rational mind of man. Hinduism never demands any undue restraint upon the freedom of human reason, the freedom of thought, feeling and will of man. It allows the widest freedom in matters of faith and worship. Hinduism is a religion of freedom.

It allows absolute freedom to the human reason and heart with regard to questions such as nature of God, soul, creation, form of worship and the goal of life. Hinduism does not lie in the acceptance of any particular doctrine, nor in the observance of some particular rituals or form of worship. It does not force anybody to accept particular dogmas or forms of worship. It allows everybody to reflect, investigate, enquire and cogitate. Hence, all sorts of religious faiths, various forms of worship or

Sadhana, and diverse kinds of rituals and customs, have found their honourable places side by side within Hinduism and are cultured and developed in harmonious relationship with one another.

Hinduism does not condemn those who deny God as the creator and ruler of the world, who do not accept the existence of an eternal soul and the state of Moksha or state of liberation. Hinduism does not render the upholders of such views unfit to be recognised as pious and honourable members of the Hindu religious society.

The religious hospitality of Hinduism is proverbial. Hinduism is extremely catholic and liberal. This is the fundamental feature of Hinduism. Hinduism pays respects to all religions. It does not revile any other religion. It accepts and honours truth—wherever it may come from and whatever garb it may put on. Despite all the differences of metaphysical doctrines, modes of religious discipline and forms of ritualistic practices and social habits prevalent in the Hindu society, there is an essential uniformity in the conception of religion and in the outlook on life and the world, among all sections of Hindus.

The Glory of Vedanta and Yoga

Vedanta, or the philosophy of the Upanishads, is lofty, sublime and unique. The Western philosophers have paid their tribute to the ancient seers of the Upanishads. They have been amazed at the lofty heights scaled by them. Schopenhauer studied the Upanishads and meditated on the thoughts of the Upanishads just before going to bed. He said: "The Upanishads are the solace of my life and they will be solace to me after my death also."

The Raja-Yoga system of Hinduism is also splendid and unique. The lessons are immensely practical and highly instructive. No system of physical exercise on the surface of the earth can compete with Hatha-Yoga. Kundalini-Yoga is wonderful. Hence the Americans and Europeans are in search of Hindu Sannyasins and Yogins. They visit the Himalayas frequently in quest of Yoga teachers. Some are living under

Hindu Yogins as disciples and are practising Yoga. Many Europeans and Americans are even now Hindus by faith and practice, though they are born Christians. They practise Raja-Yoga and Vedanta.

Emphasis on Practice

Hinduism provides spiritual food and Yoga Sadhana for all sorts of people to suit their temperaments, capacities, tastes, stages of spiritual development and conditions of life. It prescribes Yoga Sadhana even for a scavenger or a cobbler to attain God-realisation, while doing his ordinary avocation in the world. Hindu Yoga and Vedanta teachers lay great stress on self-restraint, Tapas, renunciation and practical Sadhana which is best calculated to control the mind and the senses and unfold the divinity or attain Self-realisation. Hinduism is not a religion of mere theories. It is eminently practical. In no religion you will find such a variety of practical Yoga practised and such sublime unique philosophy expounded. That is the reason why India is the only glorious land of sages, Rishis, Yogins and saints.

Religion is practical aspect of philosophy. Philosophy is rational aspect of religion. The philosophy of Hinduism is not arm-chair philosophy. It is not meant for intellectual curiosity and vain discussion. Hindu philosophy is a way of life. The philosopher of Hinduism seriously reflects after hearing the Srutis, does Atma-Vichara, constantly meditates, and then attains Self-realisation or Atma-Sakshatkara. Moksha is his goal. He attempts to attain Jivanmukti now and here.

Religion is spiritualisation of human life for a Hindu. Religious culture is really the culture of freedom for him. Religion governs all the departments of Hindu life. He must realise the freedom of the soul in every department of life. Religion affords the greatest scope for him for the culture of true freedom. Religion is the only way to him for the realisation of perfect freedom in life.

It is in India alone that every man knows something of philosophy. The cowherd who tends the cattle, the peasant who ploughs the fields, the boat-man who pulls at his oar, sing songs replete with philosophical truths. Even the barber repeats OM NAMAH SHIVAYA, SIVOHAM before he takes up the razor. The Paramahamsa Sannyasins, the itinerant monks of Hinduism, have disseminated the highest of Vedanta from door to door. In exchange for a handful of rice, they have distributed from door to door, through religious songs, the priceless gems of Hindu religion and philosophy.

Who is a Hindu?

In a meeting of the Sanatana Dharma Sabha, Lokamanya Tilak said: "A Hindu is he who believes that the Vedas contain self-evident and axiomatic truths."

The Hindu Maha Sabha has given another definition: "A Hindu is one who believes in a religion which has originated in India."

"Those who burn the dead are Hindus." This is another definition given by some.

"He who protects the cows and the Brahmins is a Hindu." This is another definition given by some.

Some define: "A Hindu is one who regards India as his motherland and the most sacred spot on earth."

Some others define: "He who calls and considers himself a Hindu is a Hindu."

Some define: "He who accepts the Vedas, the Smritis, the Puranas and the Tantras as the basis of religion and of the rule of conduct, and believes in one Supreme God (Brahman), in the Law of Karma or retributive justice, and in reincarnation *(Punarjanma)*, is a Hindu."

"He who follows the Vedic or Sanatana-Dharma is a Hindu." This is the definition by some.

"He who is a follower of the Vedanta is a Hindu." This is another definition given by some others.

"He who has perfect faith in the Law of Karma, the law of reincarnation *Avatara,* ancestor worship, *Varnashrama Dharma, Vedas* and existence of God, he who practises the instructions given in the Vedas with faith and earnestness, he who does *Sandhya, Shradha, Pitri-Tarpana* and the *Pancha-Maha-Yajnas,* he who follows the Varnashrama Dharmas, he who worships the Avataras and studies the Vedas, is a Hindu." This is the definition given by some highly cultured men. This is the only correct and complete definition.

Origin and Significance of the Term

That part of the great Aryan race which migrated from Central Asia, through the mountain passes into India, settled first in the districts near the river Sindhu, now called the Indus, on the other side of the river. The Persians pronounced the word Sindhu as Hindu, and named their Aryan brethren Hindus. *Hindu* is only a corrupt form of *Sindhu.*

The Hindu Aryans spread themselves over the plains of the Ganga. Then the Persians gave the name Hindusthan, or abode of the Hindus, to the whole of those districts between Punjab and Benaras. (Latest *historical researches have now proved that the Aryans did not come from outside India, but were the original inhabitants of India.*)

The classical name for India which is used in Sanskrit literature is *Bharata-Varsha* or *Bharata-Khanda,* after the name of Bharata who ruled over a large extent of territory in days of yore. Manu's name for the whole central region between the Himalayas and the Vindhya mountains is *Aryavarta,* Abode of the Aryans. Another name for the whole of India is *Jambu-Dvipa.* The Greeks gave the name Indu to the whole of this country. It was on account of this *India* became popular as the name of this country throughout Europe.

Hindu is not a mere name. This name *Hindu* is not only of geographical, but also of national and racial importance. The whole history of our nation from the very beginning is bound up with it. All our ideas and ideals are so intimately connected with it that it is difficult to give a simple definition of it. Poets, prophets and Avataras came to sing the praises and glory of this name. Rishis, sages and saints took their birth to compile the *Shastras* and *Darshanas* for this nation.

Heroes and warriors have fought for its honour and laid down their very lives for it. Piety, nobility, generosity, philosophy, religious bent of mind, Yoga, religious tolerance, wisdom, devotion, renunciation, Self-realisation. Ahimsa, Satya and purity are associated with the name 'Hindu'.

The Spiritual Soil of India

India is the sacred land which has given birth to countless sages, Rishis, Yogins, saints and prophets. India is the land that has produced many Acharyas or spiritual preceptors like Sri Shankara and Sri Ramanuja; many saints like Kabir, Ramdas, Tukaram and Gauranga Mahaprabhu; many Yogins like Jnana Dev, Dattatreya and Sadashiva Brahman; and many prophets like Buddha and Nanak. Buddha is our flesh and blood.

India is proud of Guru Govinda Singh and Shivaji. India is proud of king Bhoja and Vikramaditya. India is proud of Shankara and Kabir. India is proud of Valmiki and Kalidasa. Krishna, Rama and all Avataras were born in India. How sacred is India! How sublime is India!

The dust of Brindavan and Ayodhya, the land trodden by the sacred feet of Krishna and Rama, still purifies the heart of countless people. Even Jesus, during the missing period of His life, lived in Kashmir and learnt Yoga from the Indian Yogins. Glory to Mother India!

India is a spiritual country. India never conquered territories or annexed dominions. Military conquest is not her ambition. She wants her children to have *Atma-Svarajya* or Absolute Independence. She does not call upon them to rule over others. She wants them to have conquest over internal and external nature. She wants them to possess brilliant divine virtues, moral stamina and inner spiritual strength born of wisdom of the soul. Ahimsa is her weapon to have the spiritual conquest and the conquest of the minds of others.

People of India have Self-realisation as their goal. They do not, generally, bestow too much attention on material prosperity and advancement. They want Yoga or communion with the Supreme Being. They practise Ahimsa, Satya and Brahmacharya. They wish to enjoy the eternal bliss of the Absolute. They are always ready to renounce worldly possessions in order to possess or realise the inner Atman or Brahman. They will sacrifice anything and everything in order to attain the immortal Atman. They are always spiritual-minded.

India is the sacred land with several holy rivers and powerful spiritual vibrations. The hoary Himalayas attract the people of the whole world. It is a land peculiarly suitable for divine contemplation and Yogic practices. Every country has its own special attractive features. India is the land of Yogins and sages. This is the special attractive feature of India. This is the reason why people from America, England and all parts of the world come to India for the practice of Yoga.

The Facts of History

India is the most tolerant country in the world. She has a very expansive heart. She includes all nations in the embrace of her love. The Western nations are the descendents of the original Hindus or Aryans. They might have forgotten their old connections with the Aryans and Hindu culture. They might have forgotten all about their ancestors. But this cannot be effaced from the annals of history. Mother India, the repository of Hindu culture, cannot forget her children beyond the seas. They are always dear to her.

Hindu culture and Hindu civilisation were at their zenith in the days of yore. Greeks and Romans imitated the Hindus and absorbed Hindu thoughts. Even now Hindu culture and Hindu civilisation stand foremost in the world. No religion has produced so many great saints, sages, Yogins, Rishis, Maharishis, prophets, Acharyas, benefactors, heroes, poets, statesmen and kings as Hinduism. Each and every province of the country has produced intellectual giants, poets and saints. Even now India abounds in Rishis, philosophers, saints and high intellectuals. Even now she abounds in sages and great souls.

The Hindus had to undergo severe hardships and tortures. They had to face fierce battles and cruelties and yet they live today. Some mysterious power has preserved them. Some invisible force has protected them. That power will protect them for ever.

Reasons for Survival of the Hindu Religion

Hinduism is neither asceticism nor illusionism, neither polytheism nor pantheism. It is the synthesis of all types of religious experiences. It is a whole and complete view of life. It is characterised by wide toleration, deep humanity and high spiritual purpose. It is free from fanaticism. That is the reason why it has survived the attacks of the followers of some of the other great religions of the world.

No religion is so very elastic and tolerant like Hinduism. Hinduism is very stern and rigid regarding the fundamentals. It is very elastic in readjusting to the externals and non-essentials. That is the reason why it has succeeded in living through millennia. The foundation of Hinduism has been laid on the bedrock of spiritual truths. The entire structure of Hindu life is built on eternal truths, the findings of the Hindu Rishis or seers. That is the reason why this structure has lasted through scores of centuries.

Its Future: The glory of Hinduism is ineffable. It has within it all the features of a universal religion. Its Dharmas are universal. Its doctrines are sublime. Its philosophy is grand. Its ethics is soul-elevating. Its scriptures are wonderful. Its Sadhanas or Yoga-Vedantic practices are unique. Glorious has been the past of this religion; still more glorious is its future. It has a message to give to a world rent asunder by hatred, dissension and war—the message of cosmic love, truth and non-violence, the gospel of unity of Self or Upanishadic oneness.

The more you know of India and Hinduism, the more will you come to regard and love it and the more grateful to the Lord will you be in that you have got a taste for practising Yoga and that you are imbibing the teachings and spirit of Hinduism.

Glory to India! Glory to Hinduism! Glory, glory to the Rishis and the seers who have kept burning the flame of Hinduism with its extreme effulgence and splendour!

Hindu Scriptures

Sanskrit Literature: Sanskrit literature can be classified under six orthodox heads and four secular heads. The six orthodox sections form the authoritative scriptures of the Hindus. The four secular sections embody the later developments in classical Sanskrit literature.

The six scriptures are: (i) Srutis, (ii) Smritis, (iii) Itihasas, (iv) Puranas, (v) Agamas and (vi) Darshanas.

The four secular writings are: (i) Subhashitas, (ii) Kavyas, (iii) Natakas and (iv) Alankaras.

The Scriptures

The Srutis: The *Srutis* are called the *Vedas,* or the *Amnaya.* The Hindus have received their religion through revelation, the Vedas. These are direct intuitional revelations and are held to be *Apaurusheya* or entirely superhuman, without any author in particular. The Veda is the glorious pride of the Hindus, nay, of the whole world!

The term *Veda* comes from the root *Vid,* to know. The word *Veda* means knowledge. When it is applied to scripture, it signifies a book of knowledge. The Vedas are the foundational scriptures of the Hindus. The Veda is the source of the other five sets of scriptures, why, even of the secular and the materialistic. The Veda is the storehouse of Indian wisdom and is a memorable glory which man can never forget till eternity.

Revealed Truths Without Beginning or End: The Vedas are the eternal truths revealed by God to the great ancient Rishis of India. The word *Rishi* means a seer from *dris,* to see. He is the *Mantra-Drashta,* a seer of Mantra or thought. The thought was not his own. The Rishis saw the truths or heard them. Therefore, the Vedas are what are heard (Sruti). The Rishi did not write. He did not create it out of his mind. He was the seer of thought which existed already. He was only the spiritual discoverer of the thought. He is not the inventor of the Veda.

The Vedas represent the spiritual experiences of the Rishis of yore. The Rishi is only a medium or an agent to transmit to people the intuitional experiences which he received. The truths of the Vedas are revelations. All the other religions of the world claim their authority as being delivered by special messengers of God to certain persons, but the Vedas do not owe their authority to any one. They are themselves the authority as they are eternal, as they are the Knowledge of the Lord.

Lord Brahma, the Creator, imparted the divine knowledge to the Rishis or seers. The Rishis disseminated the knowledge. The Vedic Rishis were great realised persons who had direct intuitive perception of Brahman or the Truth. They were inspired writers. They built a simple, grand and perfect system of religion and philosophy from which the founders and teachers of all other religions have drawn their inspiration.

The Vedas are the oldest books in the library of man. The truths contained in all religions are derived from the Vedas and are ultimately traceable to the Vedas. The Vedas are the fountain-head of religion. The Vedas are the ultimate source to which all religious knowledge can be traced. Religion is of divine origin. It was revealed by God to man in the earliest times. It is embodied in the Vedas.

The Vedas are eternal. They are without beginning and end. An ignorant man may say how a book can be without beginning or end. By the Vedas, no books are meant. Vedas came out of the breath of the Lord. They are the words of God. The Vedas are not the utterances of persons. They are not the composition of any human mind. They were never written, never created. They are eternal and impersonal. The date of the Vedas has never been fixed. It can never be fixed. Vedas are eternal spiritual truths. Vedas are an embodiment of divine knowledge. The books may be destroyed, but the knowledge cannot be destroyed. Knowledge is eternal. In that sense, the Vedas are eternal.

The Four Vedas and Their Sub Divisions: The Veda is divided into four great books: the Rig-Veda, the Yajur-Veda, the Sama-Veda and the Atharva-Veda. The Yajur-Veda is again divided into two parts, the Sukla and the Krishna. The Krishna or the Taittiriya is the older book and the Sukla or the Vajasaneya is a later revelation to sage Yajnavalkya from the resplendent Sun-God.

The Rig-Veda is divided into twenty-one sections, the Yajur-Veda into one hundred and nine sections, the Sama-Veda into one thousand sections and the Atharva-Veda into fifty sections. In all, the whole Veda is thus divided into one thousand one hundred and eighty recenssions.

Each Veda Consists of Four Parts: the Mantra-Samhitas or hymns, the Brahmanas or explanations of Mantras or rituals, the Aranyakas and the Upanishads. The division of the Vedas into four parts is to suit the four stages in a man's life.

The Mantra-Samhitas are hymns in praise of the Vedic God for attaining material prosperity here and happiness hereafter. They are metrical poems comprising prayers, hymns and incantations addressed to various deities, both subjective and objective. The Mantra portion of the Vedas is useful for the Brahmacharins.

The Brahmana portions guide people to perform sacrificial rites. They are prose explanations of the method of using the Mantras in the Yajna or the sacrifice. The Brahmana portion is suitable for the householders.

The Aranyakas are the forest books, the mystical sylvan texts which give philosophical interpretations of the rituals. The Aranyakas are intended for the Vanaprasthas or hermits who prepare themselves for taking Sannyasa.

The Upanishads are the most important portion of the Vedas. The Upanishads contain the essence or the knowledge portion of the Vedas. The philosophy of the Upanishads is sublime, profound, lofty and soul-stirring. The Upanishads speak of the identity of the individual soul and the Supreme Soul. They reveal the most subtle and deep spiritual truths. The Upanishads are useful for the Sannyasins.

The subject matter of the whole Veda is divided into *Karma-Kanda, Upasana-Kanda* and *Jnana-Kanda*. The Karma-Kanda or Ritualistic Section deals with various sacrifices and rituals. The Upasana-Kanda or Worship-Section deals with various kinds of worship or meditation. The Jnana-Kanda or Knowledge-Section deals with the highest knowledge of Nirguna Brahman. The Mantras and the Brahmanas constitute Karma-Kanda; the Aranyakas Upasana-Kanda; and the Upanishads Jnana-Kanda.

***The Mantra-Samhitas*:** The Rig-Veda Samhita is the grandest book of the Hindus, the oldest and the best. It is the Great Indian Bible, which no Hindu would forget to adore from the core of his heart. Its style, the language and the tone are most beautiful and mysterious. Its immortal Mantras embody the greatest truths of existence, and it is perhaps the greatest treasure in all the scriptural literature of the world. Its priest is called the Hotri.

The Yajur-Veda Samhita is mostly in prose and is meant to be used by the Adhvaryu, the Yajur-Vedic priest, for superfluous explanations of the rites in sacrifices, supplementing the Rig-Vedic Mantras.

The Sama-Veda Samhita is mostly borrowed from the Rig-Vedic Samhita and is meant to be sung by the Udgatri, the Sama-Vedic priest, in sacrifices.

The Atharva-Veda Samhita is meant to be used by the Brahma, the Atharva-Vedic priest, to correct the mispronunciations and wrong performances that may accidentally be committed by the other three priests of the sacrifice.

***The Brahmanas and the Aranyakas*:** There are two Brahmanas to the Rig-Veda—the Aiteriya and the Sankhayana. "The Rig-Veda," says Max Muller, "is the most ancient book of the world. The sacred hymns of the Brahmanas stand unparalleled in the literature of the whole world; and their preservation might well be called miraculous." (History of Ancient Sanskrit Literature) The Satapatha Brahmana belongs to the Sukla Yajur-Veda. The Krishna-Yajur-Veda has the Taittiriya and the Maitrayana Brahmanas.

The Tandya or Panchavimsa, the Shadvimsa, the Chhandogya, the Adbhuta, the Arsheya and the Upanishad Brahmanas belong to the Sama-Veda. The Brahmana of the Atharva-Veda is called the Gopatha. Each of the Brahmanas has got an Aranyaka.

***The Upanishads*:** The Upanishads are the concluding portions of the Vedas or the end of the Vedas. The teaching based on them is called Vedanta. The Upanishads are the gist and the goal of the Vedas. They form the very foundation of Hinduism.

There are as many Upanishads to each Veda as there are Sakhas, branches or recenssions, *i.e.*, 21, 109, 1000 and 50 respectively to the four Vedas, the Rig-Veda, the Yajur-Veda, the Sama-Veda and the Atharva-Veda.

The different philosophers of India belonging to different schools, such as Monism, Qualified Monism, Dualism, Pure Monism, Difference-cum-non-difference, etc., have acknowledged the supreme authority of the Upanishads. They have given their own interpretations, but they have obeyed the authority. They have built their philosophy on the foundation of the Upanishads.

Even the Western scholars have paid their tribute to the seers of the Upanishads. At a time when the Westerners were clad in barks and were sunk in deep ignorance, the Upanishadic seers were enjoying the eternal bliss of the Absolute, and had the highest culture and civilisation.

The most important Upanishads are Isa, Kena, Katha, Prasna, Mundaka, Mandukya, Aiteriya, Taittiriya, Chhandogya, Brihadaranyaka, Kaushitaki and Svetasvatara and Maitrayani. These are supremely authoritative.

May the fundamental truths of the Vedas be revealed unto you all, like the Amalaka fruit in the palm of your hand. May Gayatri, the blessed Mother of the Vedas, impart to you the milk of Knowledge, the ancient wisdom of the Upanishads.

***The Upa-Vedas*:** There are four *Upa-Vedas* or subsidiary Vedas, *viz.*, the Ayurveda, the Dhanurveda, the Gandharva Veda and the Arthashastra, forming auxiliaries to the four Vedas, which mean, respectively, the science of health, the science of war, the science of music and the science of polity.

***The Vedangas*:** There are six *Angas* or explanatory limbs, to the Vedas: the *Siksha* and *Vyakarana* of Panini, the *Chhandas* of Pingalacharya, the *Nirukta* of Yaska, the *Jyotisha* of Garga, and the *Kalpas* (Srauta, Grihya, Dharma and Sulbha) belonging to the authorship of various Rishis.

Siksha is a knowledge of phonetics. Siksha deals with pronunciation and accent. The text of the Vedas is arranged in various forms or *Pathas*. The Pada-patha gives each word its separate form. The Krama-patha connects the word in pairs.

Vyakarana is Sanskrit grammar. Panini's books are most famous. Without knowledge of Vyakarana, you cannot understand the Vedas.

Chhandas is metre dealing with prosody.

Nirukta is philology or etymology.

Jyotisha is astronomy and astrology. It deals with the movements of the heavenly bodies, planets, etc., and their influence in human affairs.

Kalpa is the method of ritual. The Srauta Sutras which explain the ritual of sacrifices belong to Kalpa. The sulbha Sutras, which treat of the measurements which are necessary for laying out the sacrificial areas, also belong to Kalpa. The Grihya Sutras which concern domestic life, and the Dharma Sutras which deal with ethics, customs and laws, also belong to Kalpa.

The Pratishakhyas, Padapathas, Kramapathas, Upalekhas, Anukramanis, Daivatsamhitas, Parishishtas, Prayogas, Paddhatis, Karikas, Khilas and Vyuhas are further elaborations in the rituals of the Kalpa Sutras.

Among the Kalpa Sutras, the Asvalayana, Sankhyana and the Sambhavya belong to the Rig-Veda. The Mashaka, Latyayana, Drahyayana, Gobhila and Khadira belong to the Sama-Veda. The Katyayana and Paraskara belong to the Sukla Yajur-Veda. The Apastamba, Hiranyakesi, Bodhayana, Bharadvaja, Manava, Vaikhanasa and the Kathaka belong to the Krishna Yajur-Veda. The Vaitana and the Kaushika belong to the Atharva-Veda.

The Smritis

Next in importance to the Sruti are the Smritis or secondary scriptures. These are the ancient sacred law-codes of the Hindus dealing with the Sanatana-Varnashrama-Dharma. They supplement and explain the ritualistic injunctions called *Vidhis* in the Vedas. The Smriti Shastra is founded on the Sruti. The Smritis are based on the teachings of the Vedas. The Smriti stands next in authority to the Sruti. It explains and develops Dharma. It lays down the laws which regulate Hindu national, social, family and individual obligations.

The works which are expressly called Smritis are the law books, Dharma Shastras. Smriti, in a broader sense, covers all Hindu Shastras save the Vedas. The laws for regulating Hindu society from time to time are codified in the Smritis. The Smritis have laid down definite rules and laws to guide the individuals and communities in their daily conduct and to regulate their manners and customs. The Smritis have given detailed instructions, according to the conditions of the time, to all classes of men regarding their duties in life.

The Hindu learns how he has to spend his whole life from these Smritis. The duties of Varnashrama and all ceremonies are clearly given in these books. The Smritis prescribe certain acts and prohibit some others for a Hindu, according to his birth and stage of life. The object of the Smritis is to purify the heart of man and take him gradually to the supreme abode of immortality and make him perfect and free.

These Smritis have varied from time to time. The injunctions and prohibitions of the Smritis are related to the particular social surroundings. As these surroundings and essential conditions of the Hindu society changed from time to time, new Smritis had to be compiled by the sages of different ages and different parts of India.

***The Celebrated Hindu Law-Givers*:** From time to time, a great law-giver would take his birth. He would codify the existing laws and remove those which had become obsolete. He would make some alterations, adaptations, readjustments, additions and subtractions, to suit the needs of the time and see that the way of living of the people would be in accordance with the teachings of the Veda. Of such law-givers, Manu, Yajnavalkya and Parasara are the most celebrated persons.

Hindu society is founded on, and governed by, the laws made by these three great sages. The Smritis are named after them. We have Manu Smriti or Manava Dharma-Shastra (the Laws of Manu or the Institutes of Manu), Yajnavalkya Smriti and Parasara Smriti. Manu is the greatest law-giver of the race. He is the oldest law-giver as well. The Yajnavalkya Smriti follows the same general lines as the Manu Smriti and is next in importance to it. Manu Smriti and Yajnavalkya Smriti are universally accepted at the present time as authoritative works all over India. Yajnavalkya Smriti is chiefly consulted in all matters of Hindu Law. Even the Government of India are applying some of these laws.

There are eighteen main Smritis or Dharma Shastras. The most important are those of Manu, Yajnavalkya and Parasara. The other fifteen are those of Vishnu, Daksha, Samvarta, Vyasa, Harita, Satatapa, Vasishtha, Yama, Apastamba, Gautama, Devala, Sankha-Likhita, Usana, Atri and Saunaka.

The laws of Manu are intended for the Satya Yuga, those of Yajnavalkya are for the Treta Yuga; those of Sankha and Likhita are for the Dvapara Yuga; and those of Parasara are for the Kali Yuga.

The laws and rules which are based entirely upon our social positions, time and clime, must change with the changes in society and changing conditions of time and clime. Then only the progress of the Hindu society can be ensured.

***Need for a New Law-Code*:** It is not possible to follow some of the laws of Manu at the present time. We can follow their spirit and not the letter. Society is advancing. When it advances, it outgrows certain laws which were valid and helpful at a particular stage of its growth. Many new things which were not thought out by the old law-givers have come into existence now. It is no use insisting people to follow now those old laws which have become obsolete. Our present society has considerably changed. A new Smriti to suit the requirements of this age is very necessary. Another sage will place before the Hindus of our days a new suitable code of laws. Time is ripe for a new Smriti. Cordial greetings to this age.

***The Inner Voice of Dharma*:** He who is endowed with a pure heart through protracted Tapas, Japa, Kirtana, meditation and service of Guru and who has a very clear conscience, can be guided by the inner voice in matters of Dharma or duty or moral action. The inner voice that proceeds from a clean heart filled with Sattva is, indeed, the voice of God or Soul or Antaryamin or Inner Ruler. This voice is more than Smriti. It is Smriti of Smritis. Purify your heart and train yourself to hear this inner voice. Keep your ear in tune with the 'voice'.

The Sruti and the Smriti: The Sruti and the Smriti are the two authoritative sources of Hinduism. *Sruti* literally means what is heard, and *Smriti* means what is remembered. Sruti is revelation and Smriti is tradition. Upanishad is a Sruti. Bhagwad Gita is a Smriti.

Sruti is direct experience. Great Rishis heard the eternal truths of religion and left a record of them for the benefit of posterity. These records constitute the Vedas. Hence, Sruti is primary authority. Smriti is a recollection of that experience. Hence, it is secondary authority. The Smritis or Dharma Shastras also are books written by sages, but they are not the final authority. If there is anything in a Smriti which contradicts the Sruti, the Smriti is to be rejected.

The Itihasas

The Friendly Treatises and the Commanding Treatises: There are four books under this heading: The Valmiki-Ramayana, the Yogavasishtha, The Mahabharata and the Harivamsa. These embody all that is in the Vedas, but only in a simpler manner. These are called the Suhrit-Samhitas or the Friendly Treatises, while the Vedas are called the Prabhu-Samhitas or the Commanding Treatises with great authority. These works explain the great universal truths in the form of historical narratives, stories and dialogues. These are very interesting volumes and are liked by all, from the inquisitive child to the intellectual scholar.

The Itihasas give us beautiful stories of absorbing interest and importance, through which all the fundamental teachings of Hinduism are indelibly impressed on one's mind. The laws of Smritis and the principles of the Vedas are stamped firmly on the minds of the Hindus through the noble and marvellous deeds of their great national heroes. We get a clear idea of Hinduism from these sublime stories.

The common man cannot comprehend the high abstract philosophy of the Upanishads and the Brahma Sutras. Hence, the compassionate sages Valmiki and Vyasa wrote the Itihasas for the benefit of common people. The same philosophy is presented with analogies and parables in a tasteful form to the common run of mankind.

The two well-known Itihasas (histories) are the epics (Mahakavyas), *Ramayana* and *Mahabharata*. They are two very popular and useful Shastras of the Hindus. The Ramayana was written by the sage Valmiki, and the Mahabharata by Vyasa.

The Ramayana: The Ramayana, the Adi-Kavya or the first epic poem, relates the story of Sri Rama, the ideal man. It is the history of the family of the solar race descended from Ikshvaku, in which was born Sri Ramachandra, the Avatara of Lord Vishnu, and his three brothers. The ideal characters like Rama, Sita, Lakshmana, Bharata and Sri Hanuman that we find in Ramayana firmly establish Hindu Dharma in our minds. The story of the birth of Rama and his brothers, their education and marriages, the exile of Sri Rama, the carrying off and recovery of Sita, his wife, the destruction of Ravana, the Rakshasa King of Lanka, and the reign of Sri Rama, are described in detail in Ramayana. How a man should behave towards his superiors, equals and inferiors, how a king ought to rule his kingdom, how a man should lead his life in this world, how he can obtain his release, freedom and perfection, may be learnt from this excellent epic.

The Ramayana gives a vivid picture of Indian life. Even today our domestic, social and national ideals are copied from the noble characters in the Ramayana and the Mahabharata. The great national heroes stand even today as beacon-lights to guide and inspire the people of the whole world. The lives of Rama, Bharata and Lakshmana provide a model of fraternal affection and mutual service. Sri Hanuman stands as an ideal unique Karma Yogin. The life of Sita is regarded as the most perfect example of womanly fidelity, chastity and sweetness. The Ramayana is written in twenty-four thousand verses by Sri Valmiki.

***The Mahabharata*:** The Mahabharata is the history of the Pandavas and the Kauravas. It gives a description of the great war, the Battle of Kurukshetra, which broke out between the Kauravas and the Pandavas who were cousins and descendants of the lunar race. The Mahabharata is an encyclopaedia of Hindu Dharma. It is rightly called the fifth Veda. There is really no theme in religion, philosophy, mysticism and polity which this great epic does not touch and expound. It contains very noble moral teachings, useful lessons of all kinds, many beautiful stories and episodes, discourses, sermons, parables and dialogues which set forth the principles of morals and metaphysics. The Pandavas obtained victory through the grace of Lord Krishna. The Mahabharata is written in one hundred thousand verses by Sri Krishnadvaipayana Vyasa.

***The Bhagwad Gita*:** The most important part of the Mahabharata is the *Bhagwad Gita.* It is a marvellous dialogue between Lord Krishna and Arjuna on the battle-field, before the commencement of the great war. Bhagavan Sri Krishna became the charioteer of Arjuna. Sri Krishna explained the essentials of Hindu religion to Arjuna. Just as the Upanishads contain the cream of the Vedas, so does the Gita contain the cream of the Upanishads. The Upanishads are the cows. Lord Krishna is the cowherd. Arjuna is the calf. The Gita is the milk. The wise men are those who drink the milk of the Gita.

The Gita is the most precious jewel of Hindu literature. It is a universal gospel. The Gita teaches the Yoga of Synthesis. It ranks high in the religious literature of the world.

Arjuna saw before him his dear relatives and teachers in the battle-field. He fainted and refused to fight against them. Then Lord Krishna imparted knowledge of the Self to Arjuna and convinced him that it was his duty to fight regardless of consequences. Afterwards Arjuna gave up his *Moha,* or delusion. All his doubts were cleared. He fought against the Kauravas and achieved victory.

***Knowledge of Ancient Indian History and Culture*:** The Mahabharata contains also the immortal discourse of Bhishma on Dharma, which he gave to Yudhishthira, when he was lying on the bed of arrows. The whole Mahabharata forms an encyclopaedia of history, morals and religion unsurpassed by any other epic in the world.

The Ramayana and the Mahabharata speak to us clearly about the ancient India, about her people, her customs, her ways of living, her arts, her civilisation and culture, her manufactures, etc. If you read these two books, you will come to know how great India once was, and you will be inspired to make her great once more. No other country has produced so many great men, great teachers, great Yogins, great Rishis, great prophets, great Acharyas, great kings, great heroes, great statesmen, great patriots and great benefactors, as India. The more you know of India and Hinduism, the more you will honour and love it and the more thankful to the Lord you will be that you were born in India as a Hindu. Glory to India! Glory to Hinduism! Glory to the seers of the Upanishads! Glory, glory to Lord Krishna, the author of the Song Divine!

The Puranas

The Puranas are of the same class as the Itihasas. They have five characteristics *(Pancha-Lakshana) viz.*, history, cosmology (with various symbolical illustrations of philosophical principles), secondary creation, genealogy of kings and of Manvantaras. All the Puranas belong to the class of Suhrit-Samhitas.

Vyasa is the compiler of the Puranas from age to age; and for this age, he is Krishnadvaipayana, the son of Parasara.

The Puranas were written to popularise the religion of the Vedas. They contain the essence of the Vedas. The aim of the Puranas is to impress on the minds of the masses the teachings of the Vedas and to generate in them devotion to God, through concrete examples, myths, stories, legends, lives of saints, kings and great men, allegories and chronicles of great historical events. The sages made use of these things to illustrate the eternal principles of religion. The Puranas were meant, not for the scholars, but for the ordinary people who could not understand high philosophy and who could not study the Vedas.

The Darshanas are very stiff. They are meant only for the learned few. The Puranas are meant for the masses with inferior intellect. Religion is taught in a very easy and interesting way through these Puranas. Even to this day, the Puranas are popular. The Puranas contain the history of remote times. They also give a description of the regions of the universe not visible to the ordinary physical eye. They are very interesting to read and are full of information of all kinds. Children hear the stories from their grandmothers. Pundits and Purohits hold Kathas in temples, on banks of rivers and in other important places. Agriculturists, labourers and bazaar people hear the stories.

***The Eighteen Puranas*:** There are eighteen main Puranas and an equal number of subsidiary Puranas or Upa-Puranas. The main Puranas are: Vishnu Purana, Naradiya Purana, Srimad Bhagavata Purana, Garuda (Suparna) Purana, Padma Purana, Varaha Purana, Brahma Purana, Brahmanda Purana, Brahma Vaivarta Purana, Markandeya Purana, Bhavishya Purana, Vamana Purana, Matsya Purana, Kurma Purana, Linga Purana, Shiva Purana, Skanda Purana and Agni Purana. Of these, six are Sattvic Puranas and glorify Vishnu; six are Rajasic and glorify Brahma; six are Tamasic and they glorify Shiva.

Neophytes or beginners in the spiritual Path are puzzled when they go through Shiva Purana and Vishnu Purana. In Shiva Purana, Lord Shiva is highly eulogised and an inferior position is given to Lord Vishnu. Sometimes Vishnu is belittled. In Vishnu Purana, Lord Hari is highly eulogised and an inferior status is given to Lord Shiva. Sometimes Lord Shiva is belittled. This is only to increase the faith of the devotees in their particular Ishta-Devata. Lord Shiva and Lord Vishnu are one.

The best among the Puranas are the Srimad Bhagavata and the Vishnu Purana. The most popular is the Srimad Bhagavata Purana. Next comes Vishnu Purana. A portion of the Markandeya Purana is well known to all Hindus as *Chandi,* or Devimahatmya. Worship of God as the Divine Mother is its theme. Chandi is read widely by the Hindus on sacred days and Navaratri (Durga Puja) days.

The Srimad Bhagavata Purana and the Ten Avataras: The Srimad Bhagavata Purana is a chronicle of the various Avataras of Lord Vishnu. There are ten Avataras of Vishnu. The aim of every Avatara is to save the world from some great danger, to destroy the wicked and protect the virtuous. The ten Avataras are: Matsya (The Fish), Kurma (The Tortoise), Varaha (The Boar), Narasimha (The Man-Lion), Vamana (The Dwarf), Parasurama (Rama with the axe, the destroyer of the Kshatriya race), Ramachandra (The hero of Ramayana—the son of Dasaratha), who destroyed Ravana, Sri Krishna, The teacher of the Gita, Buddha (The prince-ascetic, founder of Buddhism) and Kalki (The hero riding on a white horse, who is to come at the end of the Kali-Yuga).

The object of the Matsya Avatara was to save Vaivasvata Manu from destruction by a deluge. The object of Kurma Avatara was to enable the world to recover some precious things which were lost in the deluge. The Kurma gave its back for keeping the churning rod when the Gods and the Asuras churned the ocean of milk. The purpose of Varaha Avatara was to rescue, from the waters, the earth which had been dragged down by a demon named Hiranyaksha. The purpose of Narasimha Avatara, half-lion and half-man, was to free the world from the oppression of Hiranyakasipu, a demon, the father of Bhakta Prahlada.

The object of Vamana Avatara was to restore the power of the gods which had been eclipsed by the penance and devotion of King Bali. The object of Parasurama Avatara was to deliver the country from the oppression of the Kshatriya rulers. Parasurama destroyed the Kshatriya race twenty-one times. The object of Rama was to destroy the wicked Ravana. The object of Sri Krishna Avatara was to destroy Kamsa and other demons, to deliver His wonderful message of the Gita in the Mahabharata war, and to become the centre of the Bhakti schools of India. The object of Buddha Avatara was to prohibit animal sacrifices and teach piety. The object of the Kalki Avatara is the destruction of the wicked and the re-establishment of virtue.

***The Tamil Puranas*:** Lord Shiva incarnated himself in the form of Dakshinamurti to impart knowledge to the four Kumaras. He took human form to initiate Sambandhar, Manikkavasagar, Pattinathar. He appeared in flesh and blood to help his devotees and relieve their sufferings. The divine Lilas of Lord Shiva are recorded in the Tamil Puranas like Shiva Purana, Periya Purana, Shiva Parakramam and Tiruvilayadal Purana.

***The Upa-Puranas*:** The eighteen Upa-Puranas are: Sanatkumara, Narasimha, Brihannaradiya, Shivarahasya, Durvasa, Kapila, Vamana, Bhargava, Varuna, Kalika, Samba, Nandi, Surya, Parasara, Vasishtha, Devi-Bhagavata, Ganesha and Hamsa.

***Utility of the Puranas*:** Study of the Puranas, listening to sacred recitals of scriptures, describing and expounding of the transcendent Lilas of the Blessed Lord—these form an important part of Sadhana of the Lord's devotees. It is most pleasing to the Lord. *Sravana* is a part of *Navavidha-Bhakti. Kathas* and *Upanyasas* open the springs of devotion in the hearts of hearers and develop *Prema-Bhakti* which confers immortality on the *Jiva.*

The language of the Vedas is archaic, and the subtle philosophy of Vedanta and the Upanishads is extremely difficult to grasp and assimilate. Hence, the Puranas are of special value as they present philosophical truths and precious teachings in an easier manner. They give ready access to the mysteries of life and the key to bliss. Imbibe their teachings. Start a new life of Dharma-Nishtha and Adhyatmic Sadhana from this very day.

The Agamas

Another class of popular scriptures are the Agamas. The Agamas are theological treatises and practical manuals of divine worship. The Agamas include the Tantras, Mantras and Yantras. These are treatises explaining the external worship of God, in idols, temples, etc. All the Agamas treat of (i) *Jnana* or Knowledge, (ii) *Yoga* or Concentration, (iii) *Kriya* or Esoteric Ritual and (iv) *Charya* or Exoteric Worship. They also give elaborate details about ontology and cosmology, liberation, devotion, meditation, philosophy of *Mantras,* mystic diagrams, charms and spells, temple-building, image-making, domestic observances, social rules, public festivals, etc.

The Agamas are divided into three sections: The *Vaishnava,* the *Shaiva* and the *Shakta.* The three chief sects of Hinduism, *viz.*, Vaishnavism, Shaivism and Shaktism, base their doctrines and dogmas on their respective Agamas. The Vaishnava Agamas or Pancharatra Agamas glorify God as Vishnu. The Shaiva Agamas glorify God as Shiva and have given rise to an important school of philosophy known as Shaiva-Siddhanta, which prevails in South India, particularly in the districts of Tirunelveli and Madurai. The Shakta Agamas or Tantras glorify God as the Mother of the Universe, under one of the many names of *Devi.*

The Agamas do not derive their authority from the Vedas, but are not antagonistic to them. They are all Vedic in spirit and character. That is the reason why they are regarded as authoritative.

***The Vaishnava Agamas*:** The Vaishnava Agamas are of four kinds: the Vaikhanasa, Pancharatra, Pratishthasara and Vijnanalalita. The Brahma, Shaiva Kaumara, Vasishtha, Kapila, Gautamiya and the Naradiya are the seven groups of the Pancharatras. The Naradiya section of the Santi-Parva of the Mahabharata is the earliest source of information about the Pancharatras. Vishnu is the Supreme Lord in the Pancharatra Agamas. The Vaishnavas regard the Pancharatra Agamas to be the most authoritative. They believe that these Agamas were revealed by Lord Vishnu Himself. Narada-Pancharatra says: "Everything from Brahma to a blade of grass is Lord Krishna." This corresponds to the Upanishadic declaration: "All this is, verily, Brahman—*Sarvam Khalvidam Brahma.*"

There are two hundred and fifteen of these Vaishnava texts. Isvara, Ahirbudhnya, Paushkara, Parama, Sattvata, Brihad-Brahma and Jnanamritasara Samhitas are the important ones.

***The Shaiva Agamas*:** The Shaivas recognise twenty-eight Agamas, of which the chief is Kamika. The Agamas are also the basis of Kashmir Shaivism which is called the Pratyabhijna system. The latter works of Pratyabhijna system show a distinct leaning to Advaitism. The Southern Shaivism, *i.e.*, Shaiva Siddhanta and the Kashmir Shaivism, regard these Agamas as their authority, besides the Vedas. Each Agama has Upa-Agamas. Of these, only fragmentary texts of twenty are extant. Lord Shiva is the central God in the Shaiva Agamas. They are suitable to this age, Kali Yoga. They are open to all castes and both the sexes.

***The Shakta Agamas*:** There is another group of scriptures known as the *Tantras.* They belong to the Shakta cult. They glorify Shakti as the World-Mother. They dwell on the Shakti (energy) aspect of God and prescribe numerous courses of ritualistic worship of the Divine Mother in various forms. There are seventy-seven Agamas. These are very much like the Puranas in some respects. The texts are usually in the form of dialogues between Shiva and Parvati. In some of these, Shiva answers the questions put by Parvati, and in others, Parvati answers, Shiva questioning. Mahanirvana, Kularnava, Kulasara, Prapanchasara, Tantraraja, Rudra-Yamala, Brahma-Yamala, Vishnu-Yamala and Todala Tantra are the important works. The Agamas teach several occult practices some of which confer powers, while the others bestow knowledge and freedom. Shakti is the creative power of Lord Shiva. Shaktism is really a supplement to Shaivism.

Among the existing books on the Agamas, the most famous are the Isvara-Samhita, Ahirbudhnya-Samhita, Sanatkumara-Samhita, Narada-Pancharatra, Spanda-Pradipika and the Mahanirvana-Tantra.

The Six Darshanas

These are the intellectual section of the Hindu writings, while the first four are intuitional, and the fifth inspirational and emotional. Darshanas are schools of philosophy based on the Vedas. The Agamas are theological. The Darshana literature is philosophical. The Darshanas are meant for the erudite scholars who are endowed with acute acumen, good understanding, power of reasoning and subtle intellect. The

Itihasas, Puranas and Agamas are meant for the masses. The Darshanas appeal to the intellect, while the Itihasas, Puranas, etc., appeal to the heart.

Philosophy has six divisions—*Shad-Darshana*—the six Darshanas or ways of seeing things, usually called the six systems or six different schools of thought. The six schools of philosophy are the six instruments of true teaching or the six demonstrations of Truth. Each school has developed, systematised and correlated the various parts of the Veda in its own way. Each system has its *Sutrakara*, *i.e.*, the one great Rishi who systematised the doctrines of the school and put them in short aphorisms or Sutras.

The Sutras are terse and laconic. The Rishis have condensed their thoughts in the aphorisms. It is very difficult to understand them without the help of commentaries by great sages or Rishis. Hence, there arose many commentators or *Bhashyakaras*. There are glosses, notes and, later, commentaries on the original commentaries.

The Shad-Darshanas (the six schools of philosophy) or the Shat-Shastras are: the NYAYA, founded by Gautama Rishi, the VAISESHIKA by Kanada Rishi, the SANKHYA by Kapila Muni, the YOGA by Patanjali Maharshi, the PURVA MIMAMSA by Jaimini, and the UTTARA MIMAMSA or VEDANTA by Badarayana or Vyasa. The Darshanas are divided into three pairs of aphoristic compositions which explain the philosophy of the Vedas in a rationalistic method of approach. They are: the Nyaya and the Vaiseshika, the Sankhya and the Yoga, and the Mimamsa and the Vedanta. Each set of Sutras has got its *Bhashya, Vritti, Varttika, Vyakhyana* or *Tika* and *Tippani.*

Sutra

Svalpaksharam-asandigdhaṃ
Saravad-visvatomukham
Astobham-anavadyam cha
Sutram sutravido viduh

A Sutra or an aphorism is a short formula with the least possible number of letters, without any ambiguity or doubtful assertion, containing the very essence, embracing all meanings, without any stop or obstruction and absolutely faultless in nature.

The Sutrakara or the composer of the aphorisms is said to be as happy as one would be while getting the first male child, if he is but able to reduce one letter in his abstruse Sutra of far-fetched words and ideas. The best example of the greatest, the tersest and the most perfect of Sutra literature is the series of aphorisms called the *Ashtadhyayi* composed by Panini. Panini is the father of all Sutrakaras from whom all others seem to have borrowed the method of composition.

The Sutras are meant to explain a big volume of knowledge in short assertions suitable to be kept in memory at all times. The six Vedangas and the six systems of Hindu philosophy form the twelve sets of Sutra literature of the world. In addition to these, there are later compositions like the Narada-Bhakti Sutras, the Sandilya-Bhakti Sutras, etc., which also wish to assume an equal form with the famous Sutras mentioned above.

Bhashya

Sutrartho varnyate yatra
Padaih sutranusaribhih
Svapadani cha varnyante
Bhashyam bhashyavido viduh

A Bhashya is an elaborate exposition, a commentary on the Sutras, with word by word meaning of the aphoristic precepts, their running translation, together with the individual views of the commentator or the Bhashyakara. The best and the exemplary Bhashya in Sanskrit literature is the one written by Patanjali on the Vyakarana Sutras of Panini. This Bhashya is so very famous and important that it is called the MAHABHASHYA and its celebrated author is specially called the BHASHYAKARA. Patanjali is the father of Bhashyakaras. The next important Bhashya is the one on the Mimamsa Sutras written by Sabara-Swamin who learnt the art from Patanjali's commentary.

The third important Bhashya was written by Shankara on the Brahma Sutras, in close following with the Sabara-Bhashya. The Bhashyas on the six sets of aphorisms dealing with Indian philosophy were written by Vatsyayana, Prasastapada, Vijnanabhikshu, Vyasa, Sabara and Shankara. On the Vedanta or Brahma Sutras, there are about sixteen Bhashyas, like those of Ramanuja, Madhva, Vallabha, Nimbarka, etc.

Vritti

Sadvrittih sannibandhana

A Vritti is a short gloss explaining the aphorisms in a more elaborate way, but not as extensively as a Bhashya. An example is Bodhayana's Vritti on the Brahma Sutras.

Varttika

Uktanuktaduruktanam
Chinta yatra pravartate
Tam grantham varttikam prahuh
Varttikajnavichakshanah

A Varttika is a work where a critical study is made of that which is said and left unsaid or imperfectly said in a Bhashya, and the ways of making it perfect by supplying the omissions therein, are given. Examples are the Varttikas of Katyayana on Panini's Sutras, of Suresvara on Shankara's Upanishad-Bhashyas, and of Kumarila Bhatta on the Sabara-Bhashya on the Karma-Mimamsa.

Vyakhyana or Tika: A Vyakhyana is a running explanation in an easier language of what is said in the original, with little elucidations here and there. A Vyakhyana, particularly of a Kavya, deals with eight different modes of dissection of the Sloka, like Pada-Chheda, Vigraha, Sandhi, Alankara, Anuvada, etc. This forms an important aspect in the study of Sanskrit Sahitya Shastra. An Anu-Vyakhyana—like the one written by Sri Madhva—is a repetition of what is already written, but in greater detail. An Anuvada is merely a running translation or statement of an abstruse text of the original. Tika is only another name for Vyakhyana. The best Vyakhyanas are of Vachaspati Mishra on the Darshanas, especially on Shankara's Brahmasutra-Bhashya.

Tippani: Tippani is just like a Vritti, but is less orthodox than the Vritti. It is an explanation of difficult words or phrases occurring in the original. Examples are Kaiyata's gloss on the

Mahabhashya of Patanjali, Nagojibhatta's gloss on Kaiyata's gloss, or Appayya's gloss on Amalananda's gloss on the Bhamati of Vachaspati Mishra.

Other Scriptures

The Tevaram and the Tiruvachakam which are the hymns of the Shaiva saints of South India, the Divya-Prabandham of the Alwar saints of South India, the songs of Kabir, the Abhangas of Tukaram and the Ramayana of Tulasi Das—all of which are the outpourings of great realised souls—are wonderful scriptures. They contain the essence of the Vedas.

The Secular Writings

The Subhashitas: The Subhashitas are wise sayings, instructions and stories, either in poetry or in prose. Examples are Bhartrihari's three centuries of verses, the Subhashita-Ratna-Bhandagara and Somadeva Bhatta's Katha-Sarit-Sagara or Kshemendra's Brihat-Katha-Manjari. The Panchatantra and the Hitopadesa also belong to this category.

The Kavyas: These are highly scholarly compositions in poetry, prose or both. The greatest of poetical Kavyas are those of Kalidas *(The Raghuvamsa* and *Kumarasambhava),* Bharavi *(The Kiratarjuniya),* Magha *(The Sisupalavadha),* Sri Harsha *(The Naishadha).* The best prose Kavyas in the whole of Sanskrit literature were written by Bhattabana *(The Kadambari* and *Harshacharita),* the great genius in classical Sanskrit. Among those containing both poetry and prose, the Champu-Ramayana and the Champu-Bharata are most famous. These are all wonderful masterpieces which will ever remain to glorify India's literary calibre.

The Natakas: These are marvellously scholastic dramas embodying the *Rasas* of Sringara, Vira, Karuna, Adbhuta, Hasya, Bhayanaka, Bibhatsa and Raudra. It is told that none can write on the ninth Rasa, *viz.*, Santi. It is attainable only on final Liberation. The best dramas are written by Kalidasa *(Sakuntala),* Bhavabhuti *(Uttara-Rama-Charita),* and Visakhadatta *(Mudrarakshasa).*

***The Alankaras*:** These are grand rhetorical texts, treating of the science of perfection and beauty of ornamental language and of effective composition with elegance and force, both in poetry and in prose. These are the fundamentals of Sanskrit Sahitya, even superior to the Kavyas and the Natakas. The best Alankara-Granthas are those of Mammata *(Kavyaprakasa)* and Jagannath *(Rasagangadhara)*.

Conclusion

These constitute the entirety of Sanskrit literature—sacred and secular. The Sruti is the root; the Smritis, Itihasas and Puranas are the trunk; the Agamas and Darshanas are the branches; and the Subhashitas, Kavyas, Natakas and Alankaras are the flowers of the tree of India's Culture.

The Smritis, the Itihasas, the Puranas, the Agamas and the Darshanas are only developments of the Veda. Their ultimate source is the Veda. Their one common aim is to enable man to annihilate his ignorance and attain perfection, freedom, immortality and eternal bliss through knowledge of God or the Eternal. Their purpose is to make man like God and one with Him.

5

Brahmin Dharma

Silent adorations to the Lord, the Embodiment of Dharma, the Controller and Protector of Dharma and the Fountain-head of Dharma. What is Dharma? Dharma is so called, because it *holds;* Dharma alone holds the people, etc. The word *Dharma* is derived from the root *Dhr*—to hold—and its etymological meaning is 'that which holds' this world, or the people of the world, or the whole creation from the microcosm to the macrocosm. It is the eternal Divine Law of the Lord. The entire creation is held together and sustained by the All-powerful Law of God. Practice of Dharma, therefore, means recognition of this Law and abidence by it.

That which brings well-being to man is Dharma. Dharma supports this world. The people are upheld by Dharma. That which secures preservation of beings is Dharma. Dharma leads to eternal happiness and immortality. That which is Dharma is verily the Truth. Therefore, whosoever speaks the truth is said to speak Dharma, and whosoever speaks Dharma is said to speak the truth. One and the same thing becomes both. Dharma includes all external deeds, as well as thoughts and other mental practices which tend to elevate the character of man. Dharma comes from the Divine and leads you to the Divine.

Definition of Dharma

No language is perfect. There is no proper equivalent word in English for the Sanskrit term *Dharma.* It is very difficult to define Dharma. Dharma is generally defined as 'righteousness' or 'duty.' Dharma is the principle of righteousness. It is the principle of holiness. It is also the principle of unity. Bhishma says in his instructions to Yudhishthira that whatever creates conflict is Adharma, and whatever puts an end to conflict and brings about unity and harmony is Dharma. Anything that helps to unite all and develop pure divine love and universal brotherhood, is Dharma.

Anything that creates discord, split and disharmony and foments hatred, is Adharma. Dharma is the cementer and sustainer of social life. The rules of Dharma have been laid down for regulating the worldly affairs of men. Dharma brings as its consequence happiness, both in this world and in the next. Dharma is the means of preserving one's self. If you transgress it, it will kill you. If you protect it, it will protect you. It is your sole companion after death. It is the sole refuge of humanity.

That which elevates one is Dharma. This is another definition. Dharma is that which leads you to the path of perfection and glory. Dharma is that which helps you to have direct communion with the Lord. Dharma is that which makes you divine. Dharma is the ascending stairway unto God. Self-realisation is the highest Dharma. Dharma is the heart of Hindu ethics. God is the centre of Dharma.

Dharma means *Achara* or the regulation of daily life. Achara is the supreme Dharma. It is the basis of Tapas or austerity. It leads to wealth, beauty, longevity and continuity of lineage. Evil conduct and immorality will lead to ill-fame, sorrow, disease and premature death. Dharma has its root in morality and the controller of Dharma is God Himself.

Maharshi Jaimini defines Dharma as that which is enjoined by the Vedas and is not ultimately productive of suffering.

Rishi Kanada, founder of the Vaiseshika system of philosophy, has given the best definition of Dharma, in his Vaiseshika Sutras: *"Yato-bhyudayanihsreyasa-siddhih sa dharmah."* "That which leads to the attainment of *Abhyudaya* (prosperity in this world) and *Nihsreyasa* (total cessation of pain and attainment of eternal bliss hereafter) is Dharma."

The Sole Authority of the Vedas

The four Vedas, the Smriti texts, the behaviour of those who have entered into their spirit and act according to their injunctions, the conduct of holy men and satisfaction of one's own self—these are the bases of Dharma, according to Manu.

In the matter of Dharma, the Vedas are the ultimate authority. You cannot know the truth about Dharma through any source of knowledge other than the Vedas. Reason cannot be the authority in the matter of Dharma. Among the scriptures of the world, the Vedas are the oldest. This is supported by all leading scholars and antiquarians of the entire civilised world. They all declare with one voice, that of all books so far written in any human language, the Rig-Veda Samhita is undoubtedly the oldest. No antiquarian has been able to fix the date when the Rig-Veda Samhita was composed or came to light.

The Changing Dharma

Just as a doctor prescribes different medicines for different people according to their constitution and the nature of their disease, so also Hinduism prescribes different duties for different people. Rules for women are different from the rules for men. The rules for different Varnas and Ashramas vary. But, non-violence, truth, non-stealing, cleanliness and control of the senses, are the duties common to all men.

Dharma depends upon time, circumstances, age, degree of evolution and the community to which one belongs. The Dharma of this century is different from that of the tenth century.

There are conditions under which Dharma may change its usual course. Apad-Dharma is such a deviation from the usual practice. This is allowed only in times of extreme distress or calamity.

What is Dharma in one set of circumstances becomes Adharma in another set of circumstances. That is the reason why it is said that the secret of Dharma is extremely profound and subtle. Lord Krishna says in the Gita: "Let the scriptures be the authority in determining what ought to be done and what ought not to be done" (Ch. XVI, 24). The truth of Dharma lies hidden. Srutis and Smritis are many. The way of Dharma open to all is that which a great realised soul has traversed.

Dharma in Other Religions

All other religions also lay stress on Dharma. Buddhism, Jainism, Christianity, Sikhism, Zoroastrianism, Islam are all remarkably alive to its value. Plato, Socrates, Aristotle, Kant, Swedenborg and Spinoza are all striking examples in the interesting history of Western philosophy for the high pedestal on which they have placed morality, duty and righteousness, and adored them all as the only means to the attainment of the goal of life. Each religion lays greater stress on certain aspects of Dharma.

Benefits of the Practice of Dharma

Of the four grand objects of human aspiration—*Purusharthas—viz.*, Dharma, Artha, Kama and Moksha, *Dharma* is given the foremost rank in the scriptures. Dharma alone is the gateway to Moksha, to immortality, infinite bliss, supreme peace and highest knowledge. Dharma alone is the primary Purushartha. Dharma is the first and foremost Purushartha. Through the practice of Dharma alone can you ever hope to achieve the crowning glory of all human endeavours, *viz.*, Moksha which is the best and the highest of all desirable things.

Practice of Dharma leads to the perfect realisation of essential unity or the final end, the highest good, namely, Moksha. The practitioner experiences peace, joy, strength and tranquillity within himself. His life becomes thoroughly disciplined. His powers and capacities are exceedingly intensified. He realises that there is one underlying homogeneous essence, a living truth, behind these names and forms. He is transmuted into divinity. His whole nature gets transformed. He becomes one with the Eternal. He beholds Brahman above, Brahman below, Brahman to the right, Brahman to the left, Brahman in front, Brahman at the back, Brahman within, Brahman without and Brahman pervading the whole world.

Kinds of Dharma

Dharma can be classified under two heads: (i) *Samanya* or the general, universal Dharma and (ii) *Visesha* or the specific, personal Dharma. Contentment, forgiveness, self-restraint, non-stealing, purity, control of senses, discrimination between right and wrong, between the real and the unreal, spiritual knowledge, truthfulness and absence of anger come under the general or universal Dharma. The rules of the castes and orders of life are specific Dharmas. These are the tenfold characteristics of Dharma according to Manu.

Dharma assumes various kinds: Sanatana Dharma (Eternal Law), Samanya Dharma (general duty), Visesha Dharma (special duty), Varnashrama Dharma (duties of Caste and Order), Svadharma (one's own duty), Yuga Dharma (duty of the Age), Kula Dharma (duty of family), Manava Dharma (duty of man), Purusha Dharma (duty of male), Stri Dharma (duty of female), Raja Dharma (duty of king), Praja Dharma (duty of subjects), Pravritti Dharma (duty in worldly life) and Nivritti Dharma (duty in spiritual life).

Sanatana Dharma

Sanatana Dharma means the Eternal Religion, the Ancient Law. This is based on the Vedas. This is the oldest of living religions. Hinduism is known by the name Sanatana Dharma. What the Vedas alone declare to be the means of attaining the *summum bonum* or the final emancipation, is the Sanatana Dharma or Hindu Dharma.

The foundation of Sanatana Dharma is Sruti; Smritis are the walls; the Itihasas and Purnas are the buttresses or supports. In ancient times, the Srutis were learnt by heart. The teacher sang them to his pupils and the pupils sang them after him. They were not written in book form. All the sects, all the philosophical systems, appeal to the Sruti as the final authority. The Smriti stands next in authority to the Sruti.

Hinduism stands unrivalled in the depth and grandeur of its philosophy. Its ethical teachings are lofty, unique and sublime. It is highly flexible and adapted to every human need.

It is a perfect religion by itself. It is not in need of anything from any other religion. No other religion has produced so many great saints, great patriots, great warriors and great Pativratas. The more you know of it, the more you will honour and love it. The more you study it, the more it will enlighten you and satisfy your heart.

India—The Home of Religions

The religious history of the world tells us that from time immemorial, India has been the home of great sages, seers and Rishis. All the grand religious ideals that have moulded the character of men, the loftiest of ethics and morality that have raised human beings to magnanimous heights of divine splendour and all the sublime truths of spirituality that have made men divine and have moulded the spiritual ideals of nations and saviours of mankind, first arose in India.

The spiritual horizon of India has always been illumined with the glory of the self-effulgent sun of wisdom of the Upanishads. Whenever there was any upheaval in any part of the world, the origin of this could be traced to the wave of spirituality caused by the birth of a great soul—a special manifestation of Divinity—in some part of India.

Hindus have had a culture, civilisation and religion millennia older than those of any other country or people. God did speak to the world through India's Rishis, Yogins, Mahatmas, Alvars, prophets, Acharyas, Sannyasins and saints. Their teachings and Puranas are really inspired. God is the one Light and Truth from whom emanate the teachings of all faiths.

India is the home and abode of religions. It occupies the proud first place in religious devotion and godliness. It is famous for its Yogins and saints. The goal of India is Self-realisation or attainment of God-consciousness, through renunciation. The history of India is a history of religion. Its social code and regulations are founded upon religion. Minus its Yoga, religion and its regulations, India will not be what it has been for millennia. Some Hindus are still not aware of the distinguishing features of Sanatana Dharma. If every Hindu knew and understood what Hinduism is, the Hindus of today would all be gods on this earth. May you all be endowed with the knowledge of Sanatana Dharma!

May you all endeavour to protect the Eternal Dharma! May the secrets of Sanatana Dharma be revealed unto you all, like a fruit in the palm of your hand, through the Grace of the Lord! May the blessings of Rishis be upon you all! Glory to the Vedas and Sanatana Dharma! Glory to Brahman, the source for all Vedas and Sanatana Dharma!

Samanya Dharma

Every religion has a generic form or *Samanya-Rupa* and a specific form or *Visesha-Rupa*. The general form remains eternally the same. It is never changed by any circumstance whatsoever. It is not affected at all by changes of time, place, surroundings and individual differences. This aspect of religion is called Sanatana or eternal. That which changes according to the change of time, place and surrounding circumstances is the external aspect or ritual, of Dharma.

Samanya Dharma is the general Dharma or law for all men. Varnashrama Dharmas are special Dharmas which are to be practised by particular castes and by men in particular stages of life. The Samanya Dharmas must be practised by all, irrespective of distinctions of Varna and Ashrama, creed or colour. Goodness is not the property of any one class, creed, sect or community. Every man should possess this virtue.

Fundamentals of Dharma

The Vishnu Samhita enumerates forgiveness, truthfulness, control of the mind, purity, practice of charity, control of the senses, non-violence, service of the Guru, visiting places of pilgrimage, compassion, simplicity, absence of greed, worship of the gods and the Brahmanas, and absence of malice as the ingredients of Samanya Dharma, the general law for all men.

The Mahabharata enumerates the performance of Shradha or offering oblations to the forefathers, religious austerity, truth, restraint of anger, satisfaction with one's own wife, purity, learning, absence of envy, knowledge of the Self and forbearance as the fundamentals of Dharma.

It is said in Padma Purana that Dharma proceeds from continence, truthfulness, austerity, charity, self-control, forbearance, purity, non-violence, serenity and non-thieving and that one should recognise Dharma by these ten factors. According to this Purana, bestowing gifts on deserving persons, fixing one's thoughts on Lord Krishna, adoration of one's parents, offering a portion of the daily meal to all creatures and giving a morsel of food to a cow are the characteristics of Dharma.

According to Matsya Purana, freedom from malice, absence of covetousness, control of the senses, austerity, celibacy, compassion, truthfulness, forbearance and fortitude constitute the fundamentals of Sanatana Dharma.

Patanjali Maharshi, the exponent of Raja Yoga philosophy, recommends that ten virtues should be practised by all men. The first five are: Ahimsa (non-violence), Satya (truthfulness), Brahmacharya (celibacy in thought, word and deed), Asteya (non-stealing) and Aparigraha (non-covetousness). These constitute Yama or self-restraint. The other five virtues are: Saucha (internal and external purity), Santosha (contentment), Tapas (austerity), Svadhyaya (study of scriptures or recitation of Mantra) and Isvara-pranidhana (consecration of the fruits of all works to the Lord). These constitute Niyama or religious observance.

The Gita enumerates the following virtues as Daivi-Sampat or divine qualities: fearlessness, cleanness of life, steadfastness in the Yoga of Wisdom, alms-giving, self-restraint, sacrifice, study of the scriptures, austerity, straightforwardness, harmlessness, truth, absence of wrath, renunciation, peacefulness, absence of crookedness, compassion to living beings, non-covetousness, mildness, modesty, absence of fickleness, vigour, forgiveness, fortitude, purity and absence of envy and pride. All these virtues are manifestations of the four fundamental virtues: (i) non-violence, (ii) truth, (iii) purity and (iv) self-control. All the above virtues come under the above four cardinal virtues. The virtues that are enumerated under the Noble Eightfold Path of Buddhism and the virtues prescribed by Lord Jesus in his Sermon on the Mount, also come under the above fundamental virtues.

The development of the divine qualities is indispensable for the attainment of Self-realisation. Brahman or the Eternal is purity. The Eternal cannot be attained without the attainment of purity. Brahman is truth. The Eternal cannot be attained without practising truth. Brahman is fearlessness. The Eternal cannot be attained unless you become absolutely fearless. Attachment to the body causes fear and Dehadhyasa. If only you become fearless, then the identification with the body will vanish.

You have rendered the heart harder than flint, steel or diamond through greed, miserliness, harshness and rudeness. You can soften it only through the practice of mercy, sympathy, charity, generosity, magnanimity, harmlessness, mildness, disinterested action and untiring service of the poor. You have made the heart crooked and narrow through hypocrisy, untruthfulness, backbiting and talebearing. You can expand it through the practice of straightforwardness, truthfulness, cleanness of life, alms-giving and non-covetousness. You have rendered the heart impure through lust. You can purify it through the practice of celibacy in thought, word and deed.

***Non-violence*:** Ahimsa or non-violence is the most important virtue. That is the reason why Patanjali Maharshi has placed it first in Yama. Practice of Ahimsa must be in thought, word and deed. Practice of Ahimsa is not impotence or cowardice or weakness. It is the highest type of heroism. The practice demands immense patience, forbearance and endurance, infinite inner spiritual strength and gigantic will-power.

Ahimsa is a modification or expression of truth only. Satyam and Ahimsa always go together. He who is established in Ahimsa can move the whole world. In his presence, all hostilities vanish; lion and cow, cobra and mongoose, live together peacefully. Hinduism, Buddhism and Jainism lay great stress on Ahimsa. Lord Jesus also has emphasised much on Ahimsa in his Sermon on the Mount. He says: "If anyone beats you on one cheek, show him the other cheek also."

He who is firmly established in Ahimsa can hope to attain Self-realisation. He who practises Ahimsa develops cosmic love to a maximum degree. Practice of Ahimsa eventually leads to realisation of oneness or unity of Self. Such a man only can attain self-restraint. Retaliation—tooth for tooth, blow for blow—is the maxim, doctrine or principle of an Asura or a man of diabolic nature. This belongs to the beastly nature. To return good for evil is divine. Constant vigilance and alertness are needed in the practice of Ahimsa. If you are careless even a bit, you will be carried away by the force of previous wrong Samskaras and impulses and will become a victim of Himsa, despite your good intentions.

***Truth*:** Brahman is Sat or Existence-Absolute. Truth must be observed in thought, word and deed. If you are established in truth, all other virtues will cling to you by themselves. Harischandra sacrificed everything for the sake of truth. He lives still in our hearts. Yudhishthira was also devoted to truth. There is no virtue higher than truth. Practice of truth and Ahimsa constitute the crown and glory of ethical life. In the Taittiriya Upanishad, the preceptor says in his convocation address to the students: "*Satyam vada*—Speak the truth." The world is rooted in truth. Dharma is rooted in truth. All religions are rooted in truth. Honesty, justice, straightforwardness and sincerity are only modifications or expressions of truth.

***Purity*:** Purity comprises both external purity and internal purity. Purity implies both purity of body and purity of mind. Purity of body is only the preliminary to purity of mind.

This body is the temple of God. It should be kept clean by daily bathing and clean dress. Cleanliness is a part of godliness.

The restriction in diet is best calculated to make the mind pure. Food exercises a direct influence on the mind.

Sattvic food makes the mind pure. Purity of food leads to purity of mind. Mind is only made up of the fine essence of food. As the food is, so is the mind.

You must be pure in thought, word and deed. Your heart must be as pure as crystal or the Himalayan snow. Then only the divine light will descend. Purity comprises such virtues as frankness, innocence, straightforwardness and absence of all evil thoughts. He who is endowed with purity will find it easy to tread the spiritual path.

Self-control: You must have perfect self-control or self-mastery. Self-control implies both control of the body and control of the mind. Self-control does not mean self-torture. You must lead a well-regulated and disciplined life. You must keep all the senses under your perfect control. The senses are like turbulent and wild horses. This body is like a chariot. Mind is the reins. Intellect is the driver.

The Atman is the Lord of the chariot. If the senses are not kept under proper control, they will throw this chariot into a deep abyss. You will come to ruin. He who keeps the reins firm and drives this chariot intelligently by controlling the horses (senses), will reach the destination (Moksha or the Abode of Eternal Bliss) safely.

Self-control implies self-sacrifice, annihilation of egoism, patience, endurance, forbearance and humility. Overcome Raga or attachment by Vairagya or dispassion. Dispassion will dawn in your mind if you look into the defects of sensual life such as birth, death, disease, old age, pain, sorrow, etc. (Mithya-Drishti and Dosha-Drishti). Overcome anger and hatred by Kshama or forgiveness, love and selfless service. Overcome evil by good. Return good for evil. Overcome lust by the practice of Brahmacharya and regular Japa and meditation. Conquer greed by charity, generosity and disinterested actions. Conquer pride by humility and delusion by discrimination and enquiry. Overcome jealousy by magnanimity, Atma-bhava and nobility. Conquer egoism by self-sacrifice, self-surrender, self-abnegation and meditation on the non-dual, eternal, self-luminous Brahman, the innermost Self, the Inner Ruler, the Immortal.

May you all attain eternal bliss and immortality through the practice of the cardinal virtues or the fundamental Dharma.

Varnashrama Dharma

The principle of Varnashrama Dharma is one of the basic principles of Hinduism. The Varnashrama system is peculiar to Hindus. It is a characteristic feature of Hinduism. It is also prevalent throughout the world according to Guna-Karma (aptitude and conduct), though there is no such distinct denomination of this kind, elsewhere.

The duties of the castes are Varna Dharma. The four castes are Brahmana, Kshatriya, Vaishya and Sudra. The duties of the stages in life are Ashrama Dharma. The four Ashramas or orders of life are Brahmacharya, Grihastha, Vanaprastha and Sannyasa.

The Principle: Human society is like a huge machine. The individuals and communities are like its parts. If the parts are weak and broken, the machine will not work. A machine is nothing without its parts. The human body also can work efficiently if its parts and organs are in sound and strong condition. If there is pain in any part of the body, if there is disease in any organ or part of the body, this human machine will go out of order. It will not perform its usual function or work.

So is the case with the human society. Every individual should perform his duties efficiently. The Hindu Rishis and sages formed an ideal scheme of society and an ideal way of individual life, which is known by the name Varnashrama Dharma. Hinduism is built on Varnashrama Dharma. The structure of the Hindu society is based on Varnashrama Dharma. Observance of Varnashrama Dharma helps one's growth and self-evolution. It is very indispensable. If the rules are violated, the society will soon perish.

The aim of Varnashrama Dharma is to promote the development of the universal, eternal Dharma. If you defend Dharma, it will defend you. If you destroy it, it will destroy you. Therefore, never destroy your Dharma. This principle holds true of the individual as much as of the nation. It is Dharma alone which keeps a nation alive. Dharma is the very soul of man. Dharma is the very soul of a nation also.

In the West and in the whole world also, there is Varnashrama, though it is not rigidly observed there. Some Western philosophers have made a division of three classes, *viz.*, philosophers, warriors and masses. The philosophers correspond to the Brahmanas, warriors to Kshatriyas and the masses to Vaishyas and Sudras. This system is indispensable to keep the society in a state of perfect harmony and order.

The Four Castes

In Purusha-Sukta of the Rig-Veda, there is reference to the division of Hindu society into four classes. It is described there that the Brahmanas came out of the face of the Lord, the Creator, Kshatriyas from His arms, Vaishyas from His thighs, and the Sudras from His feet.

This division is according to the Guna and Karma. Guna (quality) and Karma (kind of work) determine the caste of a man. This is supported by Lord Krishna in the Gita, also. He says in the Gita: "The four castes were emanated by Me, by the different distribution of qualities and actions. Know Me to be the author of them, though the actionless and inexhaustible" (Ch. IV-13).

There are three qualities or Gunas, *viz.*, *Sattva* (purity), *Rajas* (passion) and *Tamas* (inertia). Sattva is white, Rajas is red and Tamas is black. These three qualities are found in man in varying proportions. Sattva preponderates in some persons. They are Brahmanas. They are wise persons or thinkers. They are the priests, ministers or philosophers who guide kings or rulers. In some, Rajas is predominant. They are Kshatriyas. They are warriors or men of action. They fight with the enemies or invaders and defend the country. In some, Tamas is predominant. They are Vaishyas or traders. They do business and agriculture and amass wealth. Sudras are the servants. None of these qualities is highly developed in them. They serve the other three castes.

In a broad sense, a Sattvic man, who is pious and virtuous and leads the divine life, is a Brahmana, a Rajasic man with heroic quality is a Kshatriya, a Rajasic man with business tendencies is a Vaishya and a Tamasic man is a Sudra. Hitler and Mussolini were Kshatriyas. Ford was a Vaishya.

Serenity, self-restraint, austerity, purity, forgiveness, and also, uprightness, knowledge, Realisation and belief in God are the duties of the Brahmanas, born of (their own) nature. Prowess, splendour, firmness, dexterity, and also, not flying from battle, generosity and lordliness are the duties of the Kshatriyas, born of (their own) nature. Agriculture, cattle-rearing and trade are the duties of the Vaishyas, born of (their own) nature. And action consisting of service is the duty of the Sudras, born of (their own) nature.

***The Law of Spiritual Economics*:** The underlying principle in caste system or Varna Dharma, is division of labour. Rishis studied human nature carefully. They came to the conclusion that all men were not equally fit for all kinds of work. Hence, they found it necessary to allocate different kinds of duties to different classes of people, according to their aptitude, capacity or quality. The Brahmanas were in charge of spiritual and intellectual affairs. The work of political administration and defence was given to the Kshatriyas. The Vaishyas were entrusted with the duty of supplying food for the nation and administering its economic welfare. The Sudras did menial work. The Rishis felt all these needs of the Hindu nation and started the system of Varnas and Ashramas.

This division of labour began in Vedic times. The Vedas taught that the Brahmana was the brain of the society, the Kshatriya its arms, the Vaishya its stomach, and the Sudra its feet. There was a quarrel between the senses, the mind and the Prana as to who was superior. There was a quarrel amongst the different organs and the stomach. If the hands quarrel with the stomach; the entire body will suffer. When Prana departed from the body, all the organs suffered. The head or stomach cannot claim its superiority over the feet and hands. The hands and feet are as much important as the stomach or head. If there is quarrel between the different castes as to which is superior, then the entire social fabric will suffer. There will be disharmony, rupture and discord. A scavenger and a barber are as much important as a minister for the running of the society. The social edifice is built on the law of spiritual economics. It has nothing to do with superiority or inferiority. Each class contributes its best to the common weal or world-solidarity. There is no question of higher and lower here.

***Character Determines Caste*:** A Brahmana is no Brahmana if he is not endowed with purity and good character, and if he leads a life of dissipation and immorality. A Sudra is a Brahmana if he leads a virtuous and pious life. What a great soul was Vidura! What a noble, candid, straightforward student was Satyakama Jabala of Chhandogya Upanishad! Caste is a question of character. Varna is no more the colour of the skin, but the colour of one's character or quality. Conduct and character count and not lineage alone. If one is Brahmana by birth and, at the same time, if he possesses the virtues of a Brahmana, it is extremely good, because certain virtuous qualifications only determine the birth of a Brahmana.

Use and Abuse of the Caste System: The Hindus have survived many a foreign conquest on account of their caste system. But they have developed class jealousies and hatred in the name of the caste system. They have not got the spirit of cooperation. That is the reason why they are weak and disunited today. They have become sectarians in the name of the caste system. Hence there is degradation in India.

The caste system is, indeed, a splendid thing. It is quite flawless. But the defect came in from somewhere else. The classes gradually neglected their duties. The test of ability and character slowly vanished. Birth became the chief consideration in determining castes. All castes fell from their ideals and forgot all about their duties. Brahmanas became selfish and claimed superiority over others by mere birth, without possessing due qualifications.

The Kshatriyas lost their chivalry and spirit of sacrifice. The Vaishyas became very greedy. They did not earn wealth by honest means. They did not look after the economic welfare of the people. They did not give charity. They also lost the spirit of sacrifice. Sudras gave up service. They became officers. They wished that others should serve them. The greed and pride of man have created discord and disharmony.

There is nothing wrong in Varnashrama. It is arrogance and haughtiness in men that have brought troubles. Man or the little Jiva is imperfect. He is full of defects. He is simply waiting for claiming superiority over others. The Brahmana thinks that the other three castes are inferior to him. The Kshatriya thinks that the Vaishya and Sudra are inferior to him. A rich Sudra thinks that he is superior to a poor Brahmana or a poor Kshatriya or Vaishya. At the present moment, the

Varnashrama system exists in name only. It has to be rebuilt properly. Brahmanas, Kshatriyas, Vaishyas and Sudras, who have fallen from their ideals and who are not doing their respective duties, must do their respective duties properly. They must be educated on right lines. They must raise themselves to their original lofty level. The sectarian spirit must die. They should develop a new understanding heart of love and devotion, with a spirit of cooperation, sacrifice and service.

The Four Ashramas

There are four Ashramas or stages in life, *viz.*, Brahmacharya or the period of studentship, Grihastha or the stage of the householder, Vanaprastha or the stage of the forest-dweller or hermit, and Sannyasa or the life of renunciation or asceticism. Each stage has its own duties. These stages help the evolution of man. The four Ashramas take man to perfection by successive stages. The practice of the four Ashramas regulates the life from the beginning to the end. The first two Ashramas pertain to Pravritti Marga or the path of work and the two later stages—the life of Vanaprastha and that of Sannyasa—are the stages of withdrawal from the world. They pertain to Nivritti Marga or the path of renunciation.

Towards Orderly Spiritual Evolution: Life is very systematically and orderly arranged in Sanatana Dharma. There is opportunity for the development of the different sides of human activity. Due occupations and training are assigned to each period of life. Life is a great school in which the powers, capacities and faculties of man are to be evolved gradually.

Every man should pass through the different Ashramas regularly. He should not enter any stage of life prematurely. He can enter the next stage, only when each has been completed. In nature, evolution is gradual. It is not revolutionary.

Lord Manu says in his Smriti: "Having studied the Vedas or two Vedas or even one Veda in due order without breaking celibacy, let him dwell in the householder order. When the householder sees wrinkles in his skin and whiteness in his hair and the son of his son, then let him retire to the forest. Having passed the third portion of life in the forests, let him, having abandoned attachments, wander as an ascetic in the fourth portion of life."

In extraordinary cases, however, some of the stages may be omitted. Suka was a born Sannyasin. Shankara took Sannyasa without entering the stage of a householder. In rare and exceptional cases, a student is allowed to become a Sannyasin, his debts to the world having been fully paid in a previous birth. Nowadays, young Sannyasins without qualification are found in abundance. This is contrary to the ancient rules and causes much trouble.

***The Brahmacharin or the Celibate Student*:** The first stage, Brahmacharya, is the period of study and discipline. The student should not indulge in any pleasures. He stays in the house of his preceptor and studies the Vedas and the sciences. This is the period of probation. The teachers in ancient India usually lived in forest hermitages. These hermitages were the Gurukulas or forest universities. The student begged his food. The children of the rich and poor lived together. The student regarded his teacher as his spiritual father and served him with faith, devotion and reverence.

The life of the student begins with the Upanayana ceremony, his second birth. He must be hardy and simple in his habits. He rises early, bathes and does Sandhya and Gayatri Japa. He studies scriptures. He takes simple food in moderation and takes plenty of exercise. He sleeps on a hard mat and does not use soft beds and pillows. He is humble and obedient. He serves and respects elders. He attempts to be chaste in thought, word and deed.

He ever engages himself in doing services to his preceptor. He refrains from wine, meat, perfumes, garlands, tasty and savoury dishes, women, acids, spices and injury to sentient creatures; from lust, anger, greed; dancing, singing and playing on musical instruments; from dice-playing, gossip, slander and untruth. He sleeps alone. After the end of his student career, he gives a present to his preceptor according to his ability and returns home to enter the household life. The preceptor gives the final instruction and sends the student home. The teacher delivers a convocation address to the students at the conclusion of their studentship:

"Speak the truth. Do your duty. Never swerve from the study of the Veda. Do not cut off the line of progeny (after giving the preceptor the fee he desires). Never swerve away from truth. Never swerve from duty. Never neglect your welfare. Never neglect your prosperity. Never neglect the study and the teaching of the Vedas.

"Never swerve from the duties to the gods and the forefathers. Regard your mother as a god *(Matridevo Bhava).* Regard your father as a god *(Pitridevo Bhava).* Regard your teacher as a god *(Acharyadevo Bhava).* Regard your guest as god *(Atithidevo Bhava).* Let only those actions that are free from blemishes be done and not others. Only those that are good acts to us should be performed by you and not others.

"You should remove the fatigue of Brahmanas who are superior to you by serving them with seats, etc. Gift should be given with faith, in plenty, with modesty and sympathy. If there be any doubt regarding rites or conduct, then look up to the lives of great men and follow their examples. This is the injunction. This is the teaching. This is the secret of the Vedas. This is God's word of command. This should be observed. Thus is this to be meditated upon."

***The Grihastha or the Householder*:** The second stage is that of the Grihastha or householder. The household stage is entered at marriage, when the student has completed his studentship and is ready to take up the duties and responsibilities of householder life. Of all the Ashramas, this is the most important, because it supports all the others. As all creatures live supported by the air, so the other Orders exist supported by the householder. As all streams and rivers flow to rest in the ocean, so all the Ashramas flow to rest in the householder. The Grihastha is the very heart of Aryan life. Everything depends on him.

Marriage is a sacrament for a Hindu. The wife is his partner in life. She is his Ardhangini. He cannot do any religious ritual without her. She stands by his left side when he performs any religious performance. Husband and wife keep Rama and Sita as their ideal.

A householder should earn money by honest means and distribute it in the proper manner. He should spend one-tenth of his income in charity. He should enjoy sensual pleasures within the limits of the moral law. A householder is permitted to enjoy conjugal happiness on one night in a month.

The householder should perform the Pancha Maha Yajnas. The five Yajnas are:

DEVA-YAJNA—offering oblations unto Devas, with recitation of Vedic Mantras.

RISHI-YAJNA—study of Vedas and teaching of Vedas to students, and offering of oblations to Rishis.

PITRI-YAJNA—Tarpana or ablutions to departed souls and Shradha or annual religious rites performed for departed souls.

BHUTA-YAJNA—distribution of food to cows, crows and animals in general.

ATITHI-YAJNA—giving food to guests and honouring them.

Hospitality is one of the householder's chief duties. He must ever feed first his guests, Brahmanas and his relatives, and then he and his wife should eat.

When the householder sees that his sons are able to bear the burden of his duties, when his grandsons are around him, he should know that the time has come for him and his wife to retire from the world and spend their time in study and meditation.

***The Vanaprastha or the Recluse*:** The next stage is that of the Varnaprastha. Brahmacharya is a preparation for the life of the householder. Even so, Vanaprastha is a preparation for the final stage of Sannyasa. After discharging all the duties of a householder, he should retire to the forest or a solitary country place and begin to meditate in solitude on higher spiritual things. He is now free from social bonds and the responsibilities of life. He has ample time for study of scriptures. His wife may go with him or remain with her sons.

***The Sannyasin or the Renunciate*:** The next stage is that of a Sannyasin. When a man becomes a Sannyasin, he renounces all possessions, all distinctions of caste, all rites and ceremonies and all attachments to any particular country, nation, or religion. He lives alone and spends his time in meditation. He lives on alms. When he attains the sublime state of deep meditation he rejoices in his own Self. He is quite indifferent to sensual pleasures. He is free from likes and dislikes, desires, egoism, lust, anger, greed and pride.

He has equal vision and balanced mind. He loves all. He roams about happily and disseminates Brahma Jnana or Knowledge of the Self. He is the same in honour and dishonour, praise and censure, success and failure. He is now *Ativarnasrami, i.e.*, above Varna and Ashrama. He is quite a free man. He is not bound by any social customs and conventions.

Such a Sannyasin is an ideal man. He has attained perfection and freedom. He is Brahman Himself. He is a Jivanmukta or a liberated sage. Glory to such exalted personages who are living Gods on earth!

Ashrama Dharma Under Modern Conditions

At the present moment, the Ashramas cannot be exactly lived according to the details of the ancient rules, as the conditions have changed very much; but, they may be revived in their spirit, to the great improvement of modern life. In these stages, no one should do the duty of another. The student or Brahmachari should not do the duties of a householder, a recluse or a Sannyasin. The householder must not perform the duties of a Brahmacharin, Vanaprastha or a Sannyasin. A Sannyasin should not seek again the joys of the householder.

Peace and order will prevail in society, only if and when all people do their respective duties efficiently. The abolition of Varnas and Ashramas will cut at the very root of social duties. How can the nation hope to live when Varnashrama Dharma is not rigidly practised?

The students of schools, and colleges should lead a life of purity and simple living. The householder should lead the life of an ideal Grihastha. He should practise self-restraint, mercy, tolerance, non-injury, truthfulness and moderation in everything. Those who find it difficult to lead the life of the third and the fourth Ashramas should, remaining in either of the other two Ashramas, gradually withdraw themselves from worldly life and practise selfless service, study and meditation.

The Highest State

Varnashrama pertains to body alone, but not to the pure, all-pervading, immortal soul or Atman. Attain Knowledge of the Self and become an Ativarnasrami like Lord Dattatreya. Hear what he says:

Mahadadi Jagat Sarvam

Na kinchit pratibhati me
Brahmaiva kevalam sarvam
Katham varnasramasthitih

"The whole world, from Mahat downwards, does not shine in Me. Everything is Brahman only. Where then is Varnashrama?"

May you all have comprehensive understanding of Varnashrama Dharma! May you all develop universal love and brotherhood! May all barriers which are made by man for his own self-aggrandisement and self-assertion and which create discord and disunion, be broken asunder!

Yuga Dharma

In Satya-Yuga or the golden age there was a different set of Dharmas or laws; in Treta, they changed into another form; in Dvapara, the Dharmas were different from the Dharmas of other Yugas; and in Kali-Yuga, they assumed still another form. The Dharma changes according to the changes of the cycles. Man is undergoing change. His nature gets transformed through experiences. Hence, his external form of Dharmas also should change. That which is achieved through contemplation in Satya Yuga, through sacrifices in Treta Yuga, and through the worship of Lord Hari in Dvapara Yuga, may be attained through Kirtana or loud chanting of Lord Vishnu's Name in Kali Yuga or Iron age.

In the Satya Yuga, the mind of men was generally pure. They had no distraction of the mind. There were neither cinemas, nor hotels, nor dancing halls and similar other distractions. Hence, meditation was easy and natural for them. That is the reason why contemplation has been prescribed for men of Satya Yuga. In the Treta Yuga, materials for the performance of Yajnas or sacrifices were easily available. The people had active tendencies. Therefore it was easy for them to perform Agnihotra, Jyotistoma, Darsa-Paurnimas and other Yajnas.

That is the reason why Yajna has been described as the external form of Sanatana Dharma in that age. In the Dvapara Yuga, there was the manifestation of Avataras and men could easily have direct worship of God. Hence, worship was prescribed as the principal form of Sadhana in that age. In the Kali Yuga, there are many distractions for the mind. People lack in Brahmacharya, strength of will and power of enquiry or rational investigation. It is very difficult to procure materials for the performance of sacrifices. Therefore, Hari Kirtana or loud chanting of the Divine Name and selfless service of humanity have been recommended as the principal forms of Sadhana.

Conclusion

Follow your Dharma with zeal and enthusiasm. Discharge your duties faithfully. Develop all the virtues which constitute Dharma. Never deviate an inch from the path of righteousness. Stick to Dharma with all your heart, with all your mind and with all your soul. Performance of one's duties brings happiness, quick evolution and freedom. You will soon attain immortality, eternal bliss, supreme peace, perennial joy, absolute freedom and perfection. Glory to Dharma, the supreme light that leads you to the kingdom of eternal bliss and everlasting peace.

May the eternal Dharma of Hinduism be preserved for ever! May all Hindus be consolidated by the bond of true love!!

6

The Laws of Brahmanical Soceity in Ancient India

Manusmriti-the Laws of Manu

CHAPTER-I

1. The great sages approached Manu, who was seated with a collected mind, and, having duly worshipped him, spoke as follows:
2. 'Deign, divine one, to declare to us precisely and in due order the sacred laws of each of the (four chief) castes (varna) and of the intermediate ones.
3. 'For thou, O Lord, alone knowest the purport, (*i.e.*) the rites, and the knowledge of the soul, (taught) in this whole ordinance of the Self-existent (Svayambhu), which is unknowable and unfathomable.'
4. He, whose power is measureless, being thus asked by the high-minded great sages, duly honoured them, and answered, 'Listen!'
5. This (universe) existed in the shape of Darkness, unperceived, destitute of distinctive marks, unattainable by reasoning, unknowable, wholly immersed, as it were, in deep sleep.
6. Then the divine Self-existent (Svayambhu, himself) indiscernible, (but) making (all) this, the great elements and the rest, discernible, appeared with irresistible (creative) power, dispelling the darkness.

7. He who can be perceived by the internal organ (alone), who is subtile, indiscernible, and eternal, who contains all created beings and is inconceivable, shone forth of his own (will).
8. He, desiring to produce beings of many kinds from his own body, first with a thought created the waters, and placed his seed in them.
9. That (seed) became a golden egg, in brilliancy equal to the sun; in that (egg) he himself was born as Brahman, the progenitor of the whole world.
10. The waters are called narah, (for) the waters are, indeed, the offspring of Nara; as they were his first residence (ayana), he thence is named Narayana.
11. From that (first) cause, which is indiscernible, eternal, and both real and unreal, was produced that male (Purusha), who is famed in this world (under the appellation of) Brahman.
12. The divine one resided in that egg during a whole year, then he himself by his thought (alone) divided it into two halves;
13. And out of those two halves he formed heaven and earth, between them the middle sphere, the eight points of the horizon, and the eternal abode of the waters.
14. From himself (atmanah) he also drew forth the mind, which is both real and unreal, likewise from the mind egoism, which possesses the function of self-consciousness (and is) lordly;
15. Moreover, the great one, the soul, and all (products) affected by the three qualities, and, in their order, the five organs which perceive the objects of sensation.
16. But, joining minute particles even of those six, which possess measureless power, with particles of himself, he created all beings.
17. Because those six (kinds of) minute particles, which form the (creator's) frame, enter (a-sri) these (creatures), therefore the wise call his frame sarira, (the body.)

18. That the great elements enter, together with their functions and the mind, through its minute parts the framer of all beings, the imperishable one.
19. But from minute body (framing) particles of these seven very powerful Purushas springs this (world), the perishable from the imperishable.
20. Among them each succeeding (element) acquires the quality of the preceding one, and whatever place (in the sequence) each of them occupies, even so many qualities it is declared to possess.
21. But in the beginning he assigned their several names, actions, and conditions to all (created beings), even according to the words of the Veda.
22. He, the Lord, also created the class of the gods, who are endowed with life, and whose nature is action; and the subtile class of the Sadhyas, and the eternal sacrifice.
23. But from fire, wind, and the sun he drew forth the threefold eternal Veda, called Rik, Yagus, and Saman, for the due performance of the sacrifice.
24. Time and the divisions of time, the lunar mansions and the planets, the rivers, the oceans, the mountains, plains, and uneven ground.
25. Austerity, speech, pleasure, desire, and anger, this whole creation he likewise produced, as he desired to call these beings into existence.
26. Moreover, in order to distinguish actions, he separated merit from demerit, and he caused the creatures to be affected by the pairs (of opposites), such as pain and pleasure.
27. But with the minute perishable particles of the five (elements) which have been mentioned, this whole (world) is framed in due order.
28. But to whatever course of action the Lord at first appointed each (kind of beings), that alone it has spontaneously adopted in each succeeding creation.
29: Whatever he assigned to each at the (first) creation, noxiousness or harmlessness, gentleness or ferocity,

virtue or sin, truth or falsehood, that clung (afterwards) spontaneously to it.

30. As at the change of the seasons each season of its own accord assumes its distinctive marks, even so corporeal beings (resume in new births) their (appointed) course of action.

31. But for the sake of the prosperity of the worlds he caused the Brahman, the Kshatriya, the Vaishya, and the Sudra to proceed from his mouth, his arms, his thighs, and his feet.

32. Dividing his own body, the Lord became half male and half female; with that (female) he produced Virag.

33. But know me, O most holy among the twice-born, to be the creator of this whole (world), whom that male, Virag, himself produced, having performed austerities.

34. Then I, desiring to produce created beings, performed very difficult austerities, and (thereby) called into existence ten great sages, lords of created beings,

35. Mariki, Atri, Angiras, Pulastya, Pulaha, Kratu, Praketas, Vashistha, Bhrigu, and Narada.

36. They created seven other Manus possessing great brilliancy, gods and classes of gods and great sages of measureless power,

37. Yakshas (the servants of Kubera, the demons called) Rakshasas and Pisakas, Gandharvas (or musicians of the gods), Apsarases (the dancers of the gods), Asuras, (the snake-deities called) Nagas and Sarpas, (the bird-deities called) Suparnas and the several classes of the manes,

38. Lightnings, thunderbolts and clouds, imperfect (rohita) and perfect rainbows, falling meteors, supernatural noises, comets, and heavenly lights of many kinds,

39. (Horse-faced) Kinnaras, monkeys, fishes, birds of many kinds, cattle, deer, men, and carnivorous beasts with two rows of teeth,

40. Small and large worms and beetles, moths, lice, flies,

bugs, all stinging and biting insects and the several kinds of immovable things.

41. Thus was this whole (creation), both the immovable and the movable, produced by those high-minded ones by means of austerities and at my command, (each being) according to (the results of) its actions.
42. But whatever act is stated (to belong) to (each of) those creatures here below, that I will truly declare to you, as well as their order in respect to birth.
43. Cattle, deer, carnivorous beasts with two rows of teeth, Rakshasas, Pisakas, and men are born from the womb.
44. From eggs are born birds, snakes, crocodiles, fishes, tortoises, as well as similar terrestrial and aquatic (animals).
45. From hot moisture spring stinging and biting insects, lice, flies, bugs, and all other (creatures) of that kind which are produced by heat.
46. All plants, propagated by seed or by slips, grow from shoots; annual plants (are those) which, bearing many flowers and fruits, perish after the ripening of their fruit;
47. (Those trees) which bear fruit without flowers are called vanaspati (lords of the forest); but those which bear both flowers and fruit are called vriksha.
48. But the various plants with many stalks, growing from one or several roots, the different kinds of grasses, the climbing plants and the creepers spring all from seed or from slips.
49. These (plants) which are surrounded by multiform Darkness, the result of their acts (in former existences), possess internal consciousness and experience pleasure and pain.
50. The (various) conditions in this always terrible and constantly changing circle of births and deaths to which created beings are subject, are stated to begin with (that of) Brahman, and to end with (that of) these (just mentioned immovable creatures).

51. When he whose power is incomprehensible, had thus produced the universe and men, he disappeared in himself, repeatedly suppressing one period by means of the other.
52. When that divine one wakes, then this world stirs; when he slumbers tranquilly, then the universe sinks to sleep.
53. But when he reposes in calm sleep, the corporeal beings whose nature is action, desist from their actions and mind becomes inert.
54. When they are absorbed all at once in that great soul, then he who is the soul of all beings sweetly slumbers, free from all care and occupation.
55. When this (soul) has entered darkness, it remains for a long time united with the organs (of sensation), but performs not its functions; it then leaves the corporeal frame.
56. When, being clothed with minute particles (only), it enters into vegetable or animal seed, it then assumes, united (with the fine body), a (new) corporeal frame.
57. Thus he, the imperishable one, by (alternately) waking and slumbering, incessantly revivifies and destroys this whole movable and immovable (creation).
58. But he having composed these Institutes (of the sacred law), himself taught them, according to the rule, to me alone in the beginning; next I (taught them) to Mariki and the other sages.
59. Bhrigu, here, will fully recite to you these Institutes; for that sage learned the whole in its entirety from me.
60. Then that great sage Bhrigu, being thus addressed by Manu, spoke, pleased in his heart, to all the sages, 'Listen!'
61. Six other high-minded, very powerful Manus, who belong to the race of this Manu, the descendant of the Self-existent (Svayambhu), and who have severally produced created beings,
62. (Are) Svarokisha, Auttami, Tamasa, Raivata,

Kakshusha, possessing great lustre, and the son of Vivasvat.

63. These seven very glorious Manus, the first among whom is Svayambhuva, produced and protected this whole movable and immovable (creation), each during the period (allotted to him).

64. Eighteen nimeshas (twinklings of the eye, are one kashtha), thirty kashthas one kala, thirty kalas one muhurta, and as many (muhurtas) one day and night.

65. The sun divides days and nights, both human and divine, the night (being intended) for the repose of created beings and the day for exertion.

66. A month is a day and a night of the manes, but the division is according to fortnights. The dark (fortnight) is their day for active exertion, the bright (fortnight) their night for sleep.

67. A year is a day and a night of the gods; their division is (as follows): the half year during which the sun progresses to the north will be the day, that during which it goes southwards the night.

68. But hear now the brief (description of) the duration of a night and a day of Brahman and of the several ages (of the world, yuga) according to their order.

69. They declare that the Krita age (consists of) four thousand years (of the gods); the twilight preceding it consists of as many hundreds, and the twilight following it of the same number.

70. In the other three ages with their twilights preceding and following, the thousands and hundreds are diminished by one (in each).

71. These twelve thousand (years) which thus have been just mentioned as the total of four (human) ages, are called one age of the gods.

72. But know that the sum of one thousand ages of the gods (makes) one day of Brahman, and that his night has the same length.

73. Those (only, who) know that the holy day of Brahman,

indeed, ends after (the completion of) one thousand ages (of the gods) and that his night lasts as long, (are really) men acquainted with (the length of) days and nights.

74. At the end of that day and night he who was asleep, awakes and, after awaking, creates mind, which is both real and unreal.

75. Mind, impelled by (Brahman's) desire to create, performs the work of creation by modifying itself, thence ether is produced; they declare that sound is the quality of the latter.

76. But from ether, modifying itself, springs the pure, powerful wind, the vehicle of all perfumes; that is held to possess the quality of touch.

77. Next from wind modifying itself, proceeds the brilliant light, which illuminates and dispels darkness; that is declared to possess the quality of colour;

78. And from light, modifying itself, (is produced) water, possessing the quality of taste, from water earth which has the quality of smell; such is the creation in the beginning.

79. The before-mentioned age of the gods, (or) twelve thousand (of their years), being multiplied by seventy-one, (constitutes what) is here named the period of a Manu (Manvantara).

80. The Manvantaras, the creations and destructions (of the world, are) numberless; sporting, as it were, Brahman repeats this again and again.

81. In the Krita age Dharma is four-footed and entire, and (so is) Truth; nor does any gain accrue to men by unrighteousness.

82. In the other (three ages), by reason of (unjust) gains (agama), Dharma is deprived successively of one foot, and through (the prevalence of) theft, falsehood, and fraud the merit (gained by men) is diminished by one fourth (in each).

83. (Men are) free from disease, accomplish all their aims,

and live four hundred years in the Krita age, but in the Treta and (in each of) the succeeding (ages) their life is lessened by one quarter.

84. The life of mortals, mentioned in the Veda, the desired results of sacrificial rites and the (supernatural) power of embodied (spirits) are fruits proportioned among men according to (the character of) the age.

85. One set of duties (is prescribed) for men in the Krita age, different ones in the Treta and in the Dvapara, and (again) another (set) in the Kali, in a proportion as (those) ages decrease in length.

86. In the Krita age the chief (virtue) is declared to be (the performance of) austerities, in the Treta (divine) knowledge, in the Dvapara (the performance of) sacrifices, in the Kali liberality alone.

87. But in order to protect this universe He, the most resplendent one, assigned separate (duties and) occupations to those who sprang from his mouth, arms, thighs, and feet.

88. To Brahmans he assigned teaching and studying (the Veda), sacrificing for their own benefit and for others, giving and accepting (of alms).

89. The Kshatriya he commanded to protect the people, to bestow gifts, to offer sacrifices, to study (the Veda), and to abstain from attaching himself to sensual pleasures;

90. The Vaishya to tend cattle, to bestow gifts, to offer sacrifices, to study (the Veda), to trade, to lend money, and to cultivate land.

91. One occupation only the lord prescribed to the Sudra, to serve meekly even these (other) three castes.

92. Man is stated to be purer above the navel (than below); hence the Self-existent (Svayambhu) has declared the purest (part) of him (to be) his mouth.

93. As the Brahman sprang from (Brahman's) mouth, as he was the first-born, and as he possesses the Veda, he is by right the lord of this whole creation.

94. For the Self-existent (Svayambhu), having performed

austerities, produced him first from his own mouth, in order that the offerings might be conveyed to the gods and manes and that this universe might be preserved.

95. What created being can surpass him, through whose mouth the gods continually consume the sacrificial viands and the manes the offerings to the dead?

96. Of created beings the most excellent are said to be those which are animated; of the animated, those which subsist by intelligence; of the intelligent, mankind; and of men, the Brahmans;

97. Of Brahmans, those learned (in the Veda); of the learned, those who recognise (the necessity and the manner of performing the prescribed duties); of those who possess this knowledge, those who perform them; of the performers, those who know the Brahman.

98. The very birth of a Brahman is an eternal incarnation of the sacred law; for he is born to (fulfil) the sacred law, and becomes one with Brahman.

99. A Brahman, coming into existence, is born as the highest on earth, the lord of all created beings, for the protection of the treasury of the law.

100. Whatever exists in the world is, the property of the Brahman; on account of the excellence of his origin The Brahman is, indeed, entitled to all.

101. The Brahman eats but his own food, wears but his own apparel, bestows but his own in alms; other mortals subsist through the benevolence of the Brahman.

102. In order to clearly settle his duties those of the other (castes) according to their order, wise Manu sprung from the Self-existent, composed these Institutes (of the sacred Law).

103. A learned Brahman must carefully study them, and he must duly instruct his pupils in them, but nobody else (shall do it).

104. A Brahman who studies these Institutes (and) faithfully

fulfils the duties (prescribed therein), is never tainted by sins, arising from thoughts, words, or deeds.

105. He sanctifies any company (which he may enter), seven ancestors and seven descendants, and he alone deserves (to possess) this whole earth.

106. (To study) this (work) is the best means of securing welfare, it increases understanding, it procures fame and long life, it (leads to) supreme bliss.

107. In this (work) the sacred law has been fully stated as well as the good and bad qualities of (human) actions and the immemorial rule of conduct, (to be followed) by all the four castes (varna).

108. The rule of conduct is transcendent law, whether it be taught in the revealed texts or in the sacred tradition; hence a twice-born man who possesses regard for himself, should be always careful to (follow) it.

109. A Brahman who departs from the rule of conduct, does not reap the fruit of the Veda, but he who duly follows it, will obtain the full reward.

110. The sages who saw that the sacred law is thus grounded on the rule of conduct, have taken good conduct to be the most excellent root of all austerity.

111. The creation of the universe, the rule of the sacraments, the ordinances of studentship, and the respectful behaviour (towards Gurus), the most excellent rule of bathing (on return from the teacher's house),

112. (The law of) marriage and the description of the (various) marriage-rites, the regulations for the great sacrifices and the eternal rule of the funeral sacrifices,

113. The description of the modes of (gaining) subsistence and the duties of a Snataka, (the rules regarding) lawful and forbidden food, the purification of men and of things,

114. The laws concerning women, (the law) of hermits, (the manner of gaining) final emancipation and (of) renouncing the world, the whole duty of a king and the manner of deciding lawsuits,

115. The rules for the examination of witnesses, the laws concerning husband and wife, the law of (inheritance and) division, (the law concerning) gambling and the removal of (men nocuous like) thorns,

116. (The law concerning) the behaviour of Vaisyas and Sudras, the origin of the mixed castes, the law for all castes in times of distress and the law of penances,

117. The threefold course of transmigrations, the result of (good or bad) actions, (the manner of attaining) supreme bliss and the examination of the good and bad qualities of actions,

118. The primeval laws of countries, of castes (gati), of families, and the rules concerning heretics and companies (of traders and the like)-(all that) Manu has declared in these Institutes.

119. As Manu, in reply to my questions, formerly promulgated these Institutes, even so learn ye also the (whole work) from me.

CHAPTER-II

1. Learn that sacred law which is followed by men learned (in the Veda) and assented to in their hearts by the virtuous, who are ever exempt from hatred and inordinate affection.
2. To act solely from a desire for rewards is not laudable, yet an exemption from that desire is not (to be found) in this (world): for on (that) desire is grounded the study of the Veda and the performance of the actions, prescribed by the Veda.
3. The desire (for rewards), indeed, has its root in the conception that an act can yield them, and in consequence of (that) conception sacrifices are performed; vows and the laws prescribing restraints are all stated to be kept through the idea that they will bear fruit.
4. Not a single act here (below) appears ever to be done by a man free from desire; for whatever (man) does, it is (the result of) the impulse of desire.

5. He who persists in discharging these (prescribed duties) in the right manner, reaches the deathless state and even in this (life) obtains (the fulfilment of) all the desires that he may have conceived.
6. The whole Veda is the (first) source of the sacred law, next the tradition and the virtuous conduct of those who know the (Veda further), also the customs of holy men, and (finally) self-satisfaction.
7. Whatever law has been ordained for any (person) by Manu, that has been fully declared in the Veda: for that (sage was) omniscient.
8. But a learned man after fully scrutinising all this with the eye of knowledge, should, in accordance with the authority of the revealed texts, be intent on (the performance of) his duties.
9. For that man who obeys the law prescribed in the revealed texts and in the sacred tradition, gains fame in this (world) and after death unsurpassable bliss.
10. But by Sruti (revelation) is meant the Veda, and by Smriti (tradition) the Institutes of the sacred law: those two must not be called into question in any matter, since from those two the sacred law shone forth.
11. Every twice-born man, who, relying on the Institutes of dialectics, treats with contempt those two sources (of the law), must be cast out by the virtuous, as an atheist and a scorner of the Veda.
12. The Veda, the sacred tradition, the customs of virtuous men, and one's own pleasure, they declare to be visibly the fourfold means of defining the sacred law.
13. The knowledge of the sacred law is prescribed for those who are not given to the acquisition of wealth and to the gratification of their desires; to those who seek the knowledge of the sacred law the supreme authority is the revelation (Sruti).
14. But when two sacred texts (Sruti) are conflicting, both are held to be law; for both are pronounced by the wise (to be) valid law.

15. (Thus) the (Agnihotra) sacrifice may be (optionally) performed, at any time after the sun has risen, before he has risen, or when neither sun nor stars are visible; that (is declared) by Vedic texts.
16. Know that he for whom (the performance of) the ceremonies beginning with the rite of impregnation (Garbhadhana) and ending with the funeral rite (Antyeshti) is prescribed, while sacred formulas are being recited, is entitled (to study) these Institutes, but no other man whatsoever.
17. That land, created by the gods, which lies between the two divine rivers Saraswati and Drishadvati, the (sages) call Brahmavarta.
18. The custom handed down in regular succession (since time immemorial) among the (four chief) castes (varna) and the mixed (races) of that country, is called the conduct of virtuous men.
19. The plain of the Kurus, the (country of the) Matsyas, Pankalas, and Surasenakas, these (form), indeed, the country of the Brahmarshis (Brahmanical sages, which ranks) immediately after Brahmavarta.
20. From a Brahman, born in that country, let all men on earth learn their several usages.
21. That (country) which (lies) between the Himavat and the Vindhya (mountains) to the east of Prayaga and to the west of Vinasana (the place where the river Saraswati disappears) is called Madhyadesa (the central region).
22. But (the tract) between those two mountains (just mentioned), which (extends) as far as the eastern and the western oceans, the wise call Aryavarta (the country of the Aryans).
23. That land where the black antelope naturally roams, one must know to be fit for the performance of sacrifices; (the tract) different from that (is) the country of the Mlekkhas (barbarians).
24. Let twice-born men seek to dwell in those (above-

mentioned countries); but a Sudra, distressed for subsistence, may reside anywhere.

25. Thus has the origin of the sacred law been succinctly described to you and the origin of this universe; learn (now) the duties of the castes (varna).
26. With holy rites, prescribed by the Veda, must the ceremony on conception and other sacraments be performed for twice-born men, which sanctify the body and purify (from sin) in this (life) and after death.
27. By burnt oblations during (the mother's) pregnancy, by the Gatakarman (the ceremony after birth), the Kauda (tonsure), and the Maungibandhana (the tying of the sacred girdle of Munga grass) is the taint, derived from both parents, removed from twice-born men.
28. By the study of the Veda, by vows, by burnt oblations, by (the recitation of) sacred texts, by the (acquisition of the) threefold sacred science, by offering (to the gods, Rishis, and manes), by (the procreation of) sons, by the great sacrifices, and by (Srauta) rites this (human) body is made fit for (union with) Brahman.
29. Before the navel-string is cut, the Gatakarman (birth-rite) must be performed for a male (child); and while sacred formulas are being recited, he must be fed with gold, honey, and butter.
30. But let (the father perform or) cause to be performed the Namadheya (the rite of naming the child), on the tenth or twelfth (day after birth), or on a lucky lunar day, in a lucky muhurta, under an auspicious constellation.
31. Let (the first part of) a Brahman's name (denote something) auspicious, a Kshatriya's be connected with power, and a Vaishya's with wealth, but a Sudra's (express something) contemptible.
32. (The second part of) a Brahman's (name) shall be (a word) implying happiness, of a Kshatriya's (a word) implying protection, of a Vaishya's (a term) expressive of thriving, and of a Sudra's (an expression) denoting service.

33. The names of women should be easy to pronounce, not imply anything dreadful, possess a plain meaning, be pleasing and auspicious, end in long vowels, and contain a word of benediction.
34. In the fourth month the Nishkramana (the first leaving of the house) of the child should be performed, in the sixth month the Annaprasana (first feeding with rice), and optionally (any other) auspicious ceremony required by (the custom of) the family.
35. According to the teaching of the revealed texts, the Kudakarman (tonsure) must be performed, for the sake of spiritual merit, by all twice-born men in the first or third year.
36. In the eighth year after conception, one should perform the initiation (upanayana) of a Brahman, in the eleventh after conception (that) of a Kshatriya, but in the twelfth that of a Vaishya.
37. (The initiation) of a Brahman who desires proficiency in sacred learning should take place in the fifth (year after conception), (that) of a Kshatriya who wishes to become powerful in the sixth, (and that) of a Vaishya who longs for (success in his) business in the eighth.
38. The (time for the) Savitri (initiation) of a Brahman does not pass until the completion of the sixteenth year (after conception), of a Kshatriya until the completion of the twenty-second, and of a Vaishya until the completion of the twenty-fourth.
39. After those (periods men of) these three (castes) who have not received the sacrament at the proper time, become Vratyas (outcasts), excluded from the Savitri (initiation) and despised by the Aryans.
40. With such men, if they have not been purified according to the rule, let no Brahman ever, even in times of distress, form a connexion either through the Veda or by marriage.
41. Let students, according to the order (of their castes), wear (as upper dresses) the skins of black antelopes,

spotted deer, and he-goats, and (lower garments) made of hemp, flax or wool.

42. The girdle of a Brahman shall consist of a of a triple cord of Munga grass, smooth and soft; (that) of a Kshatriya, of a bowstring, made of Murva fibres; (that) of a Vaishya, of hempen threads.
43. If Munga grass (and so forth) be not procurable, (the girdles) may be made of Kusa, Asmantaka, and Balbaga (fibres), with a single threefold knot, or with three or five (knots according to the custom of the family).
44. The sacrificial string of a Brahman shall be made of cotton, (shall be) twisted to the right, (and consist) of three threads, that of a Kshatriya of hempen threads, (and) that of a Vaishya of woollen threads.
45. A Brahman shall (carry), according to the sacred law, a staff of Bilva or Palasa; a Kshatriya, of Vata or Khadira; (and) a Vaishya, of Pilu or Udumbara.
46. The staff of a Brahman shall be made of such length as to reach the end of his hair; that of a Kshatriya, to reach his forehead; (and) that of a Vaishya, to reach (the tip of his) nose.
47. Let all the staves be straight, without a blemish, handsome to look at, not likely to terrify men, with their bark perfect, unhurt by fire.
48. Having taken a staff according to his choice, having worshipped the sun and walked round the fire, turning his right hand towards it, (the student) should beg alms according to the prescribed rule.
49. An initiated Brahman should beg, beginning (his request with the word) lady (bhavati); a Kshatriya, placing (the word) lady in the middle, but a Vaishya, placing it at the end (of the formula).
50. Let him first beg food of his mother, or of his sister, or of his own maternal aunt, or of (some other) female who will not disgrace him (by a refusal).
51. Having collected as much food as is required (from several persons), and having announced it without guile

to his teacher, let him eat, turning his face towards the east, and having purified himself by sipping water.

52. (His meal will procure) long life, if he eats facing the east; fame, if he turns to the south; prosperity, if he turns to the west; truthfulness, if he faces the east.

53. Let a twice-born man always eat his food with concentrated mind, after performing an ablution; and after he has eaten, let him duly cleanse himself with water and sprinkle the cavities (of his head).

54. Let him always worship his food, and eat it without contempt; when he sees it, let him rejoice, show a pleased face, and pray that he may always obtain it.

55. Food, that is always worshipped, gives strength and manly vigour; but eaten irreverently, it destroys them both.

56. Let him not give to any man what he leaves, and beware of eating between (the two meal-times); let him not over-eat himself, nor go anywhere without having purified himself (after his meal).

57. Excessive eating is prejudicial to health, to fame, and to (bliss in) heaven; it prevents (the acquisition of) spiritual merit, and is odious among men; one ought, for these reasons, to avoid it carefully.

58. Let a Brahman always sip water out of the part of the hand (tirtha) sacred to Brahman, or out of that sacred to Ka (Pragapati), or out of (that) sacred to the gods, never out of that sacred to the manes.

59. They call (the part) at the root of the thumb the tirtha sacred to Brahman, that at the root of the (little) finger (the tirtha) sacred to Ka (Pragapati), (that) at the tips (of the fingers, the tirtha) sacred to the gods, and that below (between the index and the thumb, the tirtha) sacred to the manes.

60. Let him first sip water thrice; next twice wipe his mouth; and, lastly, touch with water the cavities (of the head), (the seat of) the soul and the head.

61. He who knows the sacred law and seeks purity shall

always perform the rite of sipping with water neither hot nor frothy, with the (prescribed) tirtha, in a lonely place, and turning to the east or to the north.

62. A Brahman is purified by water that reaches his heart, a Kshatriya by water reaching his throat, a Vaishya by water taken into his mouth, (and) a Sudra by water touched with the extremity (of his lips).

63. A twice-born man is called upavitin when his right arm is raised (and the sacrificial string or the dress, passed under it, rests on the left shoulder); (when his) left (arm) is raised (and the string, or the dress, passed under it, rests on the right shoulder, he is called) prakinavitin; and nivitin when it hangs down (straight) from the neck.

64. His girdle, the skin (which serves as his upper garment), his staff, his sacrificial thread, (and) his water-pot he must throw into water, when they have been damaged, and take others, reciting sacred formulas.

65. (The ceremony called) Kesanta (clipping the hair) is ordained for a Brahman in the sixteenth year (from conception); for a Kshatriya, in the twenty-second; and for a Vaishya, two (years) later than that.

66. This whole series (of ceremonies) must be performed for females (also), in order to sanctify the body, at the proper time and in the proper order, but without (the recitation of) sacred texts.

67. The nuptial ceremony is stated to be the Vedic sacrament for women (and to be equal to the initiation), serving the husband (equivalent to) the residence in (the house of the) teacher, and the household duties (the same) as the (daily) worship of the sacred fire.

68. Thus has been described the rule for the initiation of the twice-born, which indicates a (new) birth, and sanctifies; learn (now) to what duties they must afterwards apply themselves.

69. Having performed the (rite of) initiation, the teacher must first instruct the (pupil) in (the rules of) personal

purification, of conduct, of the fire-worship, and of the twilight devotions.

70. But (a student) who is about to begin the Study (of the Veda), shall receive instruction, after he has sipped water in accordance with the Institutes (of the sacred law), has made the Brahmangali, (has put on) a clean dress, and has brought his organs under due control.

71. At the beginning and at the end of (a lesson in the) Veda he must always clasp both the feet of his teacher, (and) he must study, joining his hands; that is called the Brahmangali (joining the palms for the sake of the Veda).

72. With crossed hands he must clasp (the feet) of the teacher, and touch the left (foot) with his left (hand), the right (foot) with his right (hand).

73. But to him who is about to begin studying, the teacher always unwearied, must say: Ho, recite! He shall leave off (when the teacher says): Let a stoppage take place!

74. Let him always pronounce the syllable Om at the beginning and at the end of (a lesson in) the Veda; (for) unless the syllable Om precede (the lesson) will slip away (from him), and unless it follow it will fade away.

75. Seated on (blades of Kusa grass) with their points to the east, purified by Pavitras (blades of Kusa grass), and sanctified by three suppressions of the breath (Pranayama), he is worthy (to pronounce) the syllable Om.

76. Pragapati (the lord of creatures) milked out (as it were) from the three Vedas the sounds A, U, and M, and (the Vyahritis) Bhuh, Bhuvah, Svah.

77. Moreover from the three Vedas Pragapati, who dwells in the highest heaven (Parameshthin), milked out (as it were) that Rik-verse, sacred to Savitri (Savitri), which begins with the word tad, one foot from each.

78. A Brahman, learned in the Veda, who recites during both twilights that syllable and that (verse), preceded by the Vyahritis, gains the (whole) merit which (the recitation of) the Vedas confers.

79. A twice-born man who (daily) repeats those three one thousand times outside (the village), will be freed after a month even from great guilt, as a snake from its slough.

80. The Brahman, the Kshatriya, and the Vaishya who neglect (the recitation of) that Rik-verse and the timely (performance of the) rites (prescribed for) them, will be blamed among virtuous men.

81. Know that the three imperishable Mahavyahritis, preceded by the syllable Om, and (followed) by the three-footed Savitri are the portal of the Veda and the gate leading (to union with) Brahman.

82. He who daily recites that (verse), untired, during three years, will enter (after death) the highest Brahman, move as free as air, and assume an ethereal form.

83. The monosyllable (Om) is the highest Brahman, (three) suppressions of the breath are the best (form of) austerity, but nothing surpasses the Savitri truthfulness is better than silence.

84. All rites ordained in the Veda, burnt oblations and (other) sacrifices, pass away; but know that the syllable (Om) is imperishable, and (it is) Brahman, (and) the Lord of creatures (Pragapati).

85. An offering, consisting of muttered prayers, is ten times more efficacious than a sacrifice performed according to the rules (of the Veda); a (prayer) which is inaudible (to others) surpasses it a hundred times, and the mental (recitation of sacred texts) a thousand times.

86. The four Pakayagnas and those sacrifices which are enjoined by the rules (of the Veda) are all together not equal in value to a sixteenth part of the sacrifice consisting of muttered prayers.

87. But, undoubtedly, a Brahman reaches the highest goal by muttering prayers only; (whether) he perform other (rites) or neglect them, he who befriends (all creatures) is declared (to be) a (true) Brahman.

88. A wise man should strive to restrain his organs which

run wild among alluring sensual objects, like a charioteer his horses.

89. Those eleven organs which former sages have named, I will properly (and) precisely enumerate in due order,

90. (*Viz.*) the ear, the skin, the eyes, the tongue, and the nose as the fifth, the anus, the organ of generation, hands and feet, and the (organ of) speech, named as the tenth.

91. Five of them, the ear and the rest according to their order, they call organs of sense, and five of them, the anus and the rest, organs of action.

92. Know that the internal organ (manas) is the eleventh, which by its quality belongs to both (sets); when that has been subdued, both those sets of five have been conquered.

93. Through the attachment of his organs (to sensual pleasure) a man doubtlessly will incur guilt; but if he keep them under complete control, he will obtain success (in gaining all his aims).

94. Desire is never extinguished by the enjoyment of desired objects; it only grows stronger like a fire (fed) with clarified butter.

95. If one man should obtain all those (sensual enjoyments) and another should renounce them all, the renunciation of all pleasure is far better than the attainment of them.

96. Those (organs) which are strongly attached to sensual pleasures, cannot so effectually be restrained by abstinence (from enjoyments) as by a constant (pursuit of true) knowledge.

97. Neither (the study of) the Vedas, nor liberality, nor sacrifices, nor any (self-imposed) restraint, nor austerities, ever procure the attainment (of rewards) to a man whose heart is contaminated (by sensuality).

98. That man may be considered to have (really) subdued his organs, who on hearing and touching and seeing,

on tasting and smelling (anything) neither rejoices nor repines.

99. But when one among all the organs slips away (from control), thereby (man's) wisdom slips away from him, even as the water (flows) through the one (open) foot of a (water-carrier's) skin.

100. If he keeps all the (ten) organs as well as the mind in subjection, he may gain all his aims, without reducing his body by (the practice) of Yoga.

101. Let him stand during the morning twilight, muttering the Savitri until the sun appears, but (let him recite it), seated, in the evening until the constellations can be seen distinctly.

102. He who stands during the morning twilight muttering (the Savitri), removes the guilt contracted during the (previous) night; but he who (recites it), seated, in the evening, destroys the sin he committed during the day.

103. But he who does not (worship) standing in the morning, nor sitting in the evening, shall be excluded, just like a Sudra, from all the duties and rights of an Aryan.

104. He who (desires to) perform the ceremony (of the) daily (recitation), may even recite the Savitri near water, retiring into the forest, controlling his organs and concentrating his mind.

105. Both when (one studies) the supplementary treatises of the Veda, and when (one recites) the daily portion of the Veda, no regard need be paid to forbidden days, likewise when (one repeats) the sacred texts required for a burnt oblation.

106. There are no forbidden days for the daily recitation, since that is declared to be a Brahmasattra (an everlasting sacrifice offered to Brahman); at that the Veda takes the place of the burnt oblations, and it is meritorious (even), when (natural phenomena, requiring) a cessation of the Veda-study, take the place of the exclamation Vashat.

107. For him who, being pure and controlling his organs,

during a year daily recites the Veda according to the rule, that (daily recitation) will ever cause sweet and sour milk, clarified butter and honey to flow.

108. Let an Aryan who has been initiated, (daily) offer fuel in the sacred fire, beg food, sleep on the ground and do what is beneficial to this teacher, until (he performs the ceremony of) Samavartana (on returning home).

109. According to the sacred law the (following) ten (persons, *viz.*) the teacher's son, one who desires to do service, one who imparts knowledge, one who is intent on fulfilling the law, one who is pure, a person connected by marriage or friendship, one who possesses (mental) ability, one who makes presents of money, one who is honest, and a relative, may be instructed (in the Veda).

110. Unless one be asked, one must not explain (anything) to anybody, nor (must one answer) a person who asks improperly; let a wise man, though he knows (the answer), behave among men as (if he were) an idiot.

111. Of the two persons, him who illegally explains (anything), and him who illegally asks (a question), one (or both) will die or incur (the other's) enmity.

112. Where merit and wealth are not (obtained by teaching) nor (at least) due obedience, in such (soil) sacred knowledge must not be sown, just as good seed (must) not (be thrown) on barren land.

113. Even in times of dire distress a teacher of the Veda should rather die with his knowledge than sow it in barren soil.

114. Sacred Learning approached a Brahman and said to him: 'I am thy treasure, preserve me, deliver me not to a scorner; so (preserved) I shall become supremely strong.'

115. 'But deliver me, as to the keeper of thy treasure, to a Brahman whom thou shalt know to be pure, of subdued senses, chaste and attentive.'

116. But he who acquires without permission the Veda from one who recites it, incurs the guilt of stealing the Veda, and shall sink into hell.

117. (A student) shall first reverentially salute that (teacher) from whom he receives (knowledge), referring to worldly affairs, to the Veda, or to the Brahman.

118. A Brahman who completely governs himself, though he know the Savitri only, is better than he who knows the three Vedas, (but) does not control himself, eats all (sorts of) food, and sells all (sorts of goods).

119. One must not sit down on a couch or seat which a superior occupies; and he who occupies a couch or seat shall rise to meet a (superior), and (afterwards) salute him.

120. For the vital airs of a young man mount upwards to leave his body when an elder approaches; but by rising to meet him and saluting he recovers them.

121. He who habitually salutes and constantly pays reverence to the aged obtains an increase of four (things), (*viz.*) length of life, knowledge, fame, (and) strength.

122. After the (word of) salutation, a Brahman who greets an elder must pronounce his name, saying, 'I am N. N.'

123. To those (persons) who, when a name is pronounced, do not understand (the meaning of) the salutation, a wise man should say, 'It is I;' and (he should address) in the same manner all women.

124. In saluting he should pronounce after his name the word bhoh; for the sages have declared that the nature of bhoh is the same as that of (all proper) names.

125. A Brahman should thus be saluted in return, 'May'st thou be long-lived, O gentle one!' and the vowel 'a' must be added at the end of the name (of the person addressed), the syllable preceding it being drawn out to the length of three moras.

126. A Brahman who does not know the form of returning a salutation, must not be saluted by a learned man; as a Sudra, even so is he.

127. Let him ask a Brahman, on meeting him, after (his health, with the word) kusala, a Kshatriya (with the

word) anamaya, a Vaishya (with the word) kshema, and a Sudra (with the word) anarogya.

128. He who has been initiated (to perform a Srauta sacrifice) must not be addressed by his name, even though he be a younger man; he who knows the sacred law must use in speaking to such (a man the particle) bhoh and (the pronoun) bhavat (your worship).

129. But to a female who is the wife of another man, and not a blood-relation, he must say, 'Lady' (bhavati) or 'Beloved sister!'

130. To his maternal and paternal uncles, fathers-in-law, officiating priests, (and other) venerable persons, he must say, 'I am N. N.,' and rise (to meet them), even though they be younger (than himself).

131. A maternal aunt, the wife of a maternal uncle, a mother-in-law, and a paternal aunt must be honoured like the wife of one's teacher; they are equal to the wife of one's teacher.

132. (The feet of the) wife of one's brother, if she be of the same caste (varna), must be clasped every day; but (the feet of) wives of (other) paternal and maternal relatives need only be embraced on one's return from a journey.

133. Towards a sister of one's father and of one's mother, and towards one's own elder sister, one must behave as towards one's mother; (but) the mother is more venerable than they.

134. Fellow-citizens are called friends (and equals though one be) ten years (older than the other), men practising (the same) fine art (though one be) five years (older than the other), Srotriyas (though) three years (intervene between their ages), but blood-relations only (if the) difference of age be very small.

135. Know that a Brahman of ten years and Kshatriya of a hundred years stand to each other in the relation of father and son; but between those two the Brahman is the father.

136. Wealth, kindred, age, (the due performance of) rites,

and, fifthly, sacred learning are titles to respect; but each later-named (cause) is more weighty (than the preceding ones).

137. Whatever man of the three (highest) castes possesses most of those five, both in number and degree, that man is worthy of honour among them; and (so is) also a Sudra who has entered the tenth (decade of his life).

138. Way must be made for a man in a carriage, for one who is above ninety years old, for one diseased, for the carrier of a burden, for a woman, for a Snataka, for the king, and for a bridegroom.

139. Among all those, if they meet (at one time), a Snataka and the king must be (most) honoured; and if the king and a Snataka (meet), the latter receives respect from the king.

140. They call that Brahman who initiates a pupil and teaches him the Veda together with the Kalpa and the Rahasyas, the teacher (akarya, of the latter).

141. But he who for his livelihood teaches a portion only of the Veda, or also the Angas of the Veda, is called the sub-teacher (upadhyaya).

142. That Brahman, who performs in accordance with the rules (of the Veda) the rites, the Garbhadhana (conception-rite), and so forth, and gives food (to the child), is called the Guru (the venerable one).

143. He who, being (duly) chosen (for the purpose), performs the Agnyadheya, the Pakayagnas, (and) the (Srauta) sacrifices, such as the Agnishtoma (for another man), is called (his) officiating priest.

144. That (man) who truthfully fills both his ears with the Veda, (the pupil) shall consider as his father and mother; he must never offend him.

145. The teacher (akarya) is ten times more venerable than a sub-teacher (upadhyaya), the father a hundred times more than the teacher, but the mother a thousand times more than the father.

146. Of him who gives natural birth and him who gives (the knowledge of) the Veda, the giver of the Veda is the more venerable father; for the birth for the sake of the Veda (ensures) eternal (rewards) both in this (life) and after death.

147. Let him consider that (he received) a (mere animal) existence, when his parents begat him through mutual affection, and when he was born from the womb (of his mother).

148. But that birth which a teacher acquainted with the whole Veda, in accordance with the law, procures for him through the Savitri, is real, exempt from age and death.

149. (The pupil) must know that man also who benefits him by (instruction in) the Veda, be it little or much, is called in these (Institutes) his Guru, in consequence of that benefit (conferred by instruction in) the Veda.

150. That Brahman who is the giver of the birth for the sake of the Veda and the teacher of the prescribed duties becomes by law the father of an aged man, even though he himself be a child.

151. Young Kavi, the son of Angiras, taught his (relatives who were old enough to be) fathers, and, as he excelled them in (sacred) knowledge, he called them 'Little sons.'

152. They, moved with resentment, asked the gods concerning that matter, and the gods, having assembled, answered, 'The child has addressed you properly.'

153. 'For (a man) destitute of (sacred) knowledge is indeed a child, and he who teaches him the Veda is his father; for (the sages) have always said "child" to an ignorant man, and "father" to a teacher of the Veda.'

154. Neither through years, nor through white (hairs), nor through wealth, nor through (powerful) kinsmen (comes greatness). The sages have made this law, 'He who has learnt the Veda together with the Angas (Anukana) is (considered) great by us.'

155. The seniority of Brahmans is from (sacred) knowledge,

that of Kshatriyas from valour, that of Vaisyas from wealth in grain (and other goods), but that of Sudras alone from age.

156. A man is not therefore (considered) venerable because his head is gray; him who, though young, has learned the Veda, the gods consider to be venerable.

157. As an elephant made of wood, as an antelope made of leather, such is an unlearned Brahman; those three have nothing but the names (of their kind).

158. As a eunuch is unproductive with women, as a cow with a cow is unprolific, and as a gift made to an ignorant man yields no reward, even so is a Brahman useless, who (does) not (know) the Rikas.

159. Created beings must be instructed in (what concerns) their welfare without giving them pain, and sweet and gentle speech must be used by (a teacher) who desires (to abide by) the sacred law.

160. He, forsooth, whose speech and thoughts are pure and ever perfectly guarded, gains the whole reward which is conferred by the Vedanta.

161. Let him not, even though in pain, (speak words) cutting (others) to the quick; let him not injure others in thought or deed; let him not utter speeches which make (others) afraid of him, since that will prevent him from gaining heaven.

162. A Brahman should always fear homage as if it were poison; and constantly desire (to suffer) scorn as (he would long for) nectar.

163. For he who is scorned (nevertheless may) sleep with an easy mind, awake with an easy mind, and with an easy mind walk here among men; but the scorner utterly perishes.

164. A twice-born man who has been sanctified by the (employment of) the means, (described above) in due order, shall gradually and cumulatively perform the various austerities prescribed for (those who) study the Veda.

165. An Aryan must study the whole Veda together with the Rahasyas, performing at the same time various kinds of austerities and the vows prescribed by the rules (of the Veda).

166. Let a Brahman who desires to perform austerities, constantly repeat the Veda; for the study of the Veda is declared (to be) in this world the highest austerity for a Brahman.

167. Verily, that twice-born man performs the highest austerity up to the extremities of his nails, who, though wearing a garland, daily recites the Veda in private to the utmost of his ability.

168. A twice-born man who, not having studied the Veda, applies himself to other (and worldly study), soon falls, even while living, to the condition of a Sudra and his descendants (after him).

169. According to the injunction of the revealed texts the first birth of an Aryan is from (his natural) mother, the second (happens) on the tying of the girdle of Munga grass, and the third on the initiation to (the performance of) a (Srauta) sacrifice.

170. Among those (three) the birth which is symbolised by the investiture with the girdle of Munga grass, is his birth for the sake of the Veda; they declare that in that (birth) the Sivitri (verse) is his mother and the teacher his father.

171. They call the teacher (the pupil's) father because he gives the Veda; for nobody can perform a (sacred) rite before the investiture with the girdle of Munga grass.

172. (He who has not been initiated) should not pronounce (any) Vedic text excepting (those required for) the performance of funeral rites, since he is on a level with a Sudra before his birth from the Veda.

173. The (student) who has been initiated must be instructed in the performance of the vows, and gradually learn the Veda, observing the prescribed rules.

174. Whatever dress of skin, sacred thread, girdle, staff, and

lower garment are prescribed for a (student at the initiation), the like (must again be used) at the (performance of the) vows.

175. But a student who resides with his teacher must observe the following restrictive rules, duly controlling all his organs, in order to increase his spiritual merit.

176. Every day, having bathed, and being purified, he must offer libations of water to the gods, sages and manes, worship (the images of) the gods, and place fuel on (the sacred fire).

177. Let him abstain from honey, meat, perfumes, garlands, substances (used for) flavouring (food), women, all substances turned acid, and from doing injury to living creatures.

178. From anointing (his body), applying collyrium to his eyes, from the use of shoes and of an umbrella (or parasol), from (sensual) desire, anger, covetousness, dancing, singing, and playing (musical instruments),

179. From gambling, idle disputes, backbiting, and lying, from looking at and touching women, and from hurting others.

180. Let him always sleep alone, let him never waste his manhood; for he who voluntarily wastes his manhood, breaks his vow.

181. A twice-born student, who has involuntarily wasted his manly strength during sleep, must bathe, worship the sun, and afterwards thrice mutter the Rik-verse (which begins), 'Again let my strength return to me.'

182. Let him fetch a pot full of water, flowers, cowdung, earth, and Kusa grass, as much as may be required (by his teacher), and daily go to beg food.

183. A student, being pure, shall daily bring food from the houses of men who are not deficient in (the knowledge of) the Veda and in (performing) sacrifices, and who are famous for (following their lawful) occupations.

184. Let him not beg from the relatives of his teacher, nor from his own or his mother's blood-relations; but if

there are no houses belonging to strangers, let him go to one of those named above, taking the last-named first;

185. Or, if there are no (virtuous men of the kind) mentioned above, he may go to each (house in the) village, being pure and remaining silent; but let him avoid Abhisastas (those accused of mortal sin).

186. Having brought sacred fuel from a distance, let him place it anywhere but on the ground, and let him, unwearied, make with it burnt oblations to the sacred fire, both evening and morning.

187. He who, without being sick, neglects during seven (successive) days to go out begging, and to offer fuel in the sacred fire, shall perform the penance of an Avakirnin (one who has broken his vow).

188. He who performs the vow (of studentship) shall constantly subsist on alms, (but) not eat the food of one (person only); the subsistence of a student on begged food is declared to be equal (in merit) to fasting.

189. At his pleasure he may eat, when invited, the food of one man at (a rite) in honour of the gods, observing (however the conditions on his vow, or at a (funeral meal) in honour of the manes, behaving (however) like a hermit.

190. This duty is prescribed by the wise for a Brahman only; but no such duty is ordained for a Kshatriya and a Vaishya.

191. Both when ordered by his teacher, and without a (special) command, (a student) shall always exert himself in studying (the Veda), and in doing what is serviceable to his teacher.

192. Controlling his body, his speech, his organs (of sense), and his mind, let him stand with joined hands, looking at the face of his teacher.

193. Let him always keep his right arm uncovered, behave decently and keep his body well covered, and when he

is addressed (with the words), 'Be seated,' he shall sit down, facing his teacher.

194. In the presence of his teacher let him always eat less, wear a less valuable dress and ornaments (than the former), and let him rise earlier (from his bed), and go to rest later.

195. Let him not answer or converse with (his teacher), reclining on a bed, nor sitting, nor eating, nor standing, nor with an averted face.

196. Let him do (that), standing up, if (his teacher) is seated, advancing towards him when he stands, going to meet him if he advances, and running after him when he runs;

197. Going (round) to face (the teacher), if his face is averted, approaching him if he stands at a distance, but bending towards him if he lies on a bed, and if he stands in a lower place.

198. When his teacher is nigh, let his bed or seat be low; but within sight of his teacher he shall not sit carelessly at ease.

199. Let him not pronounce the mere name of his teacher (without adding an honourific title) behind his back even, and let him not mimic his gait, speech, and deportment.

200. Wherever (people) justly censure or falsely defame his teacher, there he must cover his ears or depart thence to another place.

201. By censuring (his teacher), though justly, he will become (in his next birth) an ass, by falsely defaming him, a dog; he who lives on his teacher's substance, will become a worm, and he who is envious (of his merit), a (larger) insect.

202. He must not serve the (teacher by the intervention of another) while he himself stands aloof, nor when he (himself) is angry, nor when a woman is near; if he is seated in a carriage or on a (raised) seat, he must descend and afterwards salute his (teacher).

203. Let him not sit with his teacher, to the leeward or to the windward (of him); nor let him say anything which his teacher cannot hear.

204. He may sit with his teacher in a carriage drawn by oxen, horses, or camels, on a terrace, on a bed of grass or leaves, on a mat, on a rock, on a wooden bench, or in a boat.

205. If his teacher's teacher is near, let him behave (towards him) as towards his own teacher; but let him, unless he has received permission from his teacher, not salute venerable persons of his own (family).

206. This is likewise (ordained as) his constant behaviour towards (other) instructors in science, towards his relatives (to whom honour is due), towards all who may restrain him from sin, or may give him salutary advice.

207. Towards his betters let him always behave as towards his teacher, likewise towards sons of his teacher, born by wives of equal caste, and towards the teacher's relatives both on the side of the father and of the mother.

208. The son of the teacher who imparts instruction (in his father's stead), whether younger or of equal age, or a student of (the science of) sacrifices (or of other Angas), deserves the same honour as the teacher.

209. (A student) must not shampoo the limbs of his teacher's son, nor assist him in bathing, nor eat the fragments of his food, nor wash his feet.

210. The wives of the teacher, who belong to the same caste, must be treated as respectfully as the teacher; but those who belong to a different caste, must be honoured by rising and salutation.

211. Let him not perform for a wife of his teacher (the offices of) anointing her, assisting her in the bath, shampooing her limbs, or arranging her hair.

212. (A pupil) who is full twenty years old, and knows what is becoming and unbecoming, shall not salute a young wife of his teacher (by clasping) her feet.

213. It is the nature of women to seduce men in this (world); for that reason the wise are never unguarded in (the company of) females.

214. For women are able to lead astray in (this) world not only a fool, but even a learned man, and (to make) him a slave of desire and anger.

215. One should not sit in a lonely place with one's mother, sister, or daughter; for the senses are powerful, and master even a learned man.

216. But at his pleasure a young student may prostrate himself on the ground before the young wife of a teacher, in accordance with the rule, and say, 'I, N. N., (worship thee, O lady).'

217. On returning from a journey he must clasp the feet of his teacher's wife and daily salute her (in the manner just mentioned), remembering the duty of the virtuous.

218. As the man who digs with a spade (into the ground) obtains water, even so an obedient (pupil) obtains the knowledge which lies (hidden) in his teacher.

219. A (student) may either shave his head, or wear his hair in braids, or braid one lock on the crown of his head; the sun must never set or rise while he (lies asleep) in the village.

220. If the sun should rise or set while he is sleeping, be it (that he offended) intentionally or unintentionally, he shall fast during the (next) day, muttering (the Savitri).

221. For he who lies (sleeping), while the sun sets or rises, and does not perform (that) penance, is tainted by great guilt.

222. Purified by sipping water, he shall daily worship during both twilights with a concentrated mind in a pure place, muttering the prescribed text according to the rule.

223. If a woman or a man of low caste perform anything (leading to) happiness, let him diligently practise it, as well as (any other permitted act) in which his heart finds pleasure.

224. (Some declare that) the chief good consists in (the

acquisition of) spiritual merit and wealth, (others place it) in (the gratification of) desire and (the acquisition of) wealth, (others) in (the acquisition of) spiritual merit alone, and (others say that the acquisition of) wealth alone is the chief good here (below); but the (correct) decision is that it consists of the aggregate of (those) three.

225. The teacher, the father, the mother, and an elder brother must not be treated with disrespect, especially by a Brahman, though one be grievously offended (by them).

226. The teacher is the image of Brahman, the father the image of Pragipati (the lord of created beings), the mother the image of the earth, and an (elder) full brother the image of oneself.

227. That trouble (and pain) which the parents undergo on the birth of (their) children, cannot be compensated even in a hundred years.

228. Let him always do what is agreeable to those (two) and always (what may please) his teacher; when those three are pleased, he obtains all (those rewards which) austerities (yield).

229. Obedience towards those three is declared to be the best (form of) austerity; let him not perform other meritorious acts without their permission.

230. For they are declared to be the three worlds, they the three (principal) orders, they the three Vedas, and they the three sacred fires.

231. The father, forsooth, is stated to be the Garhapatya fire, the mother the Dakshinagni, but the teacher the Ahavaniya fire; this triad of fires is most venerable.

232. He who neglects not those three, (even after he has become) a householder, will conquer the three worlds and, radiant in body like a god, he will enjoy bliss in heaven.

233. By honouring his mother he gains this (nether) world, by honouring his father the middle sphere, but by obedience to his teacher the world of Brahman.

234. All duties have been fulfilled by him who honours those three; but to him who honours them not, all rites remain fruitless.

235. As long as those three live, so long let him not (independently) perform any other (meritorious acts); let him always serve them, rejoicing (to do what is) agreeable and beneficial (to them).

236. He shall inform them of everything that with their consent he may perform in thought, word, or deed for the sake of the next world.

237. By (honouring) these three all that ought to be done by man, is accomplished; that is clearly the highest duty, every other (act) is a subordinate duty.

238. He who possesses faith may receive pure learning even from a man of lower caste, the highest law even from the lowest, and an excellent wife even from a base family.

239. Even from poison nectar may be taken, even from a child good advice, even from a foe (a lesson in) good conduct, and even from an impure (substance) gold.

240. Excellent wives, learning, (the knowledge of) the law, (the rules of) purity, good advice, and various arts may be acquired from anybody.

241. It is prescribed that in times of distress (a student) may learn (the Veda) from one who is not a Brahman; and that he shall walk behind and serve (such a) teacher, as long as the instruction lasts.

242. He who desires incomparable bliss (in heaven) shall not dwell during his whole life in (the house of) a non-Brahmanical teacher, nor with a Brahman who does not know the whole Veda and the Angas.

243. But if (a student) desires to pass his whole life in the teacher's house, he must diligently serve him, until he is freed from this body.

244. A Brahman who serves his teacher till the dissolution of his body, reaches forthwith the eternal mansion of Brahman.

245. He who knows the sacred law must not present any gift to his teacher before (the Samavartana); but when, with the permission of his teacher, he is about to take the (final) bath, let him procure (a present) for the venerable man according to his ability,

246. (*Viz.*) a field, gold, a cow, a horse, a parasol and shoes, a seat, grain, (even) vegetables, (and thus) give pleasure to his teacher.

247. (A perpetual student) must, if his teacher dies, serve his son (provided he be) endowed with good qualities, or his widow, or his Sapinda, in the same manner as the teacher.

248. Should none of these be alive, he must serve the sacred fire, standing (by day) and sitting (during the night), and thus finish his life.

249. A Brahman who thus passes his life as a student without breaking his vow, reaches (after death) the highest abode and will not be born again in this world.

CHAPTER-III

1. The vow (of studying) the three Vedas under a teacher must be kept for thirty-six years, or for half that time, or for a quarter, or until the (student) has perfectly learnt them.
2. (A student) who has studied in due order the three Vedas, or two, or even one only, without breaking the (rules of) studentship, shall enter the order of householders.
3. He who is famous for (the strict performance of) his duties and has received his heritage, the Veda, from his father, shall be honoured, sitting on a couch and adorned with a garland, with (the present of) a cow (and the honey-mixture).
4. Having bathed, with the permission of his teacher, and performed according to the rule the Samavartana (the rite on returning home), a twice-born man shall marry a wife of equal caste who is endowed with auspicious (bodily) marks.

5. A damsel who is neither a Sapinda on the mother's side, nor belongs to the same family on the father's side, is recommended to twice-born men for wedlock and conjugal union.
6. In connecting himself with a wife, let him carefully avoid the ten following families, be they ever so great, or rich in kine, horses, sheep, grain, or (other) property,
7. (*Viz.*) one which neglects the sacred rites, one in which no male children (are born), one in which the Veda is not studied, one (the members of) which have thick hair on the body, those which are subject to hemorrhoids, phthisis, weakness of digestion, epilepsy, or white or black leprosy.
8. Let him not marry a maiden (with) reddish (hair), nor one who has a redundant member, nor one who is sickly, nor one either with no hair (on the body) or too much, nor one who is garrulous or has red (eyes),
9. Nor one named after a constellation, a tree, or a river, nor one bearing the name of a low caste, or of a mountain, nor one named after a bird, a snake, or a slave, nor one whose name inspires terror.
10. Let him wed a female free from bodily defects, who has an agreeable name, the (graceful) gait of a Hamsa or of an elephant, a moderate (quantity of) hair on the body and on the head, small teeth, and soft limbs.
11. But a prudent man should not marry (a maiden) who has no brother, nor one whose father is not known, through fear lest (in the former case she be made) an appointed daughter (and in the latter) lest (he should commit) sin.
12. For the first marriage of twice-born men (wives) of equal caste are recommended; but for those who through desire proceed (to marry again) the following females, (chosen) according to the (direct) order (of the castes), are most approved.
13. It is declared that a Sudra woman alone (can be) the wife of a Sudra, she and one of his own caste (the wives)

of a Vaishya, those two and one of his own caste (the wives) of a Kshatriya, those three and one of his own caste (the wives) of a Brahman.

14. A Sudra woman is not mentioned even in any (ancient) story as the (first) wife of a Brahman or of a Kshatriya, though they lived in the (greatest) distress.
15. Twice-born men who, in their folly, wed wives of the low (Sudra) caste, soon degrade their families and their children to the state of Sudras.
16. According to Atri and to (Gautama) the son of Utathya, he who weds a Sudra woman becomes an outcast, according to Saunaka on the birth of a son, and according to Bhrigu he who has (male) offspring from a (Sudra female, alone).
17. A Brahman who takes a Sudra wife to his bed, will (after death) sink into hell; if he begets a child by her, he will lose the rank of a Brahman.
18. The manes and the gods will not eat the (offerings) of that man who performs the rites in honour of the gods, of the manes, and of guests chiefly with a (Sudra wife's) assistance, and such (a man) will not go to heaven.
19. For him who drinks the moisture of a Sudra's lips, who is tainted by her breath, and who begets a son on her, no expiation is prescribed.
20. Now listen to (the) brief (description of) the following eight marriage-rites used by the four castes (varna) which partly secure benefits and partly produce evil both in this life and after death.
21. (They are) the rite of Brahman (Brahma), that of the gods (Daiva), that of the Rishis (Arsha), that of Pragapati (Pragapatya), that of the Asuras (Asura), that of the Gandharvas (Gandharva), that of the Rhashasas (Rakshasa), and that of the Pisakas (Paisaka).
22. Which is lawful for each caste (varna) and which are the virtues or faults of each (rite), all this I will declare to you, as well as their good and evil results with respect to the offspring.

23. One may know that the first six according to the order (followed above) are lawful for a Brahman, the four last for a Kshatriya, and the same four, excepting the Rakshasa rite, for a Vaishya and a Sudra.
24. The sages state that the first four are approved (in the case) of a Brahman, one, the Rakshasa (rite in the case) of a Kshatriya, and the Asura (marriage in that) of a Vaishya and of a Sudra.
25. But in these (Institutes of the sacred law) three of the five (last) are declared to be lawful and two unlawful; the Paisaka and the Asura (rites) must never be used.
26. For Kshatriyas those before-mentioned two rites, the Gandharva and the Rakshasa, whether separate or mixed, are permitted by the sacred tradition.
27. The gift of a daughter, after decking her (with costly garments) and honouring (her by presents of jewels), to a man learned in the Veda and of good conduct, whom (the father) himself invites, is called the Brahma rite.
28. The gift of a daughter who has been decked with ornaments, to a priest who duly officiates at a sacrifice, during the course of its performance, they call the Daiva rite.
29. When (the father) gives away his daughter according to the rule, after receiving from the bridegroom, for (the fulfilment of) the sacred law, a cow and a bull or two pairs, that is named the Arsha rite.
30. The gift of a daughter (by her father) after he has addressed (the couple) with the text, 'May both of you perform together your duties,' and has shown honour (to the bridegroom), is called in the Smriti the Pragapatya rite.
31. When (the bridegroom) receives a maiden, after having given as much wealth as he can afford, to the kinsmen and to the bride herself, according to his own will, that is called the Asura rite.
32. The voluntary union of a maiden and her lover one

must know (to be) the Gandharva rite, which springs from desire and has sexual intercourse for its purpose.

33. The forcible abduction of a maiden from her home, while she cries out and weeps, after (her kinsmen) have been slain or wounded and (their houses) broken open, is called the Rakshasa rite.

34. When (a man) by stealth seduces a girl who is sleeping, intoxicated, or disordered in intellect, that is the eighth, the most base and sinful rite of the Pisakas.

35. The gift of daughters among Brahmans is most approved, (if it is preceded) by (a libation of) water; but in the case of other castes (it may be performed) by (the expression of) mutual consent.

36. Listen now to me, ye Brahmans, while I fully declare what quality has been ascribed by Manu to each of these marriage-rites.

37. The son of a wife wedded according to the Brahma rite, if he performs meritorious acts, liberates from sin ten ancestors, ten descendants and himself as the twenty-first.

38. The son born of a wife, wedded according to the Daiva rite, likewise (saves) seven ancestors and seven descendants, the son of a wife married by the Arsha rite three (in the ascending and descending lines), and the son of a wife married by the rite of Ka (Pragapati) six (in either line).

39. From the four marriages, (enumerated) successively, which begin with the Brahma rite spring sons, radiant with knowledge of the Veda and honoured by the Sishtas (good men).

40. Endowded with the qualities of beauty and goodness, possessing wealth and fame, obtaining as many enjoyments as they desire and being most righteous, they will live a hundred years.

41. But from the remaining (four) blamable marriages spring sons who are cruel and speakers of untruth, who hate the Veda and the sacred law.

42. In the blameless marriages blameless children are born to men, in blamable (marriages) blamable (offspring); one should therefore avoid the blamable (forms of marriage).
43. The ceremony of joining the hands is prescribed for (marriages with) women of equal caste (varna); know that the following rule (applies) to weddings with females of a different caste (varna).
44. On marrying a man of a higher caste a Kshatriya bride must take hold of an arrow, a Vaishya bride of a goad, and a Sudra female of the hem of the (bridegroom's) garment.
45. Let (the husband) approach his wife in due season, being constantly satisfied with her (alone); he may also, being intent on pleasing her, approach her with a desire for conjugal union (on any day) excepting the Parvans.
46. Sixteen (days and) nights (in each month), including four days which differ from the rest and are censured by the virtuous, (are called) the natural season of women.
47. But among these the first four, the eleventh and the thirteenth are (declared to be) forbidden; the remaining nights are recommended.
48. On the even nights sons are conceived and daughters on the uneven ones; hence a man who desires to have sons should approach his wife in due season on the even (nights).
49. A male child is produced by a greater quantity of male seed, a female child by the prevalence of the female; if (both are) equal, a hermaphrodite or a boy and a girl; if (both are) weak or deficient in quantity, a failure of conception (results).
50. He who avoids women on the six forbidden nights and on eight others, is (equal in chastity to) a student, in whichever order he may live.
51. No father who knows (the law) must take even the smallest gratuity for his daughter; for a man who, through avarice, takes a gratuity, is a seller of his offspring.

52. But those (male) relations who, in their folly, live on the separate property of women, (*e.g.* appropriate) the beasts of burden, carriages, and clothes of women, commit sin and will sink into hell.

53. Some call the cow and the bull (given) at an Arsha wedding 'a gratuity;' (but) that is wrong, since (the acceptance of) a fee, be it small or great, is a sale (of the daughter).

54. When the relatives do not appropriate (for their use) the gratuity (given), it is not a sale; (in that case) the (gift) is only a token of respect and of kindness towards the maidens.

55. Women must be honoured and adorned by their fathers, brothers, husbands, and brothers-in-law, who desire (their own) welfare.

56. Where women are honoured, there the gods are pleased; but where they are not honoured, no sacred rite yields rewards.

57. Where the female relations live in grief, the family soon wholly perishes; but that family where they are not unhappy ever prospers.

58. The houses on which female relations, not being duly honoured, pronounce a curse, perish completely, as if destroyed by magic.

59. Hence men who seek (their own) welfare, should always honour women on holidays and festivals with (gifts of) ornaments, clothes, and (dainty) food.

60. In that family, where the husband is pleased with his wife and the wife with her husband, happiness will assuredly be lasting.

61. For if the wife is not radiant with beauty, she will not attract her husband; but if she has no attractions for him, no children will be born.

62. If the wife is radiant with beauty, the whole house is bright; but if she is destitute of beauty, all will appear dismal.

63. By low marriages, by omitting (the performance of)

sacred rites, by neglecting the study of the Veda, and by irreverence towards Brahmans, (great) families sink low.

64. By (practising) handicrafts, by pecuniary transactions, by (begetting) children on Sudra females only, by (trading in) cows, horses, and carriages, by (the pursuit of) agriculture and by taking service under a king,

65. By sacrificing for men unworthy to offer sacrifices and by denying (the future rewards for good) works, families, deficient in the (knowledge of the) Veda, quickly perish.

66. But families that are rich in the knowledge of the Veda, though possessing little wealth, are numbered among the great, and acquire great fame.

67. With the sacred fire, kindled at the wedding, a householder shall perform according to the law the domestic ceremonies and the five (great) sacrifices, and (with that) he shall daily cook his food.

68. A householder has five slaughter-houses (as it were, *viz.*) the hearth, the grinding-stone, the broom, the pestle and mortar, the water-vessel, by using which he is bound (with the fetters of sin).

69. In order to successively expiate (the offences committed by means) of all these (five) the great sages have prescribed for householders the daily (performance of the five) great sacrifices.

70. Teaching (and studying) is the sacrifice (offered) to Brahman, the (offerings of water and food called) Tarpana the sacrifice to the manes, the burnt oblation the sacrifice offered to the gods, the Bali offering that offered to the Bhutas, and the hospitable reception of guests the offering to men.

71. He who neglects not these five great sacrifices, while he is able (to perform them), is not tainted by the sins (committed) in the five places of slaughter, though he constantly lives in the (order of) house (holders).

72. But he who does not feed these five, the gods, his guests, those whom he is bound to maintain, the manes, and himself, lives not, though he breathes.

73. They call (these) five sacrifices also, Ahuta, Huta, Prahuta, Brahmya-huta, and Prasita.
74. Ahuta (not offered in the fire) is the muttering (of Vedic texts), Huta the burnt oblation (offered to the gods), Prahuta (offered by scattering it on the ground) the Bali offering given to the Bhutas, Brahmya-huta (offered in the digestive fire of Brahmans), the respectful reception of Brahman (guests), and Prasita (eaten) the (daily oblation to the manes, called) Tarpana.
75. Let (every man) in this (second order, at least) daily apply himself to the private recitation of the Veda, and also to the performance of the offering to the gods; for he who is diligent in the performance of sacrifices, supports both the movable and the immovable creation.
76. An oblation duly thrown into the fire, reaches the sun; from the sun comes rain, from rain food, therefrom the living creatures (derive their subsistence).
77. As all living creatures subsist by receiving support from air, even so (the members of) all orders subsist by receiving support from the householder.
78. Because men of the three (other) orders are daily supported by the householder with (gifts of) sacred knowledge and food, therefore (the order of) householders is the most excellent order.
79. (The duties of) this order, which cannot be practised by men with weak organs, must be carefully observed by him who desires imperishable (bliss in) heaven, and constant happiness in this (life).
80. The sages, the manes, the gods, the Bhutas, and guests ask the householders (for offerings and gifts); hence he who knows (the law), must give to them (what is due to each).
81. Let him worship, according to the rule, the sages by the private recitation of the Veda, the gods by burnt oblations, the manes by funeral offerings (Sraddha), men by (gifts of) food, and the Bhutas by the Bali offering.

82. Let him daily perform a funeral sacrifice with food, or with water, or also with milk, roots, and fruits, and (thus) please the manes.

83. Let him feed even one Brahman in honour of the manes at (the Sraddha), which belongs to the five great sacrifices; but let him not feed on that (occasion) any Brahman on account of the Vaisvadeva offering.

84. A Brahman shall offer according to the rule (of his Grihya-sutra a portion) of the cooked food destined for the Vaisvadeva in the sacred domestic fire to the following deities:

85. First to Agni, and (next) to Soma, then to both these gods conjointly, further to all the gods (Visve Devah), and (then) to Dhanvantari,

86. Further to Kuhu (the goddess of the new-moon day), to Anumati (the goddess of the full-moon day), to Pragapati (the lord of creatures), to heaven and earth conjointly, and finally to Agni Svishtakrit (the fire which performs the sacrifice well).

87. After having thus duly offered the sacrificial food, let him throw Bali offerings in all directions of the compass, proceeding (from the east) to the south, to Indra, Yama, Varuna, and Soma, as well as to the servants (of these deities).

88. Saying, '(Adoration) to the Maruts,' he shall scatter (some food) near the door, and (some) in water, saying, '(Adoration to the waters;' he shall throw (some) on the pestle and the mortar, speaking thus, '(Adoration) to the trees.'

89. Near the head (of the bed) he shall make an offering to Sri (fortune), and near the foot (of his bed) to Bhadrakali; in the centre of the house let him place a Bali for Brahman and for Vastoshpati (the lord of the dwelling) conjointly.

90. Let him throw up into the air a Bali for all the gods, and (in the daytime one) for the goblins roaming about by day, (and in the evening one) for the goblins that walk at night.

91. In the upper story let him offer a Bali to Sarvatmabhuti; but let him throw what remains (from these offerings) in a southerly direction for the manes.
92. Let him gently place on the ground (some food) for dogs, outcasts, Kandalas (Svapak), those afflicted with diseases that are punishments of former sins, crows, and insects.
93. That Brahman who thus daily honours all beings, goes, endowed with a resplendent body, by a straight road to the highest dwelling-place (*i.e.* Brahman).
94. Having performed this Bali offering, he shall first feed his guest and, according to the rule, give alms to an ascetic (and) to a student.
95. A twice-born householder gains, by giving alms, the same reward for his meritorious act which (a student) obtains for presenting, in accordance with the rule, a cow to his teacher.
96. Let him give, in accordance with the rule, to a Brahman who knows the true meaning of the Veda, even (a small portion of food as) alms, or a pot full of water, having garnished (the food with seasoning, or the pot with flowers and fruit).
97. The oblations to gods and manes, made by men ignorant (of the law of gifts), are lost, if the givers in their folly present (shares of them) to Brahmans who are mere ashes.
98. An offering made in the mouth-fire of Brahmans rich in sacred learning and austerities, saves from misfortune and from great guilt.
99. But let him offer, in accordance with the rule, to a guest who has come (of his own accord) a seat and water, as well as food, garnished (with seasoning), according to his ability.
100. A Brahman who stays unhonoured (in the house), takes away (with him) all the spiritual merit even of a man who subsists by gleaning ears of corn, or offers oblations in five fires.

101. Grass, room (for resting), water, and fourthly a kind word; these (things) never fail in the houses of good men.
102. But a Brahman who stays one night only is declared to be a guest (atithi); for because he stays (sthita) not long (anityam), he is called atithi (a guest).
103. One must not consider as a guest a Brahman who dwells in the same village, nor one who seeks his livelihood by social intercourse, even though he has come to a house where (there is) a wife, and where sacred fires (are kept).
104. Those foolish householders who constantly seek (to live on) the food of others, become, in consequence of that (baseness), after death the cattle of those who give them food.
105. A guest who is sent by the (setting) sun in the evening, must not be driven away by a householder; whether he have come at (supper) time or at an inopportune moment, he must not stay in the house without entertainment.
106. Let him not eat any (dainty) food which he does not offer to his guest; the hospitable reception of guests procures wealth, fame, long life, and heavenly bliss.
107. Let him offer (to his guests) seats, rooms, beds, attendance on departure and honour (while they stay), to the most distinguished in the best form, to the lower ones in a lower form, to equals in an equal manner.
108. But if another guest comes after the Vaisvadeva offering has been finished, (the householder) must give him food according to his ability, (but) not repeat the Bali offering.
109. A Brahman shall not name his family and (Vedic) gotra in order to obtain a meal; for he who boasts of them for the sake of a meal, is called by the wise a foul feeder (vantasin).
110. But a Kshatriya (who comes) to the house of a Brahman is not called a guest (atithi), nor a Vaishya, nor a Sudra, nor a personal friend, nor a relative, nor the teacher.

111. But if a Kshatriya comes to the house of a Brahman in the manner of a guest, (the house-holder) may feed him according to his desire, after the above-mentioned Brahmans have eaten.

112. Even a Vaishya and a Sudra who have approached his house in the manner of guests, he may allow to eat with his servants, showing (thereby) his compassionate disposition.

113. Even to others, personal friends and so forth, who have come to his house out of affection, he may give food, garnished (with seasoning) according to his ability, (at the same time) with his wife.

114. Without hesitation he may give food, even before his guests, to the following persons, (*viz.*) to newly-married women, to infants, to the sick, and to pregnant women.

115. But the foolish man who eats first without having given food to these (persons) does, while he crams, not know that (after death) he himself will be devoured by dogs and vultures.

116. After the Brahmans, the kinsmen, and the servants have dined, the householder and his wife may afterwards eat what remains.

117. Having honoured the gods, the sages, men, the manes, and the guardian deities of the house, the householder shall eat afterwards what remains.

118. He who prepares food for himself (alone), eats nothing but sin; for it is ordained that the food which remains after (the performance of) the sacrifices shall be the meal of virtuous men.

119. Let him honour with the honey-mixture a king, an officiating priest, a Snataka, the teacher, a son-in-law, a father-in-law, and a maternal uncle, (if they come) again after a full year (has elapsed since their last visit).

120. A king and a Srotriya, who come on the performance of a sacrifice, must be honoured with the honey-mixture, but not if no sacrifice is being performed; that is a settled rule.

121. But the wife shall offer in the evening (a portion) of the dressed food as a Bali-oblation, without (the recitation of) sacred formulas; for that (rite which is called the) Vaisvadeva is prescribed both for the morning and the evening.

122. After performing the Pitriyagna, a Brahman who keeps a sacred fire shall offer, month by month, on the new-moon day, the funeral sacrifice (Sraddha, called) Pindanvaharyaka.

123. The wise call the monthly funeral offering to the manes Anvaharya (to be offered after the cakes), and that must be carefully performed with the approved (sorts of) flesh (mentioned below).

124. I will fully declare what and how many (Brahmans) must be fed on that (occasion), who must be avoided, and on what kinds of food (they shall dine).

125. One must feed two (Brahmans) at the offering to the gods, and three at the offering to the manes, or one only on either occasion; even a very wealthy man shall not be anxious (to entertain) a large company.

126. A large company destroys these five (advantages) the respectful treatment (of the invited, the propriety of) place and time, purity and (the selection of) virtuous Brahman (guests); he therefore shall not seek (to entertain) a large company.

127. Famed is this rite for the dead, called (the sacrifice sacred to the manes (and performed) on the new-moon day; if a man is diligent in (performing) that, (the reward of) the rite for the dead, which is performed according to Smarta rules, reaches him constantly.

128. Oblations to the gods and manes must be presented by the givers to a Srotriya alone; what is given to such a most worthy Brahman yields great reward.

129. Let him feed even one learned man at (the sacrifice) to the gods, and one at (the sacrifice) to the manes; (thus) he will gain a rich reward, not (if he entertains) many who are unacquainted with the Veda.

130. Let him make inquiries even regarding the remote (ancestors of) a Brahman who has studied an entire (recension of the) Veda; (if descended from a virtuous race) such a man is a worthy recipient of gifts (consisting) of food offered to the gods or to the manes, he is declared (to procure as great rewards as) a guest (atithi).

131. Though a million of men, unaquainted with the Rikas, were to dine at a (funeral sacrifice), yet a single man, learned in the Veda, who is satisfied (with his entertainment), is worth them all as far as the (production of) spiritual merit (is concerned).

132. Food sacred to the manes or to the gods must be given to a man distinguished by sacred knowledge; for hands, smeared with blood, cannot be cleansed with blood.

133. As many mouthfuls as an ignorant man swallows at a sacrifice to the gods or to the manes, so many red-hot spikes, spears, and iron balls must (the giver of the repast) swallow after death.

134. Some Brahmans are devoted to (the pursuit of) knowledge, and others to (the performance of) austerities; some to austerities and to the recitation of the Veda, and others to (the performance of) sacred rites.

135. Oblations to the manes ought to be carefully presented to those devoted to knowledge, but offerings to the gods, in accordance with the reason (of the sacred law), to (men of) all the four (above-mentioned classes).

136. If there is a father ignorant of the sacred texts whose son has learned one whole recension of the Veda and the Angas, and a son ignorant of the sacred texts whose father knows an entire recension of the Veda and the Angas,

137. Know that he whose father knows the Veda, is the more venerable one (of the two); yet the other one is worthy of honour, because respect is due to the Veda (which he has learned).

138. Let him not entertain a personal friend at a funeral sacrifice; he may gain his affection by (other) valuable

gifts; let him feed at a Sraddha a Brahman whom he considers neither as a foe nor as a friend.

139. He who performs funeral sacrifices and offerings to the gods chiefly for the sake of (gaining) friends, reaps after death no reward for Sraddhas and sacrifices.

140. That meanest among twice-born men who in his folly contracts friendships through a funeral sacrifice, loses heaven, because he performed a Sraddha for the sake of friendship.

141. A gift (of food) by twice-born men, consumed with (friends and relatives), is said to be offered to the Pisakas; it remains in this (world) alone like a blind cow in one stable.

142. As a husbandman reaps no harvest when he has sown the seed in barren soil, even so the giver of sacrificial food gains no reward if he presented it to a man unacquainted with the Rikas.

143. But a present made in accordance with the rules to a learned man, makes the giver and the recipient partakers of rewards both in this (life) and after death.

144. (If no learned Brahman be at hand), he may rather honour a (virtuous) friend than an enemy, though the latter may be qualified (by learning and so forth); for sacrificial food, eaten by a foe, bears no reward after death.

145. Let him (take) pains (to) feed at a Sraddha an adherent of the Rigveda who has studied one entire (recension of that) Veda, or a follower of the Yagurveda who has finished one Sakha, or a singer of Samans who (likewise) has completed (the study of an entire recension).

146. If one of these three dines, duly honoured, at a funeral sacrifice, the ancestors of him (who gives the feast), as far as the seventh person, will be satisfied for a very long time.

147. This is the chief rule (to be followed) in offering sacrifices to the gods and manes; know that the virtuous always observe the following subsidiary rule.

148. One may also entertain (on such occasions) one's maternal grandfather, a maternal uncle, a sister's son, a father-in-law, one's teacher, a daughter's son, a daughter's husband, a cognate kinsman, one's own officiating priest or a man for whom one offers sacrifices.
149. For a rite sacred to the gods, he who knows the law will not make (too close) inquiries regarding an (invited) Brahman; but when one performs a ceremony in honour of the manes, one must carefully examine (the qualities and parentage of the guest).
150. Manu has declared that those Brahmans who are thieves, outcasts, eunuchs, or atheists are unworthy (to partake) of oblations to the gods and manes.
151. Let him not entertain at a Sraddha one who wears his hair in braids (a student), one who has not studied (the Veda), one afflicted with a skin-disease, a gambler, nor those who sacrifice for a multitude (of sacrificers).
152. Physicians, temple-priests, sellers of meat, and those who subsist by shop-keeping must be avoided at sacrifices offered to the gods and to the manes.
153. A paid servant of a village or of a king, man with deformed nails or black teeth, one who opposes his teacher, one who has forsaken the sacred fire, and a usurer;
154. One suffering from consumption, one who subsists by tending cattle, a younger brother who marries or kindles the sacred fire before the elder, one who neglects the five great sacrifices, an enemy of the Brahman race, an elder brother who marries or kindles the sacred fire after the younger, and one who belongs to a company or corporation,
155. An actor or singer, one who has broken the vow of studentship, one whose (only or first) wife is a Sudra female, the son of a remarried woman, a one-eyed man, and he in whose house a paramour of his wife (resides);
156. He who teaches for a stipulated fee and he who is taught on that condition, he who instructs Sudra pupils

and he whose teacher is a Sudra, he who speaks rudely, the son of an adulteress, and the son of a widow,

157. He who forsakes his mother, his father, or a teacher without a (sufficient) reason, he who has contracted an alliance with outcasts either through the Veda or through a marriage,

158. An incendiary, a prisoner, he who eats the food given by the son of an adulteress, a seller of Soma, he who undertakes voyages by sea, a bard, an oilman, a suborner to perjury,

159. He who wrangles or goes to law with his father, the keeper of a gambling-house, a drunkard, he who is afflicted with a disease (in punishment of former) crimes, he who is accused of a mortal sin, a hypocrite, a seller of substances used for flavouring food,

160. A maker of bows and of arrows, he who lasciviously dallies with a brother's widow, the betrayer of a friend, one who subsists by gambling, he who learns (the Veda) from his son,

161. An epileptic man, who suffers from scrofulous swellings of the glands, one afflicted with white leprosy, an informer, a madman, a blind man, and he who cavils at the Veda must (all) be avoided.

162. A trainer of elephants, oxen, horses, or camels, he who subsists by astrology, a bird-fancier, and he who teaches the use of arms,

163. He who diverts watercourses, and he who delights in obstructing them, an architect, a messenger, and he who plants trees (for money),

164. A breeder of sporting-dogs, a falconer, one who defiles maidens, he who delights in injuring living creatures, he who gains his subsistence from Sudras, and he who offers sacrifices to the Ganas,

165. He who does not follow the rule of conduct, a (man destitute of energy like a) eunuch, one who constantly asks (for favours), he who lives by agriculture, a club-footed man, and he who is censured by virtuous men,

166. A shepherd, a keeper of buffaloes, the husband of a remarried woman, and a carrier of dead bodies, (all these) must be carefully avoided.

167. A Brahman who knows (the sacred law) should shun at (sacrifices) both (to the gods and to the manes) these lowest of twice-born men, whose conduct is reprehensible, and who are unworthy (to sit) in the company (at a repast).

168. As a fire of dry grass is (unable to consume the offerings and is quickly) extinguished, even so (is it with) an unlearned Brahman; sacrificial food must not be given to him, since it (would be) offered in ashes.

169. I will fully declare what result the giver obtains after death, if he gives food, destined for the gods or manes, to a man who is unworthy to sit in the company.

170. The Rakshasas, indeed, consume (the food) eaten by Brahmans who have not fulfilled the vow of studentship, by a Parivettri and so forth, and by other men not admissible into the company.

171. He must be considered as a Parivettri who marries or begins the performance of the Agnihotra before his elder brother, but the latter as a Parivitti.

172. The elder brother who marries after the younger, the younger brother who marries before the elder, the female with whom such a marriage is contracted, he who gives her away, and the sacrificing priest, as the fifth, all fall into hell.

173. He who lasciviously dallies with the widow of a deceased brother, though she be appointed (to bear a child by him) in accordance with the sacred law, must be known to be a Didhishupati.

174. Two (kinds of) sons, a Kunda and a Golaka, are born by wives of other men; (he who is born) while the husband lives, will be a Kunda, and (he who is begotten) after the husband's death, a Golaka.

175. But those two creatures, who are born of wives of other men, cause to the giver the loss (of the rewards), both

in this life and after death, for the food sacred to gods or manes which has been given (to them).

176. The foolish giver (of a funeral repast) does not reap the reward for as many worthy guests as a man, inadmissible into company, can look on while they are feeding.

177. A blind man by his presence causes to the giver (of the feast) the loss of the reward for ninety (guests), a one-eyed man for sixty, one who suffers from white leprosy for a hundred, and one punished by a (terrible) disease for a thousand.

178. The giver (of a Sraddha) loses the reward, due for such a non-sacrificial gift, for as many Brahmans as a (guest) who sacrifices for Sudras may touch (during the meal) with his limbs.

179. And if a Brahman, though learned in the Veda, accepts through covetousness a gift from such (a man), he will quickly perish, like a vessel of unburnt clay in water.

180. (Food) given to a seller of Soma becomes ordure, (that given) to a physician pus and blood, but (that presented) to a temple-priest is lost, and (that given) to a usurer finds no place (in the world of the gods).

181. What has been given to a Brahman who lives by trade that is not (useful) in this world and the next, and (a present) to a Brahman born of a remarried woman (resembles) an oblation thrown into ashes.

182. But the wise declare that the food which (is offered) to other unholy, inadmissible men, enumerated above, (is turned into) adipose secretions, blood, flesh, marrow, and bone.

183. Now hear by what chief of twice-born men a company defiled by (the presence of) unworthy (guests) is purified, and the full (description of) the Brahmans who sanctify a company.

184. Those men must be considered as the sanctifiers of a company who are most learned in all the Vedas and in all the Angas, and who are the descendants of Srotriyas.

185. A Trinakiketa, one who keeps five sacred fires, a Trisuparna, one who is versed in the six Angas, the son of a woman married according to the Brahma rite, one who sings the Gyeshthasaman,

186. One who knows the meaning of the Veda, and he who expounds it, a student, one who has given a thousand (cows), and a centenarian must be considered as Brahmans who sanctify a company.

187. On the day before the Sraddha-rite is performed, or on the day when it takes place, let him invite with due respect at least three Brahmans, such as have been mentioned above.

188. A Brahman who has been invited to a (rite) in honour of the manes shall always control himself and not recite the Veda, and he who performs the Sraddha (must act in the same manner).

189. For the manes attend the invited Brahmans, follow them (when they walk) like the wind, and sit near them when they are seated.

190. But a Brahman who, being duly invited to a rite in honour of the gods or of the manes, in any way breaks (the appointment), becomes guilty (of a crime), and (in his next birth) a hog.

191. But he who, being invited to a Sraddha, dallies with a Sudra woman, takes upon himself all the sins which the giver (of the feast) committed.

192. The manes are primeval deities, free from anger, careful of purity, ever chaste, averse from strife, and endowed with great virtues.

193. Now learn fully from whom all these (manes derive) their origin, and with what ceremonies they ought to be worshipped.

194. The (various) classes of the manes are declared to be the sons of all those sages, Mariki and the rest, who are children of Manu, the son of Hiranyagarbha.

195. The Somasads, the sons of Virag, are stated to be the manes of the Sadhyas, and the Agnishvattas, the

children of Mariki, are famous in the world (as the manes) of the gods.

196. The Barhishads, born of Atri, are recorded to be (the manes) of the Daityas, Danavas, Yakshas, Gandharvas, Snake-deities, Rakshasas, Suparnas, and a Kimnaras,

197. The Somapas those of the Brahmans, the Havirbhugs those of the Kshatriyas, the Agyapas those of the Vaisyas, but the Sukalins those of the Sudras.

198. The Somapas are the sons of Kavi (Bhrigu), the Havishmats the children of Angiras, the Agyapas the offspring of Pulastya, but the Sukalins (the issue) of Vashistha.

199. One should know that (other classes), the Agnidagdhas, the Anagnidagdhas, the Kavyas, the Barhishads, the Agnishvattas, and the Saumyas, are (the manes) of the Brahmans alone.

200. But know also that there exist in this (world) countless sons and grandsons of those chief classes of manes which have been enumerated.

201. From the sages sprang the manes, from the manes the gods and the Danavas, but from the gods the whole world, both the movable and the immovable in due order.

202. Even water offered with faith (to the manes) in vessels made of silver or adorned with silver, produces endless (bliss).

203. For twice-born men the rite in honour of the manes is more important than the rite in honour of the gods; for the offering to the gods which precedes (the Sraddhas), has been declared to be a means of fortifying (the latter).

204. Let him first invite a (Brahman) in honour of the gods as a protection for the (offering to the manes); for the Rakshasas destroy a funeral sacrifice which is left without such a protection.

205. Let him make (the Sraddha) begin and end with (a rite) in honour of the gods; it shall not begin and end with

a (rite) to the manes; for he who makes it begin and end with a (rite) in honour of the manes, soon perishes together with his progeny.

206. Let him smear a pure and secluded place with cowdung, and carefully make it sloping towards the south.

207. The manes are always pleased with offerings made in open, naturally pure places, on the banks of rivers, and in secluded spots.

208. The (sacrificer) shall make the (invited) Brahmans, who have duly performed their ablutions, sit down on separate, prepared seats, on which blades of Kusa grass have been placed.

209. Having placed those blameless Brahmans on their seats, he shall honour them with fragrant garlands and perfumes, beginning with (those who are invited in honour of) the gods.

210. Having presented to them water, sesamum grains, and blades of Kusa grass, the Brahman (sacrificer) shall offer (oblations) in the sacred fire, after having received permission (to do so) from (all) the Brahman (guests) conjointly.

211. Having first, according to the rule, performed, as a means of protecting (the Sraddha), oblations to Agni, to Soma, and to Yama, let him afterwards satisfy the manes by a gift of sacrificial food.

212. But if no (sacred) fire (is available), he shall place (the offerings) into the hand of a Brahman; for Brahmans who know the sacred texts declare, 'What fire is, even such is a Brahman.'

213. They (also) call those first of twice-born men the ancient deities of the funeral sacrifice, free from anger, easily pleased, employed in making men prosper.

214. After he has performed (the oblations) in the fire, (and) the whole series of ceremonies in such a manner that they end in the south, let him sprinkle water with his right hand on the spot (where the cakes are to be placed).

215. But having made three cakes out of the remainder of that sacrificial food, he must, concentrating his mind and turning towards the south, place them on (Kusa grass) exactly in the same manner in which (he poured out the libations of) water.

216. Having offered those cakes according to the (prescribed) rule, being pure, let him wipe the same hand with (the roots of) those blades of Kusa grass for the sake of the (three ancestors) who partake of the wipings (lepa).

217. Having (next) sipped water, turned round (towards the north), and thrice slowly suppressed his breath, (the sacrificer) who knows the sacred texts shall worship (the guardian deities of) the six seasons and the manes.

218. Let him gently pour out the remainder of the water near the cakes, and, with fixed attention, smell those cakes, in the order in which they were placed (on the ground).

219. But taking successively very small portions from the cakes, he shall make those seated Brahman eat them, in accordance with the rule, before (their dinner).

220. But if the (sacrificer's) father is living, he must offer (the cakes) to three remoter (ancestors); or he may also feed his father at the funeral sacrifice as (one of the) Brahman (guests).

221. But he whose father is dead, while his grandfather lives, shall, after pronouncing his father's name, mention (that of) his great-grandfather.

222. Manu has declared that either the grandfather may eat at that Sraddha (as a guest), or (the grandson) having received permission, may perform it, as he desires.

223. Having poured water mixed with sesamum, in which a blade of Kusa grass has been placed, into the hands of the (guests), he shall give (to each) that (above-mentioned) portion of the cake, saying, 'To those, Svadha!'

224. But carrying (the vessel) filled with food with both

hands, the (sacrificer) himself shall gently place it before the Brahmans, meditating on the manes.

225. The malevolent Asuras forcibly snatch away that food which is brought without being held with both hands.

226. Let him, being pure and attentive, carefully place on the ground the seasoning (for the rice), such as broths and pot herbs, sweet and sour milk, and honey,

227. (As well as) various (kinds of) hard food which require mastication, and of soft food, roots, fruits, savoury meat, and fragrant drinks.

228. All this he shall present (to his guests), being pure and attentive, successively invite them to partake of each (dish), proclaiming its qualities.

229. Let him on no account drop a tear, become angry or utter an untruth, nor let him touch the food with his foot nor violently shake it.

230. A tear sends the (food) to the Pretas, anger to his enemies, a falsehood to the dogs, contact with his foot to the Rakshasas, a shaking to the sinners.

231. Whatever may please the Brahmans, let him give without grudging it; let him give riddles from the Veda, for that is agreeable to the manes.

232. At a (sacrifice in honour) of the manes, he must let (his guests) hear the Veda, the Institutes of the sacred law, legends, tales, Puranas, and Khilas.

233. Himself being delighted, let him give delight to the Brahmans, cause them to partake gradually and slowly (of each dish), and repeatedly invite (them to eat) by (offering) the food and (praising) its qualities.

234. Let him eagerly entertain at a funeral sacrifice a daughter's son, though he be a student, and let him place a Nepal blanket on the on the seat (of each guest), scattering sesamum grains on the ground.

235. There are three means of sanctification, (to be used) at a Sraddha, a daughter's son, a Nepal blanket, and sesamum grains; and they recommend three (other

things) for it, cleanliness, suppression of anger, and absence of haste.

236. All the food must be very hot, and the (guests) shall eat in silence; (even though) asked by the giver (of the feast), the Brahmans shall not proclaim the qualities of the sacrificial food.

237. As long as the food remains warm, as long as they eat in silence, as long as the qualities of the food are not proclaimed, so long the manes partake (of it).

238. What (a guest) eats, covering his head, what he eats with his face turned towards the south, what he eats with sandals on (his feet), that the Rakshasas consume.

239. A Kandala, a village pig, a cock, a dog, a menstruating woman, and a eunuch must not look at the Brahmans while they eat.

240. What (any of) these sees at a burnt-oblation, at a (solemn) gift, at a dinner (given to Brahmans), or at any rite in honour of the gods and manes, that produces not the intended result.

241. A boar makes (the rite) useless by inhaling the smell (of the offerings), a cock by the air of his wings, a dog by throwing his eye (on them), a low-caste man by touching (them).

242. If a lame man, a one-eyed man, one deficient in a limb, or one with a redundant limb, be even the servant of the performer (of the Sraddha), he must be removed from that place (where the Sraddha is held).

243. To a Brahman (householder), or to an ascetic who comes for food, he may, with the permission of (his) Brahman (guests), show honour according to his ability.

244. Let him mix all the kinds of food together, sprinkle them with water and put them, scattering them (on Kusa grass), down on the ground in front of (his guests), when they have finished their meal.

245. The remnant (in the dishes), and the portion scattered on Kusa grass, shall be the share of deceased (children)

who received not the sacrament (of cremation) and of those who (unjustly) forsook noble wives.

246. They declare the fragments which have fallen on the ground at a (Sraddha) to the manes, to be the share of honest, dutiful servants.

247. But before the performance of the Sapindikarana, one must feed at the funeral sacrifice in honour of a (recently) deceased Aryan (one Brahman) without (making an offering) to the gods, and give one cake only.

248. But after the Sapindikarana of the (deceased father) has been performed according to the sacred law, the sons must offer the cakes with those ceremonies, (described above.)

249. The foolish man who, after having eaten a Sraddha (dinner), gives the leavings to a Sudra, falls headlong into the Kalasutra hell.

250. If the partaker of a Sraddha (dinner) enters on the same day the bed of a Sudra female, the manes of his (ancestors) will lie during that month in her ordure.

251. Having addressed the question, 'Have you dined well?' (to his guests), let him give water for sipping to them who are satisfied, and dismiss them, after they have sipped water, (with the words) 'Rest either (here or at home)!'

252. The Brahman (guests) shall then answer him, 'Let there be Svadha;' for at all rites in honour of the manes the word Svadha is the highest benison.

253. Next let him inform (his guests) who have finished their meal, of the food which remains; with the permission of the Brahmans let him dispose (of that), as they may direct.

254. At a (Sraddha) in honour of the manes one must use (in asking of the guests if they are satisfied, the word) svaditam; at a Goshthi-sraddha, (the word) susrutam; at a Vriddhi-sraddha, (the word) sampannam; and at (a rite) in honour of the gods, (the word) rukitam.

255. The afternoon, Kusa grass, the due preparation of the

dwelling, sesamum grains, liberality, the careful preparation of the food, and (the company of) distinguished Brahmans are true riches at all funeral sacrifices.

256. Know that Kusa grass, purificatory (texts), the morning, sacrificial viands of all kinds, and those means of purification, mentioned above, are blessings at a sacrifice to the gods.

257. The food eaten by hermits in the forest, milk, Soma-juice, meat which is not prepared (with spices), and salt unprepared by art, are called, on account of their nature, sacrificial food.

258. Having dismissed the (invited) Brahmans, let him, with a concentrated mind, silent and pure, look towards the south and ask these blessings of the manes:

259. 'May liberal men abound with us! May (our knowledge of) the Vedas and (our) progeny increase! May faith not forsake us! May we have much to give (to the needy)!'

260. Having thus offered (the cakes), let him, after (the prayer), cause a cow, a Brahman, a goat, or the sacred fire to consume those cakes, or let him throw them into water.

261. Some make the offering of the cakes after (the dinner); some cause (them) to be eaten by birds or throw them into fire or into water.

262. The (sacrificer's) first wife, who is faithful and intent on the worship of the manes, may eat the middle-most cake, (if she be) desirous of bearing a son.

263. (Thus) she will bring forth a son who will be long-lived, famous, intelligent, rich, the father of numerous offspring, endowed with (the quality of) goodness, and righteous.

264. Having washed his hands and sipped water, let him prepare (food) for his paternal relations and, after giving it to them with due respect, let him feed his maternal relatives also.

265. But the remnants shall be left (where they lie) until the

Brahmans have been dismissed; afterwards he shall perform the (daily) domestic Bali-offering; that is a settled (rule of the) sacred law.

266. I will now fully declare what kind of sacrificial food, given to the manes according to the rule, will serve for a long time or for eternity.

267. The ancestors of men are satisfied for one month with sesamum grains, rice, barley, masha beans, water, roots, and fruits, which have been given according to the prescribed rule,

268. Two months with fish, three months with the meat of gazelles, four with mutton, and five indeed with the flesh of birds,

269. Six months with the flesh of kids, seven with that of spotted deer, eight with that of the black antelope, but nine with that of the (deer called) Ruru,

270. Ten months they are satisfied with the meat of boars and buffaloes, but eleven months indeed with that of hares and tortoises,

271. One year with cow-milk and milk-rice; from the flesh of a long-eared white he-goat their satisfaction endures twelve years.

272. The (vegetable called) Kalasaka, (the fish called) Mahasalka, the flesh of a rhinoceros and that of a red goat, and all kinds of food eaten by hermits in the forest serve for an endless time.

273. Whatever (food), mixed with honey, one gives on the thirteenth lunar day in the rainy season under the asterism of Maghah, that also procures endless (satisfaction).

274. 'May such a man (the manes say) be born in our family who will give us milk-rice, with honey and clarified butter, on the thirteenth lunar day (of the month of Bhadrapada) and (in the afternoon) when the shadow of an elephant falls towards the east.'

275. Whatever (a man), full of faith, duly gives according to

the prescribed rule, that becomes in the other world a perpetual and imperishable (gratification) for the manes.

276. The days of the dark half of the month, beginning with the tenth, but excepting the fourteenth, are recommended for a funeral sacrifice; (it is) not thus (with) the others.

277. He who performs it on the even (lunar) days and under the even constellations, gains (the fulfilment of) all his wishes; he who honours the manes on odd (lunar days) and under odd (constellations), obtains distinguished offspring.

278. As the second half of the month is preferable to the first half, even so the afternoon is better for (the performance of) a funeral sacrifice than the forenoon.

279. Let him, untired, duly perform the (rites) in honour of the manes in accordance with the prescribed rule, passing the sacred thread over the right shoulder, proceeding from the left to the right (and) holding Kusa grass in his hands, up to the end (of the ceremony).

280. Let him not perform a funeral sacrifice at night, because the (night) is declared to belong to the Rakshasas, nor in the twilight, nor when the sun has just risen.

281. Let him offer here below a funeral sacrifice, according to the rule given above, (at least) thrice a year, in winter, in summer, and in the rainy season, but that which is included among the five great sacrifices, every day.

282. The burnt-oblation, offered at a sacrifice to the manes, must not be made in a common fire; a Brahman who keeps a sacred fire (shall) not (perform) a funeral sacrifice except on the new-moon day.

283. Even when a Brahman, after bathing, satisfies the manes with water, he obtains thereby the whole reward for the performance of the (daily) Sraddha.

284. They call (the manes of) fathers Vasus, (those of) grandfathers Rudras, and (those of) great-grandfathers Adityas; thus (speaks) the eternal Veda.

285. Let him daily partake of the vighasa and daily eat amrita (ambrosia); but vighasa is what remains from the meal (of Brahman guests) and the remainder of a sacrifice (is called) amrita.

286. Thus all the ordinances relating to the five (daily great) sacrifices have been declared to you; hear now the law for the manner of living fit for Brahmans.

CHAPTER-IV

1. Having dwelt with a teacher during the fourth part of (a man's) life, a Brahman shall live during the second quarter (of his existence) in his house, after he has wedded a wife.
2. A Brahman must seek a means of subsistence which either causes no, or at least little pain (to others), and live (by that) except in times of distress.
3. For the purpose of gaining bare subsistence, let him accumulate property by (following those) irreproachable occupations (which are prescribed for) his (caste), without (unduly) fatiguing his body.
4. He may subsist by Rita (truth), and Amrita (ambrosia), or by Mrita (death) and by Pramrita (what causes many deaths); or even by (the mode) called Satyanrita (a mixture of truth and falsehood), but never by Svavritti (a dog's mode of life).
5. By Rita shall be understood the gleaning of corn; by Amrita, what is given unasked; by Mrita, food obtained by begging and agriculture is declared to be Pramrita.
6. But trade and (money-lending) are Satyanrita, even by that one may subsist. Service is called Svavritti; therefore one should avoid it.
7. He may either possess enough to fill a granary, or a store filling a grain-jar; or he may collect what suffices for three days, or make no provision for the morrow.
8. Moreover, among these four Brahman householders, each later-(named) must be considered more distinguished, and through his virtue to have conquered the world more completely.

9. One of these follows six occupations, another subsists by three, one by two, but the fourth lives by the Brahmasattra.
10. He who maintains himself by picking up grains and ears of corn, must be always intent on (the performance of) the Agnihotra, and constantly offer those Ishtis only, which are prescribed for the days of the conjunction and opposition (of the moon), and for the solstices.
11. Let him never, for the sake of subsistence, follow the ways of the world; let him live the pure, straightforward, honest life of a Brahman.
12. He who desires happiness must strive after a perfectly contented disposition and control himself; for happiness has contentment for its root, the root of unhappiness is the contrary (disposition).
13. A Brahman, who is a Snataka and subsists by one of the (above-mentioned) modes of life, must discharge the (following) duties which secure heavenly bliss, long life, and fame.
14. Let him, untired, perform daily the rites prescribed for him in the Veda; for he who performs those according to his ability, attains to the highest state.
15. Whether he be rich or even in distress, let him not seek wealth through pursuits to which men cleave, nor by forbidden occupations, nor (let him accept presents) from any (giver whosoever he may be).
16. Let him not, out of desire (for enjoyments), attach himself to any sensual pleasures, and let him carefully obviate an excessive attachment to them, by (reflecting on their worthlessness in) his heart.
17. Let him avoid all (means of acquiring) wealth which impede the study of the Veda; (let him maintain himself) anyhow, but study, because that (devotion to the Veda-study secures) the realisation of his aims.
18. Let him walk here (on earth), bringing his dress, speech, and thoughts to a conformity with his age, his occupation, his wealth, his sacred learning, and his race.

19. Let him daily pore over those Institutes of science which soon give increase of wisdom, those which teach the acquisition of wealth, those which are beneficial (for other worldly concerns), and likewise over the Nigamas which explain the Veda.
20. For the more a man completely studies the Institutes of science, the more he fully understands (them), and his great learning shines brightly.
21. Let him never, if he is able (to perform them), neglect the sacrifices to the sages, to the gods, to the Bhutas, to men, and to the manes.
22. Some men who know the ordinances for sacrificial rites, always offer these great sacrifices in their organs (of sensation), without any (external) effort.
23. Knowing that the (performance of the) sacrifice in their speech and their breath yields imperishable (rewards), some always offer their breath in their speech, and their speech in their breath.
24. Other Brahmans, seeing with the eye of knowledge that the performance of those rites has knowledge for its root, always perform them through knowledge alone.
25. A Brahman shall always offer the Agnihotra at the beginning or at the end of the day and of the night, and the Darsa and Paurnamasa (Ishtis) at the end of each half-month,
26. When the old grain has been consumed the (Agrayana) Ishti with new grain, at the end of the (three) seasons the (Katurmasya) sacrifices, at the solstices an animal (sacrifice), at the end of the year Soma-offerings.
27. A Brahman, who keeps sacred fires, shall, if he desires to live long, not eat new grain or meat, without having offered the (Agrayana) Ishti with new grain and an animal-(sacrifice).
28. For his fires, not being worshipped by offerings of new grain and of an animal, seek to devour his vital spirits, (because they are) greedy for new grain and flesh.
29. No guest must stay in his house without being honoured,

according to his ability, with a seat, food, a couch, water, or roots and fruits.

30. Let him not honour, even by a greeting, heretics, men who follow forbidden occupations, men who live like cats, rogues, logicians, (arguing against the Veda,) and those who live like herons.
31. Those who have become Snatakas after studying the Veda, or after completing their vows, (and) householders, who are Srotriyas, one must worship by (gifts of food) sacred to gods and manes, but one must avoid those who are different.
32. A householder must give (as much food) as he is able (to spare) to those who do not cook for themselves, and to all beings one must distribute (food) without detriment (to one's own interest).
33. A Snataka who pines with hunger, may beg wealth of a king, of one for whom he sacrifices, and of a pupil, but not of others; that is a settled rule.
34. A Snataka who is able (to procure food) shall never waste himself with hunger, nor shall he wear old or dirty clothes, if he possesses property.
35. Keeping his hair, nails, and beard clipped, subduing his passions by austerities, wearing white garments and (keeping himself) pure, he shall be always engaged in studying the Veda and (such acts as are) conducive to his welfare.
36. He shall carry a staff of bamboo, a pot full of water, a sacred string, a bundle of Kusa grass, and (wear) two bright golden earrings.
37. Let him never look at the sun, when he sets or rises, is eclipsed or reflected in water, or stands in the middle of the sky.
38. Let him not step over a rope to which a calf is tied, let him not run when it rains, and let him not look at his own image in water; that is a settled rule.
39. Let him pass by (a mound of) earth, a cow, an idol, a Brahman, clarified butter, honey, a crossway, and well-known trees, turning his right hand towards them.

40. Let him, though mad with desire, not approach his wife when her courses appear; nor let him sleep with her in the same bed.
41. For the wisdom, the energy, the strength, the sight, and the vitality of a man who approaches a woman covered with menstrual excretions, utterly perish.
42. If he avoids her, while she is in that condition, his wisdom, energy, strength, sight, and vitality will increase.
43. Let him not eat in the company of his wife, nor look at her, while she eats, sneezes, yawns, or sits at her ease.
44. A Brahman who desires energy must not look at (a woman) who applies collyrium to her eyes, has anointed or uncovered herself or brings forth (a child).
45. Let him not eat, dressed with one garment only; let him not bathe naked; let him not void urine on a road, on ashes, or in a cow-pen,
46. Nor on ploughed land, in water, on an altar of bricks, on a mountain, on the ruins of a temple, nor ever on an ant-hill,
47. Nor in holes inhabited by living creatures, nor while he walks or stands, nor on reaching the bank of a river, nor on the top of a mountain.
48. Let him never void faeces or urine, facing the wind, or a fire, or looking towards a Brahman, the sun, water, or cows.
49. He may ease himself, having covered (the ground) with sticks, clods, leaves, grass, and the like, restraining his speech, (keeping himself) pure, wrapping up his body, and covering his head.
50. Let him void faeces and urine, in the daytime turning to the north, at night turning towards the south, during the two twilights in the same (position) as by day.
51. In the shade or in darkness a Brahman may, both by day and at night, do it, assuming any position he pleases; likewise when his life is in danger.

52. The intellect of (a man) who voids urine against a fire, the sun, the moon, in water, against a Brahman, a cow, or the wind, perishes.

53. Let him not blow a fire with his mouth; let him not look at a naked woman; let him not throw any impure substance into the fire, and let him not warm his feet at it.

54. Let him not place (fire) under (a bed or the like); nor step over it, nor place it (when he sleeps) at the foot-(end of his bed); let him not torment living creatures.

55. Let him not eat, nor travel, nor sleep during the twilight; let him not scratch the ground; let him not take off his garland.

56. Let him not throw urine or faeces into the water, nor saliva, nor (clothes) defiled by impure substances, nor any other (impurity), nor blood, nor poisonous things.

57. Let him not sleep alone in a deserted dwelling; let him not wake (a superior) who is sleeping; let him not converse with a menstruating woman; nor let him go to a sacrifice, if he is not chosen (to be officiating priest).

58. Let him keep his right arm uncovered in a place where a sacred fire is kept, in a cow-pen, in the presence of Brahmans, during the private recitation of the Veda, and at meals.

59. Let him not interrupt a cow who is suckling (her calf), nor tell anybody of it. A wise man, if he sees a rainbow in the sky, must not point it out to anybody.

60. Let him not dwell in a village where the sacred law is not obeyed, nor (stay) long where diseases are endemic; let him not go alone on a journey, nor reside long on a mountain.

61. Let him not dwell in a country where the rulers are Sudras, nor in one which is surrounded by unrighteous men, nor in one which has become subject to heretics, nor in one swarming with men of the lowest castes.

62. Let him not eat anything from which the oil has been extracted; let him not be a glutton; let him not eat very

early (in the morning), nor very late (in the evening), nor (take any food) in the evening, if he has eaten (his fill) in the morning.

63. Let him not exert himself without a purpose; let him not drink water out of his joined palms; let him not eat food (placed) in his lap; let him not show (idle) curiosity.

64. Let him not dance, nor sing, nor play musical instruments, nor slap (his limbs), nor grind his teeth, nor let him make uncouth noises, though he be in a passion.

65. Let him never wash his feet in a vessel of white brass; let him not eat out of a broken (earthen) dish, nor out of one that (to judge) from its appearance (is) defiled.

66. Let him not use shoes, garments, a sacred string, ornaments, a garland, or a water-vessel which have been used by others.

67. Let him not travel with untrained beasts of burden, nor with (animals) that are tormented by hunger or disease, or whose horns, eyes, and hoofs have been injured, or whose tails have been disfigured.

68. Let him always travel with (beasts) which are well broken in, swift, endowed with lucky marks, and perfect in colour and form, without urging them much with the goad.

69. The morning sun, the smoke rising from a (burning) corpse, and a broken seat must be avoided. Let him not clip his nails or hair, and not tear his nails with his teeth.

70. Let him not crush earth or clods, nor tear off grass with his nails; let him not do anything that is useless or will have disagreeable results in the future.

71. A man who crushes clods, tears off grass, or bites his nails, goes soon to perdition, likewise an informer and he who neglects (the rules of) purification.

72. Let him not wrangle; let him not wear a garland over (his hair). To ride on the back of cows (or of oxen) is anyhow a blamable act.

73. Let him not enter a walled village or house except by the gate, and by night let him keep at a long distance from the roots of trees.
74. Let him never play with dice, nor himself take off his shoes; let him not eat, lying on a bed, nor what has been placed in his hand or on a seat.
75. Let him not eat after sunset any (food) containing sesamum grains; let him never sleep naked, nor go anywhere unpurified (after meals).
76. Let him eat while his feet are (yet) wet (from the ablution), but let him not go to bed with wet feet. He who eats while his feet are (still) wet, will attain long life.
77. Let him never enter a place, difficult of access, which is impervious to his eye; let him not look at urine or ordure, nor cross a river (swimming) with his arms.
78. Let him not step on hair, ashes, bones, potsherds, cotton-seed or chaff, if he desires long life.
79. Let him not stay together with outcasts, nor with Kandalas, nor with Pukkasas, nor with fools, nor with overbearing men, nor with low-caste men, nor with Antyavasayins.
80. Let him not give to a Sudra advice, nor the remnants (of his meal), nor food offered to the gods; nor let him explain the sacred law (to such a man), nor impose (upon him) a penance.
81. For he who explains the sacred law (to a Sudra) or dictates to him a penance, will sink together with that (man) into the hell (called) Asamvrita.
82. Let him not scratch his head with both hands joined; let him not touch it while he is impure, nor bathe without (submerging) it.
83. Let him avoid (in anger) to lay hold of (his own or other men's) hair, or to strike (himself or others) on the head. When he has bathed (submerging) his head, he shall not touch any of his limbs with oil.
84. Let him not accept presents from a king who is not

descended from the Kshatriya race, nor from butchers, oil-manufacturers, and publicans, nor from those who subsist by the gain of prostitutes.

85. One oil-press is as (bad) as ten slaughter-houses, one tavern as (bad as) ten oil-presses, one brothel as (bad as) ten taverns, one king as (bad as) ten brothels.

86. A king is declared to be equal (in wickedness) to a butcher who keeps a hundred thousand slaughterhouses; to accept presents from him is a terrible (crime).

87. He who accepts presents from an avaricious king who acts contrary to the Institutes (of the sacred law), will go in succession to the following twenty-one hells:

88. Tamisra, Andhatamisra, Maharaurava, Raurava, the Kalasutra hell, Mahanaraka,

89. Samgivana, Mahaviki, Tapana, Sampratapana, Samghata, Sakakola, Kudmala, Putimrittika,

90. Lohasanku, Rigisha, Pathin, the (flaming) river, Salmala, Asipatravana, and Lohakaraka.

91. Learned Brahmans, who know that, who study the Veda and desire bliss after death, do not accept presents from a king.

92. Let him wake in the muhurta, sacred to Brahman, and think of (the acquisition of) spiritual merit and wealth, of the bodily fatigue arising therefrom, and of the true meaning of the Veda.

93. When he has risen, has relieved the necessities of nature and carefully purified himself, let him stand during the morning twilight, muttering for a long time (the Gayatri), and at the proper time (he must similarly perform) the evening (devotion).

94. By prolonging the twilight devotions, the sages obtained long life, wisdom, honour, fame, and excellence in Vedic knowledge.

95. Having performed the Upakarman according to the prescribed rule on (the full moon of the month) Sravana, or on that of Praushthapada (Bhadrapada), a Brahman

shall diligently study the Vedas during four months and a half.

96. When the Pushya-day (of the month Pausha), or the first day of the bright half of Magha has come, a Brahman shall perform in the forenoon the Utsargana of the Vedas.

97. Having performed the Utsarga outside (the village), as the Institutes (of the sacred law) prescribe, he shall stop reading during two days and the intervening night, or during that day (of the Utsarga) and (the following) night.

98. Afterwards he shall diligently recite the Vedas during the bright (halves of the months), and duly study all the Angas of the Vedas during the dark fortnights.

99. Let him not recite (the texts) indistinctly, nor in the presence of Sudras; nor let him, if in the latter part of the night he is tired with reciting the Veda, go again to sleep.

100. According to the rule declared above, let him recite the daily (portion of the) Mantras, and a zealous Brahman, (who is) not in distress, (shall study) the Brahman and the Mantrasamhita.

101. Let him who studies always avoid (reading) on the following occasions when the Veda-study is forbidden, and (let) him who teaches pupils according to the prescribed rule (do it likewise).

102. Those who know the (rules of) recitation declare that in the rainy season the Veda-study must be stopped on these two (occasions), when the wind is audible at night, and when it whirls up the dust in the daytime.

103. Manu has stated, that when lightning, thunder, and rain (are observed together), or when large fiery meteors fall on all sides, the recitation must be interrupted until the same hour (on the next day, counting from the occurrence of the event).

104. When one perceives these (phenomena) all together (in the twilight), after the sacred fires have been made to

blaze (for the performance of the Agnihotra), then one must know the recitation of the Veda to be forbidden, and also when clouds appear out of season.

105. On (the occasion of) a preternatural sound from the sky, (of) an earthquake, and when the lights of heaven are surrounded by a halo, let him know that (the Veda-study must be) stopped until the same hour (on the next day), even if (these phenomena happen) in the (rainy) season.

106. But when lightning and the roar of thunder (are observed) after the sacred fires have been made to blaze, the stoppage shall last as long as the light (of the sun or of the stars is visible); if the remaining (above-named phenomenon, rain, occurs, the reading shall cease), both in the daytime and at night.

107. For those who wish to acquire exceedingly great merit, a continual interruption of the Veda-study (is prescribed) in villages and in towns, and (the Veda-study must) always (cease) when any kind of foul smell (is perceptible).

108. In a village where a corpse lies, in the presence of a (man who lives as unrighteously as a) Sudra, while (the sound of) weeping (is heard), and in a crowd of men the (recitation of the Veda must be) stopped.

109. In water, during the middle part of the night, while he voids excrements, or is impure, and after he has partaken of a funeral dinner, a man must not even think in his heart (of the sacred texts).

110. A learned Brahman shall not recite the Veda during three days, when he has accepted an invitation to a (funeral rite) in honour of one ancestor (ekoddishta), or when the king has become impure through a birth or death in his family (sutaka), or when Rahu by an eclipse makes the moon impure.

111. As long as the smell and the stains of the (food given) in honour of one ancestor remain on the body of a learned Brahman, so long he must not recite the Veda.

112. While lying on a bed, while his feet are raised (on a bench), while he sits on his hams with a cloth tied round his knees, let him not study, nor when he has eaten meat or food given by a person impure on account of a birth or a death,

113. Nor during a fog, nor while the sound of arrows is audible, nor during both the twilights, nor on the new-moon day, nor on the fourteenth and the eighth (days of each half-month), nor on the full-moon day.

114. The new-moon day destroys the teacher, the fourteenth (day) the pupil, the eighth and the full-moon days (destroy all remembrance of) the Veda; let him therefore avoid (reading on) those (days).

115. A Brahman shall not recite (the Veda) during a dust-storm, nor while the sky is preternaturally red, nor while jackals howl, nor while the barking of dogs, the braying of donkeys, or the grunting of camels (is heard), nor while (he is seated) in a company.

116. Let him not study near a burial-ground, nor near a village, nor in a cow-pen, nor dressed in a garment which he wore during conjugal intercourse, nor after receiving a present at a funeral sacrifice.

117. Be it an animal or a thing inanimate, whatever be the (gift) at a Sraddha, let him not, having just accepted it, recite the Veda; for the hand of a Brahman is his mouth.

118. When the village has been beset by robbers, and when an alarm has been raised by fire, let him know that (the Veda-study must be) interrupted until the same hour (on the next day), and on (the occurrence of) all portents.

119. On (the occasion of) the Upakarman and (of) the Vedotsarga an omission (of the Veda-study) for three days has been prescribed, but on the Ashtakas and on the last nights of the seasons for a day and a night.

120. Let him not recite the Veda on horseback, nor on a tree, nor on an elephant, nor in a boat (or ship), nor on a donkey, nor on camel, nor standing on barren ground, nor riding in a carriage,

121. Nor during a verbal altercation, nor during a mutual assault, nor in a camp, nor during a battle, nor when he has just eaten, nor during an indigestion, nor after vomiting, nor with sour eructations,

122. Nor without receiving permission from a guest (who stays in his house), nor while the wind blows vehemently, nor while blood flows from his body, nor when he is wounded by a weapon.

123. Let him never recite the Rigveda or the Yagurveda while the Saman (melodies) are heard; (let him stop all Veda-study for a day and a night) after finishing a Veda or after reciting an Aranyaka.

124. The Rigveda is declared to be sacred to the gods, the Yagurveda sacred to men, and the Samaveda sacred to the manes; hence the sound of the latter is impure (as it were).

125. Knowing this, the learned daily repeat first in due order the essence of the three (Vedas) and afterwards the (text of the) Veda.

126. Know that (the Veda-study must be) interrupted for a day and a night, when cattle, a frog, a cat, a dog, a snake, an ichneumon, or a rat pass between (the teacher and his pupil).

127. Let a twice-born man always carefully interrupt the Veda-study on two (occasions, *viz.*) when the place where he recites is impure, and when he himself is unpurified.

128. A twice-born man who is a Snataka shall remain chaste on the new-moon day, on the eighth (lunar day of each half-month), on the full-moon day, and on the fourteenth, even (if they fall) in the period (proper for conjugal intercourse).

129. Let him not bathe (immediately) after a meal, nor when he is sick, nor in the middle of the night, nor frequently dressed in all his garments, nor in a pool which he does not perfectly know.

130. Let him not intentionally step on the shadow of (images of) the gods, of a Guru, of a king, of a Snataka, of his

teacher, of a reddish-brown animal, or of one who has been initiated to the performance of a Srauta sacrifice (Dikshita).

131. At midday and at midnight, after partaking of meat at a funeral dinner, and in the two twilights let him not stay long on a cross-road.

132. Let him not step intentionally on things used for cleansing the body, on water used for a bath, on urine or ordure, on blood, on mucus, and on anything spat out or vomited.

133. Let him not show particular attention to an enemy, to the friend of an enemy, to a wicked man, to a thief, or to the wife of another man.

134. For in this world there is nothing so detrimental to long life as criminal conversation with another man's wife.

135. Let him who desires prosperity, indeed, never despise a Kshatriya, a snake, and a learned Brahman, be they ever so feeble.

136. Because these three, when treated with disrespect, may utterly destroy him; hence a wise man must never despise them.

137. Let him not despise himself on account of former failures; until death let him seek fortune, nor despair of gaining it.

138. Let him say what is true, let him say what is pleasing, let him utter no disagreeable truth, and let him utter no agreeable falsehood; that is the eternal law.

139. (What is) well, let him call well, or let him say 'well' only; let him not engage in a useless enmity or dispute with anybody.

140. Let him not journey too early in the morning, nor too late in the evening, nor just during the midday (heat), nor with an unknown (companion), nor alone, nor with Sudras.

141. Let him not insult those who have redundant limbs or are deficient in limbs, nor those destitute of knowledge,

nor very aged men, nor those who have no beauty or wealth, nor those who are of low birth.

142. A Brahman who is impure must not touch with his hand a cow, a Brahman, or fire; nor, being in good health, let him look at the luminaries in the sky, while he is impure.

143. If he has touched these, while impure, let him always sprinkle with his hand water on the organs of sensation, all his limbs, and the navel.

144. Except when sick he must not touch the cavities (of the body) without a reason, and he must avoid (to touch) the hair on the secret (parts).

145. Let him eagerly follow the (customs which are) auspicious and the rule of good conduct, be careful of purity, and control all his organs, let him mutter (prayers) and, untired, daily offer oblations in the fire.

146. No calamity happens to those who eagerly follow auspicious customs and the rule of good conduct, to those who are always careful of purity, and to those who mutter (sacred texts) and offer burnt-oblations.

147. Let him, without tiring, daily mutter the Veda at the proper time; for they declare that to be one's highest duty; (all) other (observances) are called secondary duties.

148. By daily reciting the Veda, by (the observance of the rules of) purification, by (practising) austerities, and by doing no injury to created beings, one (obtains the faculty of) remembering former births.

149. He who, recollecting his former existences, again recites the Veda, gains endless bliss by the continual study of the Veda.

150. Let him always offer on the Parva-days oblations to Savitri and such as avert evil omens, and on the Ashtakas and Anvashtakas let him constantly worship the manes.

151. Far from his dwelling let him remove urine (and ordure), far (let him remove) the water used for washing his

feet, and far the remnants of food and the water from his bath.

152. Early in the morning only let him void faeces, decorate (his body), bathe, clean his teeth, apply collyrium to his eyes, and worship the gods.

153. But on the Parva-days let him go to visit the (images of the) gods, and virtuous Brahmans, and the ruler (of the country), for the sake of protection, as well as his Gurus.

154. Let him reverentially salute venerable men (who visit him), give them his own seat, let him sit near them with joined hands and, when they leave, (accompany them), walking behind them.

155. Let him, untired, follow the conduct of virtuous men, connected with his occupations, which has been fully declared in the revealed texts and in the sacred tradition (Smriti) and is the root of the sacred law.

156. Through virtuous conduct he obtains long life, through virtuous conduct desirable offspring, through virtuous conduct imperishable wealth; virtuous conduct destroys (the effect of) inauspicious marks.

157. For a man of bad conduct is blamed among people, constantly suffers misfortunes, is afflicted with diseases, and short-lived.

158. A man who follows the conduct of the virtuous, has faith and is free from envy, lives a hundred years, though he be entirely destitute of auspicious marks.

159. Let him carefully avoid all undertakings (the success of) which depends on others; but let him eagerly pursue that (the accomplishment of) which depends on himself.

160. Everything that depends on others (gives) pain, everything that depends on oneself (gives) pleasure; know that this is the short definition of pleasure and pain.

161. When the performance of an act gladdens his heart, let him perform it with diligence; but let him avoid the opposite.

162. Let him never offend the teacher who initiated him, nor him who explained the Veda, nor his father and mother, nor (any other) Guru, nor cows, nor Brahmans, nor any men performing austerities.

163. Let him avoid atheism, cavilling at the Vedas, contempt of the gods, hatred, want of modesty, pride, anger, and harshness.

164. Let him, when angry, not raise a stick against another man, nor strike (anybody) except a son or a pupil; those two he may beat in order to correct them.

165. A twice-born man who has merely threatened a Brahman with the intention of (doing him) a corporal injury, will wander about for a hundred years in the Tamisra hell.

166. Having intentionally struck him in anger, even with a blade of grass, he will be born during twenty-one existences in the wombs (of such beings where men are born in punishment of their) sins.

167. A man who in his folly caused blood to flow from the body of a Brahman who does not attack him, will suffer after death exceedingly great pain.

168. As many particles of dust as the blood takes up from the ground, during so many years the spiller of the blood will be devoured by other (animals) in the next world.

169. A wise man should therefore never threaten a Brahman, nor strike him even with a blade of grass, nor cause his blood to flow.

170. Neither a man who (lives) unrighteously, nor he who (acquires) wealth (by telling) falsehoods, nor he who always delights in doing injury, ever attain happiness in this world.

171. Let him, though suffering in consequence of his righteousness, never turn his heart to unrighteousness; for he will see the speedy overthrow of unrighteous, wicked men.

172. Unrighteousness, practised in this world, does not at

once produce its fruit, like a cow; but, advancing slowly, it cuts off the roots of him who committed it.

173. If (the punishment falls) not on (the offender) himself, (it falls) on his sons, if not on the sons, (at least) on his grandsons; but an iniquity (once) committed, never fails to produce fruit to him who wrought it.

174. He prospers for a while through unrighteousness, then he gains great good fortune, next he conquers his enemies, but (at last) he perishes (branch and) root.

175. Let him always delight in truthfulness, (obedience to) the sacred law, conduct worthy of an Aryan, and purity; let him chastise his pupils according to the sacred law; let him keep his speech, his arms, and his belly under control.

176. Let him avoid (the acquisition of) wealth and (the gratification of his) desires, if they are opposed to the sacred law, and even lawful acts which may cause pain in the future or are offensive to men.

177. Let him not be uselessly active with his hands and feet, or with his eyes, nor crooked (in his ways), nor talk idly, nor injure others by deeds or even think of it.

178. Let him walk in that path of holy men which his fathers and his grandfathers followed; while he walks in that, he will not suffer harm.

179. With an officiating or a domestic priest, with a teacher, with a maternal uncle, a guest and a dependant, with infants, aged and sick men, with learned men, with his paternal relatives, connexions by marriage and maternal relatives,

180. With his father and his mother, with female relatives, with a brother, with his son and his wife, with his daughter and with his slaves, let him not have quarrels.

181. If he avoids quarrels with these persons, he will be freed from all sins, and by suppressing (all) such (quarrels) a householder conquers all the following worlds.

182. The teacher is the lord of the world of Brahman, the

father has power over the world of the Lord of created beings (Pragapati), a guest rules over the world of Indra, and the priests over the world of the gods.

183. The female relatives (have power) over the world of the Apsarases, the maternal relatives over that of the Visve Devas, the connexions by marriage over that of the waters, the mother and the maternal uncle over the earth.

184. Infants, aged, poor and sick men must be considered as rulers of the middle sphere, the eldest brother as equal to one's father, one's wife and one's son as one's own body,

185. One's slaves as one's shadow, one's daughter as the highest object of tenderness; hence if one is offended by (any one of) these, one must bear it without resentment.

186. Though (by his learning and sanctity) he may be entitled to accept presents, let him not attach himself (too much) to that (habit); for through his accepting (many) presents the divine light in him is soon extinguished.

187. Without a full knowledge of the rules, prescribed by the sacred law for the acceptance of presents, a wise man should not take anything, even though he may pine with hunger.

188. But an ignorant (man) who accepts gold, land, a horse, a cow, food, a dress, sesamum-grains, (or) clarified butter, is reduced to ashes like (a piece of) wood.

189. Gold and food destroy his longevity, land and a cow his body, a horse his eye (sight), a garment his skin, clarified butter his energy, sesamum-grains his offspring.

190. A Brahman who neither performs austerities nor studies the Veda, yet delights in accepting gifts, sinks with the (donor into hell), just as (he who attempts to cross over in) a boat made of stone (is submerged) in the water.

191. Hence an ignorant (man) should be afraid of accepting any presents; for by reason of a very small (gift) even a fool sinks (into hell) as a cow into a morass.

192. (A man) who knows the law should not offer even water to a Brahman who acts like a cat, nor to a Brahman who acts like a heron, nor to one who is unacquainted with the Veda.

193. For property, though earned in accordance with prescribed rules, which is given to these three (persons), causes in the next world misery both to the giver and to the recipient.

194. As he who (attempts to) cross water in a boat of stone sinks (to the bottom), even so an ignorant donor and an ignorant donee sink low.

195. (A man) who, ever covetous, displays the flag of virtue, (who is) a hypocrite, a deceiver of the people, intent on doing injury, (and) a detractor (from the merits) of all men, one must know to be one who acts like a cat.

196. That Brahman, who with downcast look, of a cruel disposition, is solely intent on attaining his own ends, dishonest and falsely gentle, is one who acts like a heron.

197. Those Brahmans who act like herons, and those who display the characteristics of cats, fall in consequence of that wicked mode of acting into (the hell called) Andhatamisra.

198. When he has committed a sin, let him not perform a penance under the pretence (that the act is intended to gain) spiritual merit, (thus) hiding his sin under (the pretext of) a vow and deceiving women and Sudras.

199. Such Brahmans are reprehended after death and in this (life) by those who expound the Veda, and a vow, performed under a false pretence, goes to the Rakshasas.

200. He who, without being a student, gains his livelihood by (wearing) the dress of a student, takes upon himself the guilt of (all) students and is born again in the womb of an animal.

201. Let him never bathe in tanks belonging to other men; if he bathes (in such a one), he is tainted by a portion of the guilt of him who made the tank.

202. He who uses without permission a carriage, a bed, a seat, a well, a garden or a house belonging to an (other man), takes upon himself one fourth of (the owner's) guilt.

203. Let him always bathe in rivers, in ponds, dug by the gods (themselves), in lakes, and in waterholes or springs.

204. A wise man should constantly discharge the paramount duties (called yama), but not always the minor ones (called niyama); for he who does not discharge the former, while he obeys the latter alone, becomes an outcast.

205. A Brahman must never eat (a dinner given) at a sacrifice that is offered by one who is not a Srotriya, by one who sacrifices for a multitude of men, by a woman, or by a eunuch.

206. When those persons offer sacrificial viands in the fire, it is unlucky for holy (men) it displeases the gods; let him therefore avoid it.

207. Let him never eat (food given) by intoxicated, angry, or sick (men), nor that in which hair or insects are found, nor what has been touched intentionally with the foot,

208. Nor that at which the slayer of a learned Brahman has looked, nor that which has been touched by a menstruating woman, nor that which has been pecked at by birds or touched by a dog,

209. Nor food at which a cow has smelt, nor particularly that which has been offered by an invitation to all comers, nor that (given) by a multitude or by harlots, nor that which is declared to be had by a learned (man),

210. Nor the food (given) by a thief, a musician, a carpenter, a usurer, one who has been initiated (for the performance of a Srauta sacrifice), a miser, one bound with fetters,

211. By one accused of a mortal sin (Abhisasta), a hermaphrodite, an unchaste woman, or a hypocrite, nor (any sweet thing) that has turned sour, nor what has been kept a whole night, nor (the food) of a Sudra, nor the leavings (of another man),

212. Nor (the food given) by a physician, a hunter, a cruel man, one who eats the fragments (of another's meal), nor the food of an Ugra, nor that prepared for a woman in childbed, nor that (given at a dinner) where (a guest rises) prematurely (and) sips water, nor that (given by a woman) whose ten days of impurity have not elapsed,
213. Nor (food) given without due respect, nor (that which contains) meat eaten for no sacred purpose, nor (that given) by a female who has no male (relatives), nor the food of an enemy, nor that (given) by the lord of a town, nor that (given) by outcasts, nor that on which anybody has sneezed;
214. Nor the food (given) by an informer, by one who habitually tells falsehoods, or by one who sells (the rewards for) sacrifices, nor the food (given) by an actor, a tailor, or an ungrateful (man),
215. By a blacksmith, a Nishada, a stage-player, a goldsmith, a basket-maker, or a dealer in weapons,
216. By trainers of hunting dogs, publicans, a washerman, a dyer, a pitiless (man), and a man in whose house (lives) a paramour (of his wife),
217. Nor (the food given) by those who knowingly bear with paramours (of their wives), and by those who in all matters are ruled by women, nor food (given by men) whose ten days of impurity on account of a death have not passed, nor that which is unpalatable.
218. The food of a king impairs his vigour, the food of a Sudra his excellence in sacred learning, the food of a goldsmith his longevity, that of a leather-cutter his fame;
219. The food of an artisan destroys his offspring, that of a washerman his (bodily) strength; the food of a multitude and of harlots excludes him from (the higher) worlds.
220. The food of a physician (is as vile as) pus, that of an unchaste woman (equal to) semen, that of a usurer (as vile as) ordure, and that of a dealer in weapons (as bad as) dirt.

221. The food of those other persons who have been successively enumerated as such whose food must not be eaten, the wise declare (to be as impure as) skin, bones, and hair.

222. If he has unwittingly eaten the food of one of those, (he must) fast for three days; if he has eaten it intentionally, or (has swallowed) semen, ordure, or urine, he must perform a Krikkhra penance.

223. A Brahman who knows (the law) must not eat cooked food (given) by a Sudra who performs no Sraddhas; but, on failure of (other) means of subsistence, he may accept raw (grain), sufficient for one night (and day).

224. The gods, having considered (the respective merits) of a niggardly Srotriya and of a liberal usurer, declared the food of both to be equal (in quality).

225. The Lord of created beings (Pragapati) came and spake to them, 'Do not make that equal, which is unequal. The food of that liberal (usurer) is purified by faith; (that of the) of the) other (man) is defiled by a want of faith.'

226. Let him, without tiring, always offer sacrifices and perform works of charity with faith; for offerings and charitable works made with faith and with lawfully-earned money, (procure) endless rewards.

227. Let him always practise, according to his ability, with a cheerful heart, the duty of liberality, both by sacrifices and by charitable works, if he finds a worthy recipient (for his gifts.)

228. If he is asked, let him always give something, be it ever so little, without grudging; for a worthy recipient will (perhaps) be found who saves him from all (guilt).

229. A giver of water obtains the satisfaction (of his hunger and thirst), a giver of food imperishable happiness, a giver of sesamum desirable offspring, a giver of a lamp a most excellent eyesight.

230. A giver of land obtains land, a giver of gold long life, a giver of a house most excellent mansions, a giver of silver (rupya) exquisite beauty (rupa),

231. A giver of a garment a place in the world of the moon, a giver of a horse (asva) a place in the world of the Asvins, a giver of a draught-ox great good fortune, a giver of a cow the world of the sun;

232. A giver of a carriage or of a bed a wife, a giver of protection supreme dominion, a giver of grain eternal bliss, a giver of the Veda (brahman) union with Brahman;

233. The gift of the Veda surpasses all other gifts, water, food, cows, land, clothes, sesamum, gold, and clarified butter.

234. For whatever purpose (a man) bestows any gift, for that same purpose he receives (in his next birth) with due honour its (reward).

235. Both he who respectfully receives (a gift), and he who respectfully bestows it, go to heaven; in the contrary case (they both fall) into hell.

236. Let him not be proud of his austerities; let him not utter a falsehood after he has offered a sacrifice; let him not speak ill of Brahmans, though he be tormented (by them); when he has bestowed (a gift), let him not boast of it.

237. By falsehood a sacrifice becomes vain, by self-complacency (the reward for) austerities is lost, longevity by speaking evil of Brahmans, and (the reward of) a gift by boasting.

238. Giving no pain to any creature, let him slowly accumulate spiritual merit, for the sake (of acquiring) a companion to the next world, just as the white ant (gradually raises its) hill.

239. For in the next world neither father, nor mother, nor wife, nor sons, nor relations stay to be his companions; spiritual merit alone remains (with him).

240. Single is each being born; single it dies; single it enjoys (the reward of its) virtue; single (it suffers the punishment of its) sin.

241. Leaving the dead body on the ground like a log of wood,

or a clod of earth, the relatives depart with averted faces; but spiritual merit follows the (soul).

242. Let him therefore always slowly accumulate spiritual merit, in order (that it may be his) companion (after death); for with merit as his companion he will traverse a gloom difficult to traverse.

243. (That companion) speedily conducts the man who is devoted to duty and effaces his sins by austerities, to the next world, radiant and clothed with an ethereal body.

244. Let him, who desires to raise his race, ever form connexions with the most excellent (men), and shun all low ones.

245. A Brahman who always connects himself with the most excellent (ones), and shuns all inferior ones, (himself) becomes most distinguished; by an opposite conduct he becomes a Sudra.

246. He who is persevering, gentle, (and) patient, shuns the company of men of cruel conduct, and does no injury (to living creatures), gains, if he constantly lives in that manner, by controlling his organs and by liberality, heavenly bliss.

247. He may accept from any (man), fuel, water, roots, fruit, food offered without asking, and honey, likewise a gift (which consists in) a promise of protection.

248. The Lord of created beings (Pragapati) has declared that alms freely offered and brought (by the giver himself) may be accepted even from a sinful man, provided (the gift) had not been (asked for or) promised beforehand.

249. During fifteen years the manes do not eat (the food) of that man who disdains a (freely-offered gift), nor does the fire carry his offerings (to the gods).

250. A couch, a house, Kusa grass, perfumes, water, flowers, jewels, sour milk, grain, fish, sweet milk, meat, and vegetables let him not reject, (if they are voluntarily offered.)

251. He who desires to relieve his Gurus and those whom he is bound to maintain, or wishes to honour the gods and guests, may accept (gifts) from anybody; but he must not satisfy his (own hunger) with such (presents).

252. But if his Gurus are dead, or if he lives separate from them in (another) house, let him, when he seeks a subsistence, accept (presents) from good men alone.

253. His labourer in tillage, a friend of his family, his cowherd, his slave, and his barber are, among Sudras, those whose food he may eat, likewise (a poor man) who offers himself (to be his slave).

254. As his character is, as the work is which he desires to perform, and as the manner is in which he means to serve, even so (a voluntary slave) must offer himself.

255. He who describes himself to virtuous (men), in a manner contrary to truth, is the most sinful (wretch) in this world; he is a thief who makes away with his own self.

256. All things (have their nature) determined by speech; speech is their root, and from speech they proceed; but he who is dishonest with respect to speech, is dishonest in everything.

257. When he has paid, according to the law, his debts to the great sages, to the manes, and to the gods, let him make over everything to his son and dwell (in his house), not caring for any worldly concerns.

258. Alone let him constantly meditate in solitude on that which is salutary for his soul; for he who meditates in solitude attains supreme bliss.

259. Thus have been declared the means by which a Brahman householder must always subsist, and the summary of the ordinances for a Snataka, which cause an increase of holiness and are praiseworthy.

260. A Brahman who, being learned in the lore of the Vedas, conducts himself in this manner and daily destroys his sins, will be exalted in Brahman's world.

Bibliography

Apte, M.: *Brama Sutra Shankara Bhasya,* Popular Book Dept, Bombay, 1960.

Archer, W. G.: *The Loves of Krishna in Indian Painting and Poetry*, MacMillan, New York, 1987.

Arthur, A.: *Hymn to Kali (Karpuradi-Stotra)*, Ganesh and Co., Madras, 1965.

Baba, P: *Temple of the Phallic King: The Mind of India*, Simon and Schuster, New York, 1973.

Bhattacharjee, M.: *Hindu Law and the Constitution*, Eastern Law House, Calcutta 1994.

Biardeau, M.: *Hinduism: The Anthropology of a Civilization,* Oxford, Allahabad, 1997.

Bromley, D.: *Krishna Consciousness in the West,* Bucknell University Press, Lewisburg, 1989.

Buhler, G.: *The Laws of Manu,* Clarendon Press, Oxford, 1886.

Chandrakanta, T.: *Hindu Philosophy,* Basu Mallik Press, Calcutta, 1922.

Chaturvedi, M.D.: *Hinduism, The Eternal Religion,* Bharatiya Vidya Bhavan, Bombay, 1992.

Chaturvedi, S.: *Technology in Vedic Literature*, Books and Books, New Delhi, 1993.

Danielou, A.: *The Complete Kama Sutra*, Park Street Press, Rochester, 2000.

Dasgupta, S.: *Obscure Religious Cults,* Firma KLM, Calcutta, 1969.

David, J.: *Shiva's Other Children: Religion and Social Identity amongst Overseas Indians,* Sage, Walnut Creek, 1995.

David, M.: *Hinduism: Experiments in the Sacred*, Harper, San Francisco, 1991.

David, R.: *Hindu Goddesses: Visions of the Divine Feminine in the Hindu Religious Tradition*, University of California Press, Berkeley, 1988.

Dimock, E.: *In Praise of Krishna: Songs from the Bengali,* Anchor Books, New York, 1967.

Eliade, M.: *Yoga: Immortality and Freedom,* Princeton/ Bollingen, New York, 1970.

Flood, G.: *An Introduction to Hinduism*, Cambridge University Press, Cambridge, 1996.

Fuller, C. J.: *The Camphor Flame: Popular Hinduism and Society in India,* Princeton, London, 1992.

Gandhi, M. K.: *The Bhagavad Gita According to Gandhi*, Berkeley Hills Books, New York, 2000.

Gavin, F.: *An Introduction to Hinduism,* Cambridge University Press, England, 1996.

Glyn, G.: *A Source of Modern Hinduism*, Curzon Press, London, 1985.

Goldman, R.: *The Ramayana of Valmiki*, Berkeley Hills Books, New York, 2000.

Gurumurthy, S.: *Hindu Heritage, Assimilative, Not Divisive.* Vigil, Madras 1993.

Harlan, B.: *From the Margins of Hindu Marriage*, Oxford University Press, New York, 2000.

Iyengar, S.: *Light on the Yoga Sutras of Patanjali*, Aquarian Press, London 1993.

Jacobs, H.: *Western Psychotherapy and Hindu Sadhana*, George Allen and Unwin, London, 1961.

Jaiswal, S.: *The Origin and Development of Vaisnavism,* Munshiram Manoharlal, Delhi, 1967.

Kane, P. V.: *History of Dharmasastra,* Bhandarkar Oriental Research Institute, Poona, 1930.

Kantikar, H.: *Kalidasa's Abhijnana Shakuntala*, Popular Prakashan, Bombay, 1974.

Kenneth, W: *The Religion of the Hindus,* The Ronald Press Company, New York, 1953.

Krishna, W.: *Srimad Bhagavad Gita Bhashya of Sri Sankaracarya*, Ramakrishna Math, Madras, 1983.

Lipner, J.: *Hindus: Their Religious Beliefs and Practices,* Routledge, Delhi, 1994.

Manmatha, N.: *Outlines of Hindu Metaphysics*, Kali Ram Press, Calcutta, 1910.

Marglin, F: *Wives of the God-King: The Rituals of the Devadasis of Puri*, Oxford Univ. Press, Delhi, 2000.

Mitchell, S.: *Bhagavad Gita: A New Translation, ,* Bantam Books, Varanasi, 2002.

Narasimhan, C.V.: *The Mahabharata: An English Version Based on Selected Verses*, Columbia University Press, New York, 1965.

Narayan, R. K.: *The Ramayana,* Viking, New York, 1980.

Panikkar, M.: *Himdnism and the West*, Panjab University Publication, Chandigarh, 1964.

Prime, R.: *Hinduism and Ecology*, Motilal Banarsidass, Delhi 1994.

Ramakrishnananda, S.: *Life of Sri Ramanuja*, Sai Kalyani Press, Madras, 1959.

Ramana, M.: *Talks with Sri Ramana Maharshi,* T. N. Venkataraman, Sri Ramanasrama, Tiruvannamalai, 1987.

Ravindra, S.: *The Hindu Hearth and Home*, Carolina Academic, Durham, 1976.

Rocher, L.: *The Puranas, ,* Motilal Banarsidass, Delhi, 1984.

Samsookha, P.: *Lord Mahavira*, Kali Ram Press, Calcutta, 1957.

Sanjukta, G.: *Lakshmi Tantra*, E. J. Brill, Leiden, 1972.

Sen, C.: *The Book of Pilgrimages*, Kali Ram Press, Calcutta, 1940.

Sharma, K.: *Hindu Religion and Ethics,* Asian Publication Services, New Delhi, 1997.

Shraddhananda, S.: *Hindu Sangathan, Saviour of the Dying Race*, MacMillan, Delhi 1926.

Sivaramamurti, C.: *Sri Lakshmi in Indian Art and Thought*, Kanak, New Delhi, 1982.

Subrahmanya, S.: *Upadesasahasri, with the Sahasrivivrti of Anandagiri*, Mahesanusandhana Samsthanam, Mt. Abu, 1978.

Swami, R.: *Science and Religion*, Advaita Ashram, Calcutta, 1978.

Swami, T.: *Hindu Culture: An Introduction,* Chinmaya Publications, Piercy, 1993.

Thomas, J.: *The Hindu Religious Tradition*, Dickenson, California, 1971.

Thomas, P.: *Kama Kalpa or the Hindu Ritual of Love,* D. B. Taraporevala Sons, Bombay, 1965.

Trilok, C.: *Sadhus and Saints of India and Nepal*, Tecpress, Bangkok, 1996.

Vable, D.: *The Arya Samaj. Hindu without Hinduism*. Vikas Publ., Delhi, 1983.

van Buitenen, J. A. B.: *The Mahabharata*, University of Chicago Press, Chicago, 1973.

Visvantha, K.: *Essentials of Hinduism,* Narosa Pub. House, New Delhi, 1989.

Williams, R. B.: *A New Face of Hinduism: The Swaminarayan Religion,* Cambridge University, Cambridge, 1984.

Woods, J.: *The Yoga-System of Patanjali,* Motilal Banarsidass, Delhi, 1966.

Index

A

B

C

D

E

F

G

L

M

N

O

P

R

W

Y

Z

❑❑❑